I0975231

Mildred Wyatt-Wold Series in Ornithology

Roger Tory Peterson

ROGER TORY PETERSON

A BIOGRAPHY

by Douglas Carlson

UNIVERSITY OF TEXAS PRESS, AUSTIN

A portion of chapter 11 appeared in the June/July 2005 issue of *Birding*.

Requests for permission to reproduce material
from this work should be sent to:
Permissions
University of Texas Press
P.O. Box 7819
Austin, TX 78713-7819
www.utexas.edu/utpress/about/bpermission.html

∞ The paper used in this book meets the minimum requirements
of ANSI/NISO Z39.48-1992 (R1997) (Permanence of Paper).

LIBRARY OF CONGRESS CATALOGING-IN-PUBLICATION DATA

Carlson, Douglas, 1943–
Roger Tory Peterson : a biography / by Douglas Carlson. — 1st ed.
p.   cm. — (Mildred Wyatt-Wold series in ornithology)
Includes bibliographical references and index.
ISBN 978-0-292-71680-3 (cl. : alk. paper)
1. Peterson, Roger Tory, 1908–1996.   2. Ornithologists—
United States—Biography.   I. Title.
QL31.P45C37   2007
598.092—dc22
[B]
2007017838

To the memory of my parents, who took me outdoors
and helped me to watch, listen, and learn

Contents

Preface

"Birds have occupied my daily thoughts, filled my dreams, dominated my reading." With these words from a speech delivered in Houston two years before his death in 1996, Roger Tory Peterson summed up a life given over to an obsession. Although friends and colleagues tell of a man who was generous, funny, and kind, Peterson did, indeed, live in a world apart. All of the people interviewed for this project would link Peterson's monumental accomplishments to his "focus." He was a complex man, plagued with self-doubt, but somehow excelling in the often-conflicting cultures of artist and naturalist. Yet his letters reveal his own brand of humility; in spite of honors and accolades, he always deferred to birds.

In the thousands of letters in the Peterson correspondence housed in the Roger Tory Peterson Institute of Natural History, personal references are uncommon, and when they do occur, they usually appear within the context of his work. When he began work on his autobiography, which was never completed, he planned to avoid the details of his personal life and focus, rather, on his *life with birds:* writing about bird people, bird adventures, bird population shifts, changes in the bird-watching world. His work *was* his life.

His outlook, however, was not so narrow as might be expected. By temperament he was a world citizen, interested in cultural as well as natural history. What he called the "environmental ethic," which he expanded to include the "humane ethic," provided the link. As he explained in the Houston speech, "Watching birds has sharpened my senses, made my hearing more acute than most, my eyes more perceptive, my reactions quicker. This awareness radiated far beyond the birds, embracing nearly everything that is alive, from my fellow humans to the least beetle or cricket." It engendered "a reverence for life."

Nevertheless, a subject's reticence to talk about private things makes a biographer's task more difficult. And this reticence is compounded by the nature of Peterson's prolific writing career. As his younger son, Lee, points out, Peterson was a great assimilator of ideas and a lover of phrases that encapsulated these ideas. For example, after his friend James Fisher coined the phrase "birds are the litmus paper of the environment," it appeared in countless Peterson articles and speeches. And because of the focus of his life, he wrote on a narrow range of topics. Thus, at the very essence of his published work, despite its excellence there is a sameness. Stories and catchphrases reappear regularly over the decades. The same can be said of his correspondence.

Fortunately for those of us interested in a deeper understanding of the "personal" Peterson, he was a man of passions, given to powerful statements when moved. And as a man given to moodiness, he was often moved. Therefore it may be assumed that his personality was, in some ways, rather transparent. Readers are welcomed to share in this assumption, and to share in the intriguing process of analysis. Personality, however, must be secondary here.

While this book employs the obvious organizational devices of time and place, each section examines the varied facets of Peterson's remarkable career: as painter, writer, teacher, and environmentalist. Taking a cue from Peterson's autobiography plans, the emphasis here is on a body of work that spanned nearly the entire twentieth century. Because his death is so recent, there are many who have a personal investment in his story; beyond a request for an interview, no attempts have been made to invade the privacy of any of them. Through Peterson's painting and writing, and in the work of the Roger Tory Peterson Institute, the truths of his life are revealed.

Acknowledgments

In expressing gratitude here, my first acknowledgment is to the humbling doctrine of dependent origination. Any event is merely the brief coming together of all its causes, the interconnectedness of countless events and people. A list of persons who made it possible for me to write this book will always be incomplete. Writing mentors from years past, colleagues, friends and family, editors past and present, and spiritual guides have read chapters, offered encouragement, and shared their wisdom. My heartfelt thanks to each of you.

The following people have supplied information about Roger Tory Peterson. Sincere thanks to all for your time and generosity: Peter Alden, Mark Baldwin, Robert Bateman, Paul Benke, James Berry, Mary Beacom Bowers, William Burt, Mary Dowdell, Victor Emanuel, Thomas Erlandson, Judith Feith, Harry Foster, Liz Gentile, Robert Hernandez, Don Hudson, Greg Lasley, Richard Lewin, Robert Lewin, Elaine Lillis, Jeremy Linden, Michael Male, Helen Moe, Marlene Mudge, Lee A. Peterson, Tory C. Peterson, Noble Proctor, Robert Sundell, William Thompson III, and Rick Wright.

Thanks also to the research staff of the Carl B. Ylvisaker Library of Concordia College, Moorhead, Minnesota; to the staff of the Roger Tory Peterson Institute of Natural History in Jamestown, New York; to the McKnight Foundation, the Lake Agassiz Arts Council, and the Jerome Foundation; and to William Bishel of the University of Texas Press and copy editor Rosemary Wetherold.

Special thanks to Jim Berry and Barbara Coulter Peterson.

Very special thanks to S.A., R.J., and T.W.T.

1908–1926

Jamestown, New York

1

In a lifetime, it is a fortunate person who has one good idea. Roger Tory Peterson had one. It grew into *A Field Guide to the Birds,* which was published in 1934 and became one of the most important and influential books about the natural world written in the twentieth century.

When Peterson died in 1996, tributes focused on the three ways that his *Field Guide* had led a large segment of American society into the green movement of the century's last decades. David Clapp, a director of sanctuaries for the Massachusetts Audubon Society, suggested, "Those field guides opened a door and, culturally, all of America has walked through it. By becoming aware of birds, we essentially opened up all of our environmental thinking."[1] Clapp was referring to an awareness that there were more types of birds than just crows, robins, and little brown ones. The guide encouraged a closer look by rewarding it.

Since the guide made the names of birds accessible, awareness turned to knowledge—knowing the names of things, an essential step toward involvement. According to ornithologist Noble Proctor, "It was his [Peterson's] field guides that really started the conservation movement. Through his field guides, people obtained the knowledge to identify the plants and animals and birds. That really is the foundation. Before you can go out and save anything, you have to know what it is. His field guides did that."[2]

Finally came concern. As Frank Graham Jr. wrote in *Audubon Magazine,* "Rachel Carson's *Silent Spring* may have jolted Americans into the Age of Ecology in the 1960s, but they had been prepared for the transition by a succession of Peterson field guides over the previous three decades. . . . By the time Carson revealed the extent of the threats to wildlife, millions had already been primed by Peterson to defend the natural heritage that he had helped them know and cherish."[3] In other words, Peterson's contribution was to change the way his readers saw the natural world, to establish and prepare an audience for the David Browers and Ralph Naders—activists and polemicists who were trying to save it. And along the way, Peterson changed bird study from a rich man's pastime into a hobby for anyone.

Peterson's good idea began in the loneliness of his childhood in Jamestown, New York. The facts of his early life are rather typical for a first-generation American. His father, Charles Peterson, came to this country from Sweden as an infant and was sent to work in the mills by the time he was ten, when his own father died of appendicitis. He eventually earned his living as a traveling salesman. Peterson's mother, Henrietta Badar, came to the United States from Germany at age four and grew up in Rochester, New York. She attended a teachers' college and was teaching in Elmira, New York, when she met Charles.

The couple married and moved to Jamestown, a small industrial city in the far southwestern corner of New York State, where Charles took a job in one of the city's numerous furniture factories. Roger Tory Peterson was born there on 28 August 1908 and grew up in the chaos of his maternal grandparents' home, living with his sister, Margaret, and as many as six cousins off and on. His parents played out typical early twentieth-century gender roles, and Peterson clearly favored his mother. Charles Peterson was a Democrat; his wife was a Republican. He thought churches were filled with hypocrites; she taught Sunday school. He liked his schnapps; she objected to his drinking. The father administered the punishment, earned what money he could, and scorned all things impractical. The mother nurtured, kept house, took menial jobs to help pay the bills, and was unwavering in her support of her son. She took him to the Lutheran Church, where he was baptized and confirmed. "This gave me a rather structured life," he would write later, "but it also put the fear of God into me and made me feel rather guilty about having too much fun."[4]

Barbara Coulter Peterson, who was married to Peterson for thirty years, recalled that he seldom spoke of his childhood, relieved to put it behind him. She was able to infer, however, that it was "grim."[5] He was in constant conflict with his father, who may have had a drinking problem and whose factory job wasn't sufficient to feed the extended family. In 1943, Barbara wrote a letter to her mother, announcing her plans to marry Peterson and making some observations about him. In it, she mentions the poverty of his youth: "He

ROGER TORY PETERSON

shows, I think, the effects of malnutrition. He tells sometimes of not having enough to eat."[6] However, Peterson saw it from another angle. After he received the Horatio Alger Award, he said that he had never realized that he had been deprived as a youth. "I thought the other kids were deprived—I had the birds."[7]

"As a boy," Peterson remembered, "I found my most faithful friends in books."[8] And that's where his idea began—with one of his books. Most of his classmates had little use for him. He was younger; he managed to skip a grade and entered high school when he was twelve. "For some reason," he wrote, "I was able to skip the second grade. Why, I have never known, because I gave no evidence of brilliance, unless my habit of day-dreaming was misconstrued as perception. I suspect that skipping a grade did not help me any. I never quite caught up with my classmates and rebellion was inevitable."[9] In fact, he lacked those attributes that privilege a school child: athletic ability, good looks, social graces. And he was obsessed with nature study—which branded him, as he recalled later, a "kook."[10]

The book Peterson drew his idea from was called *Two Little Savages*, written in 1903 by Ernest Thompson Seton, a promoter of nature studies who also coauthored the first Boy Scout manual. In the book, Seton had tapped into the turn-of-the-century fashion of appropriating American Indian culture as an example of an untarnished connection with the natural world. The main character, Yan, could have been Roger Peterson; he is enthralled with nature and wants nothing but to learn all about it and escape into it, which he does by learning Native ways. Instruction in nature studies, from how to identify leaves to how to build a tipi, is embedded within a loose narrative. One story tells about how Yan learned to identify ducks; it's a story that Peterson retold in numerous interviews and articles. This is how it appears in the preface to the 1934, 1939, and 1947 editions of the *Field Guide:* "This lad had a book that showed him how to tell ducks when they were *in the hand*, but since he only saw the live birds at a distance, he was frequently at a loss for their names. He noticed, however, that all ducks were different—all had little blotches or streaks that were their labels or identification tags. He deduced then, that if he could put their labels or 'uniforms' down on paper, he would know the ducks as soon as he saw them on the water."[11] The hero finds mounted duck specimens and makes sketches of them with their patterns. Seton included two pages of

| 1. Shelldrake | 2. Red-breasted Merganser | 3. Hooded Merganser |

The Fish-Ducks, Sawbills or Mergansers

| 4. Mallard | 5. Black Duck | 6. Gadwell |

7. Widgeon

6. Green-winged Teal

| 10. Shoveller | 11. Pintail | 12. Wood Duck |

The River Ducks

(See description on page 386.)

Far-sketches showing common Ducks as seen on the water at about 50 yards distance, The pair is shown in each square, the male above.
N. B. The wings are rarely seen when the bird is swimming.

THE FISH-DUCK, SAWBILLS OR MERGANSERS

Largely white and all are crested, wings with large white areas in flight.

1. The Shelldrake or Goosander (*Merganser americanus*). Bill, feet and eye red.
2. The Sawbill or Red-breasted Merganser (*Merganser serrator*). Bill and feet red.
3. Hooded Merganser (*Lophodytes cucullatus*). Bill and feet dark ; paddle-box buff.

River duck plate from Ernest Thompson Seton's Two Little Savages, *1903.*

6

ROGER TORY PETERSON

what he called "far-sketches" of ducks; they look strikingly similar to Peterson's renderings in the early editions of the *Field Guide*.

But the drawings alone would not have been enough without the passions that Peterson and Yan shared—for the natural world and its implicit freedoms. In speeches and articles, Peterson would trace the roots of that passion to his seventh-grade teacher, Blanche Hornbeck. In the often-told story, Miss Hornbeck started a Junior Audubon Club that met after school. For a dime, students received a monthly packet containing a bird leaflet, usually written by Dr. Gilbert Pearson, president of the National Association of Audubon Societies at the time; a bird portrait by Bruce Horsfall, Allan Brooks, or Louis Agassiz Fuertes; and a bird drawing to color. The one activity that Peterson remembered best was when Miss Hornbeck gave the students a watercolor box and a Fuertes color plate to copy from Eaton's *The Birds of New York State*. He was given a blue jay, and he claimed that from then on, he wanted to be a bird painter.

Peterson and Miss Hornbeck would rediscover each other in an exchange that clearly reveals his sincerity concerning the importance of the Junior Audubon Club and provides a rather touching footnote to the story. In 1950, Miss Hornbeck read a magazine profile of Peterson in which he acknowledged his debt to her. She wrote him enthusiastically to say that she had discovered "that a former pupil was the great and honored Roger Peterson! . . . My joy and satisfaction in your wonderful achievement is unlimited and I am more happy than I can tell you to have played some small part in helping you to discover your life's work."[12] She remembered a rainy morning bird walk when she expressed surprise that anyone came. "I can still hear you say, 'You can count on me, no matter what the weather.'"[13] Peterson sent her two inscribed books, including his collection of birding recollections, *Birds over America,* which prompted her to write about her joy in "participating vicariously in events which I would like to have had."[14] Peterson continued to send books to her until he learned of her death.

The Junior Audubon Club led to another story Peterson would tell over and over—the turning point in his life. The versions vary little—he was eleven years old and on his first field trip, when he and a friend wandered into a wooded area on the south side of Jamestown:

We came across a flicker, just a few feet off the ground on the trunk of a tree. Its head was tucked under its wing coverts. It was probably exhausted from migration, but we thought it was dead. We stood and stared at it for a while, examining its beautiful plumage. When I reached out to touch its back it exploded with life—a stunning sight, flying away with its golden underwings and the red crescent on its nape—I can see it now—the way it was transformed from what we thought was death into intense life. I was tremendously excited with the feeling which I have carried ever since, of the intensity of a bird's life, and its apparent freedom, with this wonderful ability to fly.[15]

It is easy to see how such an experience could have so profound an effect on a sensitive and searching youth.

Interestingly, however, this passion for birds began to wane after a year or two and was replaced by a love for butterflies and moths. One reason was Peterson's natural curiosity and desire to learn everything about the natural world. Another might be a simple need for companionship. As he wrote later, catching butterflies and moths was something he could share with buddies, who liked it "especially around the streetlights adjoining the cemetery."[16] One of these friends, Clarence Beal, was to become a friend for life. As Beal remembered, "Roger was definitely an entomologist at that period back in 1922 or 1923 when I first began hiking with him through the hills."[17]

In trying to understand the powerful hold that the natural world had on him as an adolescent, Peterson often implied a need for sexual control. In an unpublished manuscript Peterson told a story about capturing his first luna moth, a creature that epitomized to him "everything that is fragile, elusive, and ephemeral." He netted it and examined his catch. "Nothing I had ever seen before—bird or butterfly—could match the evocative, breathtaking beauty of this, my first luna," he wrote. And it *is* remarkable: a pale green collection of shapes and curves that seems to float like a wind-borne leaf rather than flying. Years later, Peterson revisited the event in a dream—exactly as it happened, except that when he peered into his capture net, he saw "a delicate, nymphlike creature. I cannot remember whether it had wings, but it (or she) was quite naked." In Peterson's take on the dream, he wondered: "Could it be that the symbolism of butterflies (and moths) is rather like that of Rima in Hudson's *Green Mansions*—an adolescent dream of maidenhood—not of flesh and blood womanhood, but an elusive gossamer and floss vision to be pursued and, hopefully, possessed."[18] In a 1983 interview, he suggested that boys have a special "male-oriented" interest in bird-watching and spoke of birds in a similar way: "a vision of something possibly unattainable but which should be pursued and if possible captured, much the same as a boy regards a girl."[19] What better tool for such a pursuit than the camera, with its ads that invite you "to capture the moment"? Soon after his bird infatuation began, Peterson saved enough money to buy his first camera. He was fourteen.

The camera was a Premo No. 9, a drop-bed view camera that used glass plate negatives. It had an expandable bellows that opened when the front of the camera was lowered, and the photographer looked into a viewfinder on the top. Although it could be handheld, it was used primarily on a tripod. Besides camera and tripod, Peterson would have to carry the four-by-five-inch glass plates to the site, expose them, then haul them back to a darkroom at his cousin Allen's house. In a bird study journal Peterson kept when he was fifteen, called "Fourth Year of Bird Study," he mentions bringing his camera on many walks and writes about the satisfaction and frustration of his newfound obsession. Some of the difficulty can be seen in an entry about trying to photograph a goldfinch at one of his feeders. The plan was to aim the camera at the feeder, tie a string to the shutter, hide behind a bank, and wait for the bird. But the shutter got tripped accidentally; a new glass plate had to be loaded; then the bird didn't cooperate; and so on.[20] Capturing a bird on film in 1922 took time, effort, patience, and a tremendous desire.

The photographs that Peterson made in those early days were true captures. Given the limitations of his equipment, they simply record the birds. Some of the early exposures made around his home are housed in the Roger Tory Peterson Institute in Jamestown; the birds in them are identifiable, but the pictures show no awareness of composition or light and dark values. Yet they were something to hold, to pore over at night, to possess.

Even in these post-Freudian times, it's hard to resist an interpretation of a boy's suppressed desires channeled into love for his natural surroundings. Another attractive reading, however, allows for a gathering of natural passions incubating in a naturally passionate man. These passions formed Peterson's expressive side, which found a voice, to a greater or lesser degree and at various periods, in his work. In his early obsession for birds, however, it was dominant. As he wrote in *Birds over America,* an often-autobiographical collection of essays about the avocation of bird study, "In my teens, the mere glimpse of a bird would change my listlessness to fierce intensity. I lived for birds. It was exciting just to see them move, to watch them fly. There was nothing thoughtful or academic in my interest; it was so spontaneous I could not control it."[21]

Opposing this expressive side was another combination of influences — of early twentieth-century cultural demands placed upon young males and, more important, the expectations of Peterson's father. Charles Peterson was an immigrant who was accustomed to hard work — according to Roger, a "properly puritanical Swede,"[22] who had no sympathy for his son's impractical interests. Peterson wrote little about his father, and when he did, it wasn't complimentary. His reconstruction of a childhood scene in an autobiographical chapter from *Birds over America* probably accurately portrays the relationship: "'So you've been out after birds again!' my father snorted. 'Haven't you seen them all before? And look at your clothes — nobody with any sense would stay out in the rain.' Puzzled, he shook his head. 'I swear, I don't understand you,' he added reproachfully."[23]

The tension in the Peterson house was understandable: a father who had worked since he was ten years old had a son who shunned everything else to chase butterflies, study wildflowers, and watch birds. And it is clear that Peterson was completely absorbed by birds. His prized possession was a pair of four-power binoculars he bought with his paper-route money. His "Fourth Year of Bird Study" journal holds records for almost-daily bird walks. It also contains his list for the year (153 species), where each bird was first seen, and the second spring arrival date. There's a nesting survey and diary entries that include attempts to translate birdsongs into language — something he would do to great effect in his field guides. Each winter he maintained a string of feeding stations on the outskirts of town with his friend Clarence Beal. He would fill them each morning before school and then take his camera in the afternoon to photograph the chickadees, nuthatches, and other feeder birds that visited. During all this, he somehow found time to establish a bird network called the Nature Correspondence Association, which grew eventually to about sixty members in seventeen states. With three other young birders, he produced a biannual publication, *The Passenger Pigeon*. Gustav Swanson, one of the charter members and later the head of the Conservation Department at Cornell University, recalled that Peterson did a line drawing of a passenger pigeon for the cover and led the effort to contribute notes and articles about birds.[24]

The Passenger Pigeon became, as Peterson wrote in 1957, "as extinct as its namesake."[25] However, an entry from his bird study journal, a passage that was obviously worked over, suggests the flavor of Peterson's contributions to the journal. It is imitative—hardly the style of a fifteen-year-old—and, in its detail, foreshadows the first edition of the *Field Guide:*

> While I was walking along the railroad track I caught a faint strain of bird melody. The wind was strong, hushing most all the music of the commoner birds so that one had to listen very intently in order to catch their notes. It came from the side of the hill by the wilderness road. I listened again to the wild sweet strains. It was undoubtedly a hermit thrush. I went carefully up through the woods, but I could not exactly locate the sound. Sometimes it seemed farther up the hill, again to one side, and lastly I ascertained that it came from the direction I had just come. I saw a bird silently fly up from the ground, its rufous tail plainly telling that it was a hermit thrush. It well deserves its name, for in truth no other bird seems so solitary. It walks among the leaves robin-like, hunting for insects, or flying into the low branches of a small hemlock, makes an occasional 'chuck.' It need not be confused with the fox sparrow, the size is larger. The tail is not so bright, while the back is a uniform drab color, or olive brown, in contrast to the fox sparrow's striped chestnut and gray back. The chief difference is in the breast. The hermit's breast is distinctly spotted in the manner of the wood thrush, while the fox sparrow is blotched and striped with chestnut brown.[26]

Obviously when he wasn't watching birds, Peterson was thinking, reading, and writing about them.

Entomology continued to absorb him as well. His moth study was hindered by an 8:45 p.m. Jamestown city curfew, so, Peterson recalled, he went to city hall and explained the problem to the chief

A youthful Peterson examining pileated woodpecker excavations in Chautauqua County, New York.

of police, who wrote a note permitting Peterson and his "assistant, Benny Shapiro, to catch moths around street lights until 11 p.m."[27]

In 1942, Peterson's good friend Edwin Way Teale gave *Audubon* readers a sense of what it was like to have a young Peterson around the house. According to stories Peterson told Teale about himself, he pressed hundreds of plants by placing them between newspapers and slipping them under the carpets. That winter he brought home several hundred promethea moth cocoons, which emerged and laid eggs in his mother's curtains, gluing the egg clusters to the curtains with a brown secretion.[28] And in an unpublished piece, Peterson recalled an irruption of pipevine swallowtails, a species normally found in small numbers that far north. Entranced, Peterson collected eight hundred (by his estimate) caterpillars. They eat Dutchman's-pipe, a vine native to areas south of western New York but common as an ornamental in Jamestown. As a result he spent hours sneaking onto porches all over Jamestown, stealing leaves to feed his caterpillars.[29]

But ultimately it was the world of birds that engaged him. He continued to haunt the woods and fields around Jamestown, and with Beal, he rode his bicycle to the outlet of Chautauqua Lake, which remained open in the winter, to watch ducks and on longer trips of twenty-five miles or more to the ravines of Chautauqua Gorge. And they saved their pennies to take the trolley to the Lake Erie shore.

The gateway to all this birding came from *Bird-Lore* magazine, the popular bird publication of the day. It is easy to imagine Peterson poring over each issue, leaving Jamestown behind for the virtual bird world that the magazine offered. And through its pages, he was introduced to the more scientifically inclined elements of bird study. In a letter to *Bird-Lore* in 1924, he wrote, "I have become interested in the magazines, 'The Auk,' and 'The Condor.' I would like to subscribe to those magazines but I do not know where to send."[30] This interest in professional bird journals indicates that he had quickly outgrown *Bird-Lore*'s cute, anthropocentric articles about "adopted" wild birds that were inevitably named and given human attributes. For him, the magazine's fact-filled educational pieces by Gilbert Pearson and Arthur Allen were more appropriate. And writing about *Bird-Lore* as an adult, he would remember editor Frank Chapman's notes on bird plumages and the migration data compiled by Frederick Lincoln, material that he eagerly memorized. Meanwhile, his artistic side was being nourished by the frontispieces—full-color bird portraits by his boyhood idol Louis Agassiz Fuertes and others. He was so enthralled by *Bird-Lore* that when his class was asked to make believe they were the persons they most admired, Peterson eschewed world leaders and athletes, pretending he was Gilbert Pearson and delivering a lecture on bird protection.

There was fodder for planning and dreaming as well. In 1922, Frank Chapman wrote a short piece that set out the "requirements of the profession of ornithology." Among them was "an inborn love for the study of nature with so intense an interest in birds that they, more than any other forms of life, demand one's attention." Here Peterson could surely see himself and allow his imagination to dream a different life, as he often did. In this context, Chapman's words become prophetic. He describes the advantages of ornithology as "opportunity to follow one's chosen calling; to gratify an insatiable desire for research; to make work play; and, whether indoors or out, daily to renew one's joy in life." And his accounting of the service an ornithologist might provide outlines the life Peterson was to lead. The ornithologist is "limited only by one's belief in the value to man of contact with Nature and by one's ability to prove that Nature's beauty, joy, and freedom are most eloquently expressed in the lives of birds."[31] Such pronouncements would satisfy Peterson's will to believe and would provide his thoughtful nature with an abstract sense of the rightness of what he was doing. They were, in his conflict with his father, words to live by.

Peterson was eager to join such an attractive fraternity, and he officially began when he broke into print for the first time. In *Bird-Lore*'s "Notes from Field and Study" section, he recorded, anecdotally, two sight records from 1925: a Carolina wren and a tufted titmouse. His prose, in the style of such reports, reveals the wonder and excitement that would never diminish in the thousands and thousands of encounters with birds that he would publish over a lifetime. It reads, in part:

> As I was reclining on the ground in a woods 6 miles southwest of Jamestown, I became aware of an unusual voice among the wave of Chickadees, Creepers, and Warblers that was passing at the time. My ears detected a distinct *Peto-peto,* so I jumped to my feet, all alert, for I had read that this was the call of the Titmouse. . . . Among its numerous notes . . . I found that its whistled, *here-here-here-here* was easiest to imitate. It was not long before I had enticed it within 4 feet of me by imitating its call.[32]

And it closes with the necessary contextual information that this was the third record of a titmouse in Chautauqua County. Peterson must have been ecstatic over his emergence into the ornithological world; what the elder Peterson thought of it can only be assumed.

The more the father criticized, the more recalcitrant the son became. But it seems that rather than being malicious, the elder Peterson was simply acting as most fathers of his time would; he was mostly interested in Roger's getting ahead, making a good living. According to Beal, Charles Peterson once "accosted" his son's mathematics teacher on the street, insisting that "the teacher speak to Roger, showing him the futility of a career based on bird study."[33]

The teacher promised he would, but he never did. Beal himself was asked to intervene, but since he was smitten with nature study himself, it was a pointless request. And while the father professed no interest in his son's hobbies, he did offer occasional support. One recollection by an acquaintance has the elder Peterson smashing Roger's jars of butterflies and moths and throwing them away.[34] But Margaret Peterson Lager, Peterson's younger sister, tells of her father making "exquisitely mitered display boxes" for Peterson's butterfly and moth collection and fabricating steel storage boxes for his negatives. She also tells of her father proudly carrying around the note signed by the chief of police that permitted Peterson to stay out past curfew to collect moths.[35]

2

With the exception of a few good grades in art and mechanical drawing, Peterson's educational experience at Jamestown High School was a disaster. The system of the day seemed to be designed to do whatever it could to prevent individual growth. In the last quarter of the nineteenth century, the establishment of a strict hierarchical and institutional business model—presidents and deans, departments and department chairs, faculty rank—provided an "efficient" structure for education, while layers of bureaucratic procedures ensured accountability. A credit system was installed to promote standardization. Public schools adopted the same model with superintendents, principals, vice-principals, and a grade system. The intent was to create the "factory school," as evidenced in this 1916 statement by Ellwood P. Cubberly, an education professor at Stanford and a leading educationist of the time:

> Every manufacturing establishment that turns out a standard product . . . maintains a force of efficiency experts to study methods of procedure and to measure and test the output of its works. . . . Our schools are, in a sense, factories in which the raw products (children) are to be shaped and fashioned into products to meet the various demands of life. . . . This

demands good tools, specialized machinery, continuous management of production . . . the elimination of waste in manufacture, and a large variety in the output.[1]

Such a system was hardly suited for a dreamy individualist such as Peterson; he was far from a "standard product." His biology lab workbook illustrates this. The book is filled with routine write-ups of traditional, "cookbook" experiments such as tests for sugars and starches, an osmosis demonstration, and the liberation of oxygen by a water plant. Some of Peterson's descriptions are incomplete. His own interests, not about to be "shaped and fashioned," are evident though. On the last page is a list from an early spring bird walk that includes towhee, kingfisher, horned lark, and meadowlark. And inside the front cover and below his name is a drawing he labeled "trade mark." It consists of a pair of field glasses and a butterfly net alongside two signs of spring in western New York: a mourning cloak butterfly and a robin.[2] Clearly, his mind was anywhere but on school. He had already realized that the system was not made for him, and in his later years, he enjoyed telling stories of his failures. He claimed to have nearly failed history because he doodled bird pictures in the margins of his text and biology because he argued with the teacher about bird populations (she claimed that snowy egrets were becoming extinct; he knew better). He often called himself the "school non-conformist" and the "school rebel," traits he would lay claim to throughout his life.[3]

The *Jamestown High School Handbook* for 1925, the year Peterson graduated, shows a lockstep path toward a degree, with little room for individual choice. A total of five art electives were offered, in "representation," drawing, and design. Biology was taught, but comprehensive exams for college entrance covered only physics and chemistry.

The 1925 commencement address, given by John J. Tigert, the U.S. Commissioner of Education, offers a clear view of what Peterson faced. Tigert blasted "cultural education" at the expense of educating for "efficiency in trades and industries." "A majority of the people," he said, "must engage in pursuits which involve the use of the hands. Manual and industrial arts must be recognized as being truly honorable. . . . Otherwise education will eventually become destructive and a handicap to progress."[4]

In other words, Peterson was given a dilemma: either take a college entrance course of study for which he was not suited, or learn a trade in which he was not interested. As Tigert said, education should fit a student's talents—but within the confining limits of the factory school system. To illustrate, he closed his speech with a flawed analogy: "You wouldn't teach a fish to fly, a squirrel to swim, or a bird to gather nuts." Most likely, Peterson, if he was listening at all, was thinking about art school and his father's insistence that he take a job in mechanical drawing—and then daydreaming about acorn woodpeckers, which gather nuts and store them in holes that they excavate in posts and trees. Peterson recalled the baccalaureate sermon, in which the preacher said, "Many of you will be going to college and you will be offered such courses as biology where you will be taught the theory of evolution. . . . Try to avoid these courses."[5] Peterson couldn't believe what he was hearing.

After Peterson got good grades in mechanical drawing, his father saw some hope for him. And when a draftsman's job opened up at the Union Furniture Company after his graduation, he bowed to paternal pressure and took the job—proper man's work. The job lasted a week. He would later say that even though his father was displeased, the decision to quit was the right one; he might easily have remained a draftsman all his life. He called it a turning point because the job he moved to was far better suited for a young man who thought that he might want to be an artist. A cousin, Allen Jones, showed one of Peterson's bird paintings to a friend at the factory, and Peterson was offered a position painting decorative subjects on furniture. It was the first of many choices that he would have to make between his two selves—the nature lover and the immigrant's son, the romantic and the pragmatist, the artist and the scientist.

In a 1941 essay in *Audubon* titled "Symbols of Nature in Art," Peterson, at age thirty-four, provided a glimpse of his struggles as a young man and perhaps some lingering frustration:

> Bird study is a product of a highly civilized world—a world where life is becoming increasingly complex, with a multitude of laws, restrictions and community obligations, as well as inescapable restraints imposed by the household in which one has been brought up. The bird symbolizes a kind of freedom

from these restraints; it can go where it wants to, when it wants to. It acts as a vicarious and much-needed release for certain people to whom the burden has become irksome but who feel duty bound not to throw it off.[6]

There is little doubt that Peterson is one of those "certain people" to whom he refers.

Later, he would write that this metaphor that connected birds with freedom moved, in typical cases, to what he called an "intellectual pursuit." Knowledge intervened. He learned that birds aren't "free" at all but rather are captives of environmental factors and genetically encoded behaviors. To accept this knowledge was to accept any number of other "realities" outside and beyond the world of birds. A poem he published in his high school yearbook in 1925 shows how his ideas were growing.

CLOUDS

You lovely clouds that float and sail
    So very soft and white and pale,
Across the sky you seem to trail
    Like fairy coaches new and frail.

On your soft sides the stars may rest
    In their new, shining garments dressed.
The very moon has fondled and caressed
    You, as you glide on, calm and blessed.

I long to rise up and to fly
    Beyond the sight of mortal eye
To sink into your dewy depths and lie
    There, calm and peaceful 'til I die.

But lo, white clouds, you're turning black;
    The winds are chasing you far, far back!
They seem to cluster and to stack
    Great billows on your swelling back.

No longer do I wish to fly,
    Or in your gloomy depth to lie;
I'll stay right here until I die
    On this fair earth beneath the sky.[7]

In spite of some awkward lines and forced rhymes, "Clouds" is quite skillful with its enjambment and its careful argument. Although a piece of juvenilia, it represents an important accommodation, which Peterson later explained this way: "Reluctant at first to accept the strait jacket of a world which I did not comprehend, I finally, with the help of my hobby, made some sort of peace with society. The birds, which started as an escape from the unreal, bridged the gap to reality and became a key whereby I might unlock eternal things."[8] Above all, he developed a more biocentric understanding of his place in the natural world; respect for scientific fact turned a dreamy and self-referential escapism into a sustaining passion for his life's work.

3

Essential to the peace Peterson was able to make was his development as an artist. His first mentor was his first boss: Willem Dieperink von Langereis, the master artist at the furniture-decorating department. He took a liking to Peterson and encouraged him to leave Jamestown to study art in New York City. Peterson's first step in that direction came in 1925 when he attended his first American Ornithologists' Union convention. At the AOU's annual conventions, ornithologists from around the world gather to exchange news, share academic papers, and refocus the field of bird study. At seventeen, Peterson had saved up enough money to travel to the convention in New York with two paintings for the bird art exhibit: the kingbird that got him the job at Union Furniture and a hummingbird. With some embarrassment, Peterson later wrote of the kingbird effort, "My eyes were far more acute then, and with a fine oo brush I tried to paint in every barb of every feather as I imagined John James Audubon had done. . . . It was a disaster."[1] The painting may have been a disaster—enthusiasm without training will go only so far—but the convention wasn't. It was the time when the self-described "hick from the boondocks" entered the world of professional ornithology and met the men who would steer his professional life, a who's who in ornithology—Louis Agassiz Fuertes,

Ludlow Griscom, Arthur Allen, Robert Cushman Murphy, Edward Howe Forbush, Frank Chapman, Francis Lee Jaques. He was able to get Griscom's recommendation for his associate AOU membership and also got to see him in action in the field, an experience he recalled with some awe in his unpublished autobiography:

> Ludlow Griscom was the first ornithologist I ever met, when as a lad of 17 I came to New York in 1925 to attend my first meeting of the A.O.U. . . . I was to see him in action the following Saturday when he led the field trip to Long Beach on Long Island. On that day 13 new birds went down on my life list, and I particularly recall the Brunnich's Murre [now thick-billed murre] that flew over near the inlet.[2]

And the wonder over Griscom's skills was compounded by the fact that the trip was Peterson's first to the ocean:

> I grew up in the hills of western New York. When I thought of the ocean I envisioned it as a large lake, with woodlands and farms coming down to the shore like the lake at home. The largest sand beach on our lake was at an amusement park, a beach that had been dumped there by sand trucks, a strip a few feet wide for bathers to lie on. . . . So when I took the train out of New York's Pennsylvania Station for the south shore of Long Island . . . a new world opened to me.[3]

The memory of his newly discovered master at work in this wondrous setting wouldn't diminish over the years. "Ludlow was our God," he would write later.[4]

While Peterson traced his obsession with birds to the 1919 encounter with a flicker when he was eleven, he also located the source of his desire to become a bird artist that same year when he painted his version of a blue jay from a painting by Fuertes, and he never stopped painting birds from that time on. Fuertes was considered second only to Audubon among American bird painters; some place him first. Peterson would write later:

> Of those who have gone before, we can be sure of only two who will be remembered far into the future — John James Audubon, who took birds out of the glass case for all time, and Louis Agassiz Fuertes, who really brought them to life. Whereas

Audubon invariably reflected Audubon in his spirited compositions, Fuertes reflected more of the character of the bird, less of himself. No illustrator or artist has done it better.[5]

The teenager must have been starstruck when he met his idol at the AOU painting exhibition. Peterson remembered the meeting fondly, and although he couldn't recall what Fuertes said about the kingbird or the hummingbird, he remembered good conversation about painting and invaluable advice about countershading as they strolled through the American Museum of Natural History that day. When they parted, Fuertes gave Peterson, as a token of encouragement and welcome to the bird-painting fraternity, one of his own brushes. A measure of how important the gesture was to Peterson lies in the number of times he repeated the story in articles and interviews. He never used the brush and, in the most compelling version of the story, eventually lost it under some floorboards when he was a camp counselor in Maine. Retrieving it later, he found that mice had taken the bristles to line their nests. This conclusion, Peterson recalled, "was an early lesson in how everything in life is interconnected."[6] It also served as an emblem for a sad postscript to the meeting. Fuertes generously offered to look at some of Peterson's work. Peterson deferred, modestly, waiting until he felt his painting was worthy. Before that happened, Fuertes had died in an accident. To mingle with the men he most admired and to have his work hanging alongside those of the greatest bird artists of the day was a signal event in Peterson's life. It encouraged him to submit two works to the Cooper Ornithological Club's "First American Bird Art Exhibition" in Los Angeles.

The catalog for that show must have been heady stuff for Peterson. The entry for him read: "Roger Tory Peterson . . . is but 17 years of age and has barely launched upon his artistic career which has the promise of being a notable one." It went on to say, "He used his camera as an ally in recording attitudes and postures, and this early training will stand him in good stead when he comes to a mature mastery of his technique."[7] In fact, the two pieces—a Chinese ink drawing of a screech owl with a captured mouse and an oil portrait of a great horned owl—reveal that he had a great deal of work to do before any "mastery" would be evident; his technique bears all the signs of juvenilia. Perched on a bare branch, the great horned owl seems disproportionate and at odds with the painting's environment, looking like a cutout that has been pasted in. The design of the screech owl piece is better; however, the bird itself, which is slightly suggestive of a house cat, is unconvincing. But both pieces show a nascent skill and a strong understanding of his subjects. Buoyed by his Los Angeles success, his AOU experiences, and the encouragement of Langereis, Peterson realized that art school, less expensive than college, might be his way out.

In 1925, when Peterson graduated from high school, Chapman published a letter from a young man about to enter college who wanted to know "something about the career and work of the ornithologist." There is no evidence that Peterson was the author of the letter, but he could very well have been. And Chapman's response certainly spoke to him. The writer's background and Peterson's are identical: "I have spent a great deal of my spare time for the last three or four years in studying birds. At present, of all my pursuits, bird study gives me the greatest pleasure and I am more keenly interested in that than any other subject." He goes on to ask questions that would please a father as practical as Peterson's. Are opportunities available? How does one begin? Must one teach? And more to the point, "About what is the professional ornithologist paid in the various stages of his development from a beginner to an expert? Is the remuneration able to support the worker or is it necessary that he have financial means before he starts his work?"[8] Chapman's response was one that would have given courage to someone in Peterson's position. "The born bird student does not select his calling, it selects him. One becomes a professional naturalist through the force of an overpowering desire. You don't weigh the chances of future advancement pro and con—you seek only for opportunity to gratify an inherent trait which inevitably and unmistakably points your course." Chapman's assessment of an ornithologist's financial future, while buoying Peterson's spirits, would have left his father grumbling. "I cannot give you the scale of remuneration which a professional ornithologist may expect to receive; but if, to quote Thoreau again, a man is rich 'in proportion to what he can afford to do without,' then the ornithologist is rich from the start. Having through his position opportunity to follow his chosen calling, what is there left to ask beyond the mere necessities of life?"[9]

Inspired by ideas such as these, Peterson wanted more than anything to attend Cornell and study ornithology, but on his own financially, he would have faced a daunting time. His father again stood in the way, denying him any financial support in favor of his sister, Margaret. In the face of this perceived injustice, Peterson was even more determined to escape his oppressive existence in Jamestown. The choice between art and science was a critical one. He was by nature an academic, as his younger son, Lee, suggests, and if there had been money for college, Peterson would have been a scientist only.[10]

In the end, however, he chose the alternative he could afford and made his move—in a direction that made the *Field Guide* possible. Not only did his art training begin the development of Peterson's prodigious craftsmanship, but it also dictated how he approached field identification of birds. As he often pointed out, because of his art background he approached things visually rather than phylogenetically. Grouping birds by their appearance rather than their taxonomic relationships emphasized visual differences among similar species and helped with field identification. Vireos, for example, fit taxonomically between shrikes and jays, for which they could never be mistaken. Peterson's guide shows them next to the warblers, which they resemble and with which they often migrate—another example of how he reconciled the binary worlds of art and science.

More important, however, than Peterson's choice of art school over an academic career was his deliverance from Jamestown. As Beal wrote, "He never regretted leaving town and often chided me for staying put when there were so many opportunities elsewhere."[11] Throughout his life, he would find ways to be, at once, an artist and naturalist, but until the freedom of a bird's flight was made manifest in his own life, he was a captive of culture, family, and circumstance. For the courage and strength to enter a world beyond his ken and beyond his means, Peterson must have drawn profoundly on his passion for freedom, for expression, and for birds.

1926–1934

New York City and Boston

4

In 1926, Peterson moved to New York City. He was just eighteen, the prototypical hayseed: innocent, preoccupied, inexperienced, and broke. Luckily for him, he was not alone. When he attended the AOU convention the year before, he had met Bernard Nathan, a young bird student from Brooklyn. Nathan had told Peterson that he would help him find a place to live when Peterson enrolled at the Art Students League. The YMCA nearby was full, however, and the Nathan family took pity on him and invited him to stay with them. They were a family of six, kind and generous, and Nathan, a Boy Scout leader with a specialty of leading scouts on bird walks, showed Peterson all the good birding spots in and around Brooklyn, such as Prospect Park and the dump at Dyker Heights. But Peterson was out of place and lonely. He wrote home to Jamestown that he missed walking in the quiet and beauty of the hills of his Chautauqua County home instead of being "lulled to sleep by the squealing of German bands and squalling of barge whistles." He complained about "cold and sophisticated New Yorkers" and how he longed to "mingle with good, genial Chautauquans again."[1] Yet in the same letter, he seemed genuinely excited about and open to his new experiences, like eating kosher and riding the subway and battling the crowds. He soon got work decorating furniture at Deutsch Bros. Furniture in the Bronx, which entailed a long and tiresome subway ride (he claimed he learned to sleep standing up, hanging onto the straps) but provided him with the money he desperately needed.

His mother remained a strong presence in his life at this time, with frequent affectionate letter and postcard exchanges between them. He sent news of bird walks along with his dirty laundry; she asked nervous questions while giving motherly advice. In March 1927, for example, she wrote, "Just keep on having confidence in yourself, then others will too. Sometimes that is half the success. Then when success comes, we get still more confidence in ourselves and that gives power. Only we should not loose [sic] our heads with the first sign of success. That is where many make a mistake and fail in the end. It's keeping on trying in spite of success or failure that brings us somewhere."[2] Other times, she returned to an area where she perhaps felt more comfortable: "Take your bath regularly and be sure to keep your neck and ears clean."[3] Although Peterson's busy schedule later on in life kept him from the close contact with his mother that she needed and desired, he never lost his strong emotional attachment to her. He dedicated his 1949 book, *How to Know the Birds,* to her, and after her death he wrote, "When a man's mother dies, no matter how old he is, he becomes a vulnerable boy again."[4]

His birding ties with his hometown lingered as well. He worked Jamestown Christmas Bird Counts with Clarence Beal in 1926 and 1927, and in 1927 one in Youngstown, Ohio. Another carryover from western New York was Peterson's first real article in *Bird-Lore.* It was published in 1929, but it is set in Chautauqua County and, doubtless, composed from notes made earlier. Entitled "Warbler Ways," and illustrated with three of his photographs, it makes a case for the appeal of studying and photographing warblers during their nesting period as well as during migration. The job is harder, he wrote, but the rewards are worth it: "It is not easy to find their nest in the first place, but the camera-worker, more persistent than the rest, makes a game of it, searching until he finally finds his prize. So it is that the bird photographer discovers many a thing about bird behavior that others often overlook." He details nesting and feeding behavior, especially in mourning warblers. The tone is straightforward and relaxed, and one can sense a slight wistfulness when he recalls birding the hills around Jamestown:

> Here, in Chautauqua County, New York, where rugged ravines, brushy hillsides, and wet bottom-lands all offer their attractions, we are blessed with at least seventeen species of breeding Warblers. We could hardly wish for more. One soon learns to associate various songs with the birds' habitat. No matter where it is heard, the Chestnut-sides' ditty is always reminiscent of hot summer days on dry, brushy hillsides. The songs of the Magnolia and the Black-throated Green bring thoughts of cool, hemlock-clad gullies where orchids grow;—one might go right down the list, linking treasured memories with each bird.[5]

But despite the hint of nostalgia, gradually Peterson's own strong spirit and his two passions—art and birds—began to ease the difficulties of the big city.

Artistically, New York was as exciting as at any time in its history when Peterson arrived; interesting choices awaited him because of the simultaneous presence there of three distinct artistic approaches: traditional, realistic, and abstract. Representing traditional European artistic values was the National Academy of Design, founded in 1825 to provide a central place for artists to study, work, and exhibit. In 1870, another school, the Art Students League, was founded by students unhappy with the inflexible conservatism of the academy. Further, the art world itself was divided. The beginnings of the revolt against traditional art were creeping into America, and the Armory Show of 1913 allowed New Yorkers their first real look at what came to be called modernism. It revealed change on two fronts: in subject matter and in form. American realist painters turned to gritty, urban subjects—ordinary people, common scenes. Meanwhile, abstract painters began to abandon objects altogether and looked to their own minds and feelings for the sources of their work.

That Peterson would pass up experimenting with abstraction isn't surprising. Someone so profoundly in touch with the natural world could never embrace such a self-referential mode as abstract art. After all, Jackson Pollock, the best-known of the abstract painters, when asked why he didn't paint objects from nature, replied, "I am nature." Nor is it difficult to understand how Peterson could abandon the realists who dominated the Art Students League. He wanted to paint birds; they dominated his life. Social, political, and other human-centered issues simply didn't matter to him at the time. His priorities are revealed when later in life he wrote about the anthropocentric treatment of wildlife by the art world:

> Wildlife painting was not [considered] art unless it had something to do with an animal's relationship to humans. Domestic animals such as horses, dogs, and cattle were satisfactory subject matter . . . as were paintings of the chase—a hunted stag or a boar being attacked by dogs, for example. Ducks or other waterfowl were usually shown dead, hung by their feet as still lifes. Songbirds were acceptable subjects only if given some

religious or symbolic significance. The European goldfinch
. . . , a symbol of good luck or happiness, might be shown in
the hands of a child who was lovingly squeezing it to death.[6]

Peterson enrolled in the Art Students League in 1927. Reflecting on his studies there, he wrote that the most influential teacher he ever had was Kimon Nikolaides. Author of the classic text *The Natural Way to Draw*, Nikolaides insisted that his students draw what they actually saw rather than what they thought they should see. "He taught us," Peterson wrote later, "to keep our eyes on the model, scarcely dropping them to our paper, while feeling things out, first tentatively, with light delineation, then more positively, with stronger confirming lines."[7] Elsewhere he described the process as "boiling, boiling, boiling, modifying and bearing on harder with bolder lines until the form reasserted itself."[8] This was a dramatic change from painting each barb on each feather; it allowed Peterson to express what *he* saw in a bird and what *he* understood about it. As he wrote to his mother,

> We are not supposed to get a photographic likeness, either as
> to drawing or color tones, but to achieve a sense of third dimensional activity. It's exasperating at times. Art in its first
> sense is not seeing a thing as a picture but attaining a sense of
> feeling thru sculptural brush handling rather than mere paint
> spread over a flat canvas. 99 of 100 painters fail in this. I know,
> however, that if I work conscientiously I'll get a great deal out
> of this class.[9]

This new freedom began to open up the possibility of putting his profound feelings about birds into his art.

A second influence at the League was John Sloan. Sloan was a leading "realist" of the time, but his paintings are far from photographic. His technique was loose and painterly, his strokes broad and rapid. From him, Peterson developed his use of color: cool colors—greens and blues—receding into the background and warm colors—reds, oranges, and yellows—advancing from the canvas. He learned to see his subject in relation to its surroundings, to create movement in his composition, and to achieve a three-dimensional sense with color.

Through both teachers, then, he was exposed to an approach that could be called gestural, a technique that began the composition of a work in brief and general terms—an impression—and worked toward detail. It is an approach that is more painter-centered than subject-centered, one that reminded Peterson that when painting a kingbird he was not recreating a kingbird; he was putting marks on canvas. In his two years at the Art Students League, he discovered that the passion for birds that he carried from his childhood could figure into his painting, along with his ornithological knowledge.

But then he quit and enrolled in the National Academy of Design. It may have been simply a financial decision: the academy charged no fees to the artists it accepted. The reason Peterson gave for the change, however, was that Sloan was so vehement in his condemnation of the academy that Peterson's curiosity was piqued. At the time, he wrote to his mother, "I think, that next fall, I'd like to get into the National Academy. It's quite an honor to get in, but one has to enter in competition with others to gain admittance. The tuition is free, as it is a government institution. As a bird artist, it would help me a lot more than the League would, because of the manner of teaching there."[10] In 1928, he submitted some charcoal sketches and was accepted for the fall semester.

What he found there was what is termed academic realism, a style of painting concerned not only with composition and movement in space but also with more polished and finished work. He studied with portrait painters Edwin Dickinson and Raymond Neilson, drawing first from plaster casts and then graduating to live models, while progressing from charcoal to oils. Doing this fine work, he learned how to express the way shadows fell on shapes, an important concept that was ignored at the Art Students League. Peterson put it simply: "When I switched from the League to the Academy, it was because the realistic academic approach was best for a naturalist."[11] During his time at the academy, Peterson, by his own admission, could draw the human figure better than he could draw birds. But by practicing on the birds in the Bronx Zoo, he easily applied the "realistic academic," portrait approach to bird painting. It came easily because his paintings were just that: "bird portraits" rather than realistic landscapes containing birds. Birds, as we actually see them, are elusive and camouflaged. The naturalist and teacher in Peterson wanted to share the beauty and essence of birds, not with the precision of the photographer or through the private vision of the modernist. It was another accommodation, but one that would prove profitable. At the art show held at the AOU convention in 1933, seventy-five painters exhibited; Peterson showed both field guide plates and paintings. Five paintings sold; four were Peterson's. He recalled that one was a group of five egrets in flight, and another, a group of three Arctic terns. They sold, he suggested, because he had underpriced them at about $100 each. His style, a synthesis of what he had learned at both schools, was set, and his success at the convention showed that it was a style that promised to gain wide acceptance.

5

While Peterson was learning his craft in art school, he was gradually becoming more independent. Because the subway ride to and from work was so long and tiring, he moved to the Harlem YMCA. Without any financial help from home, he was making ends meet by carefully budgeting the proceeds from his $17-a-week furniture-painting job. He wrote to his mother from the Harlem YMCA that he was cleaning his paintings so that he could use the canvases again. He also enclosed a weekly budget from his last year at the Art Students League. It was a tight budget with no room for anything but the essentials.

Room—$4.25
Food—$7.00
Tuition—$3.50
Coat check—$.10
Subway fare—$.70
Materials—$3.50
Added cost for bird trips—$.50 or more[1]

He was spending all of his free time observing birds in the New York City area. It was during these days that he fell in with the Bronx County Bird Club, a group of young amateur ornithologists, and with their mentor, Ludlow Griscom. Behind many of the accolades heaped upon Peterson toward the end of his career was the assumption that he had democratized the pastime of bird study. Without the Bronx County Bird Club and Ludlow Griscom, it's doubtful that he could have accomplished this.

About Griscom it can be said that he began the move in ornithology from the museum to the field and from systematics to ecology, that he changed an ornithologist's tool from a shotgun to a pair of field glasses, that he eased away the control of ornithology from rich, white males, and most significantly, that he prepared the world of bird study for Peterson's field guide. He did all this by developing a phenomenal skill at identifying living birds.

Before Griscom, the process of identification of birds involved first shooting the bird and then comparing its carcass to detailed descriptions that appeared in the principal bird books of the day—such as *Key to North American Birds,* by Elliot Coues, and Frank M. Chapman's *Handbook of Birds of Eastern North America.* Here is a description of a robin as found in Chapman: "Top and sides of the head black, a white spot above and below the eye; rest of the upperparts grayish slate-color; margins of wings slightly lighter; tail blackish, the outer feathers with white spots at their tips; throat white, streaked with black; rest of the underparts rufous."[2] Two things stand out. It isn't until near the end that he mentions the only field mark anyone needs to identify a robin. And such a description is obviously meant for a bird "in the hand"—a dead bird. Coues himself wrote, "The double-barreled shotgun is your main reliance. Under some circumstances you may trap or snare birds, catch them with bird-line, or use other devices, but such cases are the exceptions to the rule that you will *shoot* birds."[3]

Griscom was a prodigiously gifted individual who had mastered ten languages as a teenager and was being groomed for a career as a concert pianist. He was that sort of person who could have done nearly anything he wanted. But, like Peterson, he carried a passion for birds, so he turned to ornithology. He was able to learn all the specific descriptions in Coues and Chapman and, by watching birds in the field, decided which characteristics were the keys to identification, that is, the "field marks"—a phrase coined by Edward Forbush and featured in his *Birds of Massachusetts.* Armed with this information, Griscom "invented" the technique of field identification. He could identify a bird at a glance; he knew hundreds by their flight patterns alone. But he was more than proficient; he aggressively defended and demonstrated his skills, and he passed along his techniques to anyone willing to learn. Among those willing learners were Roger Tory Peterson and the other members of the Bronx County Bird Club.

The club was a small group of extraordinary kids from the Bronx who happened to be nuts about birds. Many of them—such as Joseph Hickey, Allan Cruickshank, Richard Herbert, Irving Kassoy, and William Vogt—went on to make significant contributions in the fields of nature study and ecology. In the 1920s, however, they weren't interested in museums or publishing in scientific journals; they just wanted to find and identify as many different species of birds as they could. The club was founded in the attic of John and Richard Kuerzi on 29 November 1924. John Kuerzi was elected chairman, whose duty it was to run the meetings. Joe Hickey, as secretary, had the most important job, that of keeping the bird records. Allen Thomas, who joined the group later, identified the main characteristics of the group as enthusiasm, cohesiveness, and a lack of rivalry. The young men were genuinely helpful, sharing their expertise gladly—the better to garner a larger list. Their approach to birdwatching was nothing less than revolutionary; no one had conceived of this quiet, staid hobby with its scientific overtones as a game, and an exciting one at that. They shared a couple of pairs of cheap binoculars. Their "field guide" comprised pages torn from a copy of E. H. Eaton's *Birds of New York State* they found in the trash and Chester A. Reed's *Bird Guide: Land Birds East of the Rockies*. They even pooled their money to buy an old Buick for chasing birds. They birded all through the Bronx—the borough still held marshes, large estates, and wooded parks in the 1920s—and raced anywhere birds could be found, including sewer outfalls and garbage dumps. As Peterson said, "We were addicted to the Hunts Point Dump, and one winter we found four snowy owls feeding on rats."[4] He was one of the two significant outsiders (the other was Ernst Mayr) accepted into the group—they called him Roger Tory Jamestown Peterson because he talked so much about the birds he had seen in his hometown. He had met Cruickshank in Van Cortland Park marsh when Cruickshank was looking for rail nests. The reeds parted, Cruickshank wrote, "and there knee-deep was the Big Swede."[5] Peterson began to attend the Linnaean Society meetings with Cruickshank and Hickey, and his birding allegiances shifted from Bernie Nathan to the Bronx County boys. And he began to feel at home. In a 1927 letter to friends back home in Jamestown, Peterson was able to enthuse expertly about hot birding spots in the Bronx as well as on Long Island and in New Jersey and all the other boroughs.

Ludlow Griscom was a perfect choice for a guide. Even so, Peterson soon became Griscom's near equal in quick field identification, which he explained as a split-second reaction. "We see a bird. With an instinctive movement we center it in our glass. All the thousands of fragments we know about birds—locality, season, habitat, voice, actions, field marks, and likelihood of occurrence—flash across the mirrors of the mind and fall into place—and we have the name of our bird."[6] Through discussions at bimonthly meetings of the prestigious Linnaean Society and during weekly field trips, Peterson proved that he was becoming exceptionally adept at the process he so insightfully described.

It was during these early New York City years that Peterson realized that bird-watching could also be an organized game, even a sport, with its competitions to see how many birds could be recorded in one day or to see who had the longest list. The huge event of every year was the Christmas Bird Count. A circle with a fifteen-mile diameter was imposed on all teams, but the Bronx Club actually observed in two circles and reported the best result. That something so scientifically useful could be just plain fun came as joyful knowledge to a young man whose life was so often conflicted. This is the man who once said that his mother's Lutheran influence gave him guilty feelings that he could never overcome but who would often call himself a hedonist.

A revealing image of Peterson at this time can be found in a memoir by Alexander Sprunt Jr., who later became a colleague at the Audubon Society. When Peterson finished the school year in 1927, he was completely broke; he had barely enough money to get home to Jamestown. But he had planned his first trip south—to see birds he had never seen before—and nothing could stop him. He found a job at a furniture shop in Yonkers, decorating end tables at a dollar apiece, eighty tables to be painted with roses and Chinese figures. Peterson rushed through the job and bought himself a round-trip ticket in steerage on the Clyde Line ship that ran from New York to Charleston, South Carolina. He had written to the noted ornithologist Arthur Trezevant Wayne, who lived outside of Charleston, and had been granted a visit. After a day's birding on Isle of Palms—where he saw few birds, got into ticks, and got soaked in a rainstorm—he walked the ten miles to Wayne's house, staying for three ecstatic days of bird discussion with a man he called "legendary."

Wayne put him in touch with the Charleston Museum, where Sprunt was preparing to leave with a colleague on a three-day boat trip to local nesting colonies on Bull Island, which later became the Cape Romain National Wildlife Refuge. The first morning, Peterson disappeared with one of the skiffs and didn't return until sundown, wet and hungry. Each day was the same, except that Sprunt saw to it that Peterson had food and dry clothing. "He lived in a sort of trance the entire time and after dinner usually sat on deck, staring with a rapt expression across the waters," Sprunt wrote. Peterson's childlike sense of wonder and joy can be seen in a postcard he wrote to his mother: "I saw wondrous numbers of rare waterbirds and took 43 pictures. Talk about birds!—all kinds of terns, willets, Oyster Catchers, Atlantic Skimmers, Snowy Egrets, Louisiana Herons, and everything."[7]

Sprunt was struck by Peterson's uncanny ability to be totally absorbed in his world, to live oblivious to discomfort and ordinary need. And Sprunt was perhaps the first to comment on the remarkably single-minded, obsessive behavior that would make such an undertaking as the first *Field Guide* possible while it made the simple daily tasks of living nearly impossible: "He knew he was living in a world where other men had some kind of place; they supplied his necessities for continued existence, but it was with birds that he was really living."[8] It was a trait that would continue, unchanged, throughout Peterson's life. Whether it was one of his three wives or a friend from the bird-watching world, he could always count on someone to help him get through the mundane.

This time also saw the beginnings of Peterson's environmentalist ethic, which, as with everything else in his life, began and ended with his love for birds. An example of its beginnings can be seen in a 1927 letter. In it, he tells of coming upon a sleeping northern saw-whet owl in a pine woods in New Jersey. He climbed the tree the owl was sleeping in and held the bird in his hand. When he came back with his camera two weeks later, both bird and habitat were gone: "The woods had been half cut down and six streets cut thru!" The episode reminded him of an earlier trip to the Great Kills marsh on Staten Island. He had been warned not to go there unaccompanied because it was "very treacherous." "I went anyway," he wrote. "Half way across the marsh, and still alive, I caught sight of something white among the reeds and on investigating I found a white post marked 'Lot 112—sold.' Further on among the rushes was a sign reading 'Brook Street' and in a pool of water still another; '12th Avenue'—such a world!"[1] More of a shrug than a polemic against habitat destruction, to be sure, but this early letter, written when he was eighteen, marks an awareness of the precarious state and future of his beloved birds. The progression from sighing "such a world!" to being a leader in the conservation movement would not be merely a matter of growing awareness and increasing involvement. The nature of Peterson's environmentalism was deeply felt, sometimes conflicted, and exclusively his own.

Early publications contain statements that mainline environmentalists would find difficult to accept. But Peterson was never one to follow a party line. He measured the health of the environment by the health of its bird populations and simply reported the news—good and bad.

The first of Peterson's published conservation articles appeared in the *New York State Bulletin* in April 1930. Under the ponderous title "An American Tragedy—A Plea for Our Birds of Prey," he sets out a strong anti-gunning stance based on dwindling raptor populations and public misinformation. Peterson's evidence for population loss is anecdotal and focuses on indiscriminate hunting. The public misinformation deals with distinguishing between "beneficial" and "harmful" hawks. Peterson points out that the beneficial hawks feed on rodents and therefore should be protected. The so-called harmful hawks are defended as predators, which actually strengthen game bird populations by weeding out the weak. Although Peterson accedes to the idea of "definitely harmful species" and his defense of them is deferential, his conclusion, although a bit overwritten, is strong: "If the grave misapprehension concerning these birds is not soon dispelled, there may come a time when the hooting and calling of owls will no longer sound from the woodlands; and the circling buteo, the dashing accipiter and the plunging falcon will be but a memory. If such time comes, no power on earth can bring them back."[2]

In February 1930, Peterson wrote his sister, Margaret, asking her to type a chapter of a book he was working on. That book was apparently put aside for work on the *Field Guide* or, more likely, it was a precursor, but part of the chapter found its way into a 1932 article, "Half a Mile Away." Margaret wrote back to say she had typed and enjoyed the chapter, and she made some suggestions. For stationery, she used the reverse side of Peterson's handwritten manuscript. Peterson had written, in part, "There are in all, about a dozen kinds of terns and a goodly number of gulls on our Atlantic coast. Not so long ago it was feared that the bird protectionist had come too late to save some of the species from complete extermination at the hands of the plume hunter. The situation was uncertain. The very marked increase in bird life in recent years, especially in the last decade, is certainly a fine tribute to the efforts of organized conservation to which wild life is always quick to respond. We can assume that the future of these most graceful of feathered creatures is now secure."[3] It was a device Peterson would often employ: to report good news about bird populations while maintaining an environmental tension by emphasizing that such news was gained only through diligent work.

Still incubating was the idea that would bring together so many of Peterson's conflicts: his love of painting and his father's desire that he "succeed," his passion for birds and his methodical nature, the contradiction implied in the phrase often used to describe him—"artist-naturalist." The idea must have been on his mind as he and other Bronx County Bird Club members raced from park to marsh to dump to beach, listing birds. Or when they tried to emulate Griscom's uncanny abilities. Or when they had to resort to Reed's *Bird Guide*. As valuable as they were, Chapman's book and Griscom's own *Birds of the New York City Region* were too big to be useful in the field. Reed's book was the most widely used guide before Peterson's. Originally published in 1906, it was small, checkbook-sized, and contained 208 of Reed's paintings, one species—a male in summer plumage—per page, along with a text that listed visual cues, songs, nest and egg information (egg collecting was still legal then), and range. Following the paintings, which were amateurish by today's standards and sometimes downright misleading, was a cumbersome "field key" that separated species by such categories as "birds proximately marked with blue" or "birds with red or orange markings." For what it was worth, Peterson had memorized the book by the time he was in high school, but he knew that for the general birder a new and better guide was needed. Yet it wasn't until he became a teacher that he knew he was the person to write it.

Knowing a great deal about a subject and having a desire and ability to impart that knowledge are two entirely different things. Until 1929, Peterson's nature study and bird-watching were largely self-serving. They provided a means for escape, an outlet for his competitive nature, a boost for his ego, and occupation for his active mind. Slowly, but significantly, the next five years began to change that.

Peterson began his teaching career in the summer of 1929 at a YMCA camp on Stony Lake, in Jackson County, Michigan. His official title was "nature study instructor." Inexperienced as he was, he knew enough to seek out advice, which came in a letter from Allan Cruickshank. Make it fun, play games, do hunting parties, and, above all, "don't get scientific."[1]

Some letters that he got after camp indicate that he did, indeed, make it fun and that he was well-liked. But he also made time to discover a new landscape. The area still had a bit of prairie, and Peterson was able to watch prairie chickens and establish the first documented breeding record in Michigan for the Wilson's phalarope by capturing a fledgling. At any rate, camp directors liked him well enough to offer him the job the following March. But it was too late. Peterson had already been hired as a counselor and nature study teacher at Camp Chewonki in Wiscasset, Maine, by its founder and director, Clarence Allen. The job came about in a way that would become a familiar pattern for Peterson; he was already on his way to developing a network that became legend in the world of natural history and environmentalism. He did this by being quietly aggressive in his pursuit of birds. While he was still in school, Peterson had written John Aldrich, then working at the Buffalo Museum of Science, asking to see the museum's bird collection. Aldrich was so impressed with Peterson's knowledge and enthusiasm that he recommended him for the nature counselor's job at Chewonki, which Aldrich had to leave.

Clarence Allen was a schoolmaster in the old tradition. He taught at the Country Day School for Boys of Greater Boston for nineteen years. In 1929 he became headmaster at Rivers School, another private day school, in Brookline. He was also a nature enthusiast. As he wrote in his letter hiring Peterson, "All outdoors is in fact our best museum . . . and the whole subject is my particular joy and hobby."[2] His love of the outdoors and his dedication to teaching young boys led him to found Camp Chewonki in northeastern New York State, on the shore of Lake Champlain. There were three counselors and fifteen boys in 1915, the camp's first year. Three years later, Allen bought 125 acres of woods, farmland, and saltwater marsh on Chewonki Neck in coastal Maine and relocated the camp. There the camp has grown impressively—in size and scope. Through a series of acquisitions and donations, Camp Chewonki, which became the nonprofit Chewonki Foundation in 1962, now owns most of the neck, about 400 acres. The original farmhouse, barn, outbuildings, and tents have developed into a campus that includes the huge Center for Environmental Education, the new C. E. Allen Natural History Center, a working saltwater farm, and an infrastructure carefully designed on environmental principles. Three counselors have become 110, supported by a year-round staff of 70. And even Clarence Allen would be overwhelmed by the camp's influence today. In addition to 475 summer campers, Chewonki runs a dozen wilderness experiences; The Center for Environmental Education works with 4,000 students, and 45,000 more in its traveling natural science programs.[3] This expansion is due to good leadership, generous contributors, and a shared vision. The vision was shaped, in part, by Roger Tory Peterson.

In the summer of 1930, Peterson went to work for Allen; what he accomplished there over the next five summers was nothing short of remarkable. Don Hudson, president of the Chewonki Foundation, asserts that Peterson gave the camp its current direction. The mission statement declares, in part, that Chewonki is "dedicated to helping people grow individually and in community with others by providing educational experiences that foster understanding and appreciation of the natural world." Although the statement was drafted in 1970, decades after Peterson's time at Chewonki, his influence on Clarence Allen and the drafters of the mission statement was always present. As Hudson put it, "the boys Peterson influenced became men who had influence, and they helped to insure an environmental legacy for Chewonki."[4] In the final analysis, Peterson helped turn Chewonki from a typical summer camp for boys into a powerful educational institution for the environment. In the early years, he did it without trying to; he did it by simply being himself.

His arrival at camp set the tone. After he managed to lose his train ticket when he stopped off on his way north to Maine to chase birds with Joe Hickey at a camp on the Hudson where Hickey was working, he immediately wired Clarence Allen: "If you want your camp naturalist, send me $39.40 for rail fare. I'm broke."[5] That was Peterson's version; in Allen's retelling, less compelling but probably accurate, the telegram was the same, but it came from Buffalo, New York. In yet another version, Peterson remembered that it was his uncle, not Allen, who cabled the money. Whatever the details, Peterson arrived at camp, exhausted after having walked six miles from the train station with his baggage because he lacked even a nickel to make a telephone call. His first night at camp was notable too. Eager to impress his fellow counselors and happy to find whip-poor-wills in the woods outside his cabin, he demonstrated his skill at whip-poor-will calling, which set off a chorus that lasted well past midnight.

In spite of its quirky beginning, a relationship between the two men began that grew over their lifetimes to a surrogate father-son relationship that Peterson honored by dedicating the *Field Guide* to Allen (with William Vogt). As the years passed, the two men shared a profound and mutual respect. As Allen would write later, "How little did I know that I had made the best investment of my life. The dividends were to be in lasting friendship with one of the world's kindest and most generous of men, acclaimed throughout the world and recognized for the four-fold genius that he is."[6] Alexander Maley, Peterson's close friend and another counselor, would later comment on Allen's influence and support: "Clarence Allen had the foresight to give Roger anything he wanted in the way of help and so on. . . . [He] took a profound interest in Roger and his field guide. He knew exactly what Roger was trying to get at. He recognized the value of it immediately."[7]

Although stories persist that Peterson was absent-minded and even had to be awakened to go to work each morning, former campers tell of different assigned activities that he prepared for his students each day. Beyond that, however, he had no teaching tricks; he simply went about doing what he wanted to do: watching and sketching birds, collecting moths, immersing himself in the Maine coast's natural environment. But he did it with such passion and focus that the campers were drawn to him, to the extent that all but one of the years he worked there they voted him the counselor who did most for the camp. Allen called Peterson "a pied piper":

> Boys gladly plugged along after him through swamps and thickets. Now they were explorers, new worlds opened up to them. Here was a vigorous leader, and bird-watching became a sport demanding sharp eyes and staying powers no less rigorous than that demanded by football. Following the new counselor up hill and over gullies, going up trees and up to your middle in swamps—that was man's work, and they soon found out that every foot of the way revealed something new.[8]

That learning from Peterson could be construed as sport was not a pedagogical trick; it was simply Peterson's gift. One of his campers during the early 1930s, Sinclair Hart, offers this persuasive appraisal of an effective teacher, unencumbered by artifice or pedagogy: "He was the epitome of the best in teaching, so inspired by his subject that it was infectious, and speaking to us, not as kids, but as if we were fellow specialists."[9] Bart Chapin, another camper from that era, characterized Peterson and his influence nicely when he remembered Peterson's total absorption with birds, which allowed him to be oblivious to discomfort and custom: "The intensity of his concentration on birds just absolutely paralyzed us kids. We used to have a Sunday service, and counselors in those days wore white sailor suits. After the service on one Sunday, we went by a pond to observe birds and he walked straight through the pond to the other side to see something. Your ordinary guy doesn't do that."[10]

When Maley and Peterson sat down to reminisce years later, they remembered how Allen challenged Peterson by his choice of Peterson's campers. Each counselor had four to six boys for the summer. One summer Peterson had a boy who was already an authority on grasshoppers, one who knew all the land snails by their scientific names, and the two Atkins brothers, who had memorized all three volumes of Forbush's *Birds of Massachusetts*. As Peterson said, "Clarence Allen had put all the sharks in my tent."[11]

Two issues of the 1933 *Chewonki Chronicle*, a camp newspaper, contain stories of typical Peterson-led field trips. On one trip, he and his students swam to an offshore island to watch birds. In the story about the second trip, a camper writes of studying birds and flowers at a turtle pond and, in obvious awe, of Peterson getting two "blood suckers" on his leg and refusing to take them off. Allen writes that Peterson's trips were vigorous and sometimes risky—but always popular. Nature study took its place beside athletic games as a preferred and respected activity. "The voting at season's end proclaimed 'nature' as the most popular activity," Allen recalled. "It had become just as respectable to win credits in nature as to win a tennis championship."[12]

On the campgrounds was an old chicken coop that John Aldrich had fitted out with shelves and cupboards and a north-light skylight. Peterson adopted it for his classroom, studio, and "nature museum." Here he kept specimens of wildflowers and such to talk about with his students. And here he painted. He did a portrait of an osprey that Allen commissioned to provide Peterson with a little extra money and that now hangs in Don Hudson's office. And most likely, he worked on some of the plates for the 1934 *Field Guide*.

Peterson remains a physical presence at Chewonki. Although the nature museum has been moved, it remains much as it must have been when Peterson taught and painted there. Electric lights and a green chalkboard are obvious changes, but a bleached set of moose antlers in the rafters, a stuffed osprey specimen on one of Aldrich's shelves, and a table by the door for the day's nature activity evoke the time when Peterson worked there. The Roger Tory Peterson Library of Natural History was dedicated in 1985 in a ceremony that Peterson attended. And when the new classrooms were built, the art and science rooms were deliberately situated side by side, in honor of Chewonki's artist-naturalist and his belief that those two areas of thought could be combined. As another lasting contribution, he designed and drew the logo for the Chewonki Foundation in 1983. These physical symbols acknowledge how the camp changed over the five years that Peterson was a counselor there and how it continued to change under his influence as a director of the Chewonki Foundation from 1964 to 1977 and as Allen's lifelong confidant.

Also significant is the change in Peterson over those years from 1930 to 1934—from a penniless kid to a member of the administrative staff of the National Audubon Society, with his first, and already successful, book in hand. It is simplistic to say that he grew up, yet that is indeed partly the case. His growing maturity can be seen in a letter he wrote back to a high school classmate, who wrote often from Jamestown. The friend's letters were immature and shallow, filled with puerile remarks about girls, booze, and small-town ennui. In one, he wrote Peterson about a vague desire to become an artist himself; Peterson's response shows the separation he had made from adolescence. "An artist's life," he advised, "is *not* the easiest life—It is perhaps the most marvelous life—It is a life that hurts—a continued groping for the unattainable."[13] Although Peterson's tone could be considered affected, even a bit sophomoric, there is no mistaking the earnestness and the wonder at finding a purpose in life: to be a serious artist and, as he discovered at Chewonki, to be a teacher.

Much of this maturity can be attributed to Clarence Allen and Chewonki. First came Peterson's health. He arrived at camp, according to Allen, "not particularly well." Peterson himself put his weight at 156 pounds. Two years of self-imposed deprivation as a student had taken their toll. The cure, of course, was food and fresh air—and Peterson's natural vitality. Next came, in Allen's words, "balance and polish which at that time was far from his thoughts."[14] Allen and his staff worked on Peterson's manners and dress, while introducing him to a circle of people who lived in ways the self-styled "hick" could only imagine. This education would continue at the Rivers School.

By the summer of 1931, Peterson realized that the deepening Depression was going to end his student and New York birding days. He needed a job. Deutsch Bros. had failed, and Peterson had landed a job decorating furniture for Jan DoRio, who allowed him to live in his apartment. But DoRio went under too, and Peterson was faced with the real possibility of having to return to Jamestown. Once again Clarence Allen, who was by this time headmaster at the Rivers School, lent a hand. The same intractable mind-set that created an educational system so inimical to Peterson's development would not recognize him as a teacher either. He failed at those measures that the system deems important; he never held a degree or earned a teaching certificate. He was a teacher of the purest definition: one who teaches. Recognizing this, Allen offered him a job teaching natural history and art—two courses apparently not "academic" enough to require teacher certification. It turned out to be a boon for both men.

Peterson received a small salary and weekday meals. Rivers was a day school, and Peterson and Alexander Maley lived on the deserted campus for free—Maley over the cafeteria and Peterson in a tiny room above the administration building. Moreover, Peterson received a time and place to work and grow. Evenings, he had begun work in earnest on the *Field Guide,* using specimens from the Boston Museum of Science and the Museum of Comparative Zoology in Cambridge. Eventually he showed Maley his work, of which the latter said, "The infinite capacity for taking pains was all there, and I marveled at the accuracy of both the black and white and water-colored pictures."[15] Days were filled with good teaching experiences, for the first time synthesizing and simplifying natural science for the inexperienced. Peterson enjoyed leading frequent field trips: to the woods around Brookline, to the ocean, and to the Brookline Botanical Gardens. He found a cache of mounted birds—including an Eskimo curlew and a heath hen—in an attic and commandeered an unused room for a museum. He brought live birds to class and told their stories as he had done at Chewonki. And he was a friend to his students, not being that far from his difficult high school days and his own reaction to the oppression of strict discipline. At the graduation ceremony of his last year at Rivers, Peterson was presented with a plaque with the following inscription: "Roger Tory Peterson—June 7, 1934. From the boys and masters of The Rivers School—A tribute to friendship, industry, and skill and an acknowledgement of our pride in 'A Field Guide To the Birds.'"

A peripheral, but important, benefit was the "balance and polish" that he had begun to attain at Chewonki. Rivers was basically a preparatory school for Harvard. Peterson admitted to his mother that he was settling in to become a "straight-laced New Englander" and wrote numerous letters home telling about sailing on huge yachts and dining in lavish mansions. He hoped, he wrote, that some of this would have an effect because "I could use a little polish."[16] And he had a plan, as he wrote to his sister. After bragging a little about his dinner with a millionaire in a house "like a castle," he admitted, "My interest in birds is the doorway to all these acquaintances. . . . That is why I make these trips—to keep myself before these big men. The money spent is really an investment."[17]

A former ambassador to Britain and one of the honorable players in the Watergate scandal, Elliott Richardson, later wrote of his time as Peterson's student: "I learned from him things about the linkage between vision and communication that have stayed with me ever since. Not only did he love the subjects he taught and take a personal interest in my schoolmates and me, but he also rejoiced in enlarging our knowledge and arousing our curiosity."[18] Peterson was teaching about more than birds and flowers and rocks; he was teaching awareness and cultivating an interest in the environment. And beyond painting and drawing, according to Richardson, his students were learning how to see and how to respond.

Allen got an excellent teacher indeed. In 1974, Richardson nominated Peterson for the Teacher of the Year award, given by the American Association of School Administrators to a teacher who had helped shape the career of a prominent American. Richardson once wrote, "He was . . . a wonderful teacher in the sense that he was able to communicate his enthusiasm and focus his art and interest on his students. I got a lot out of his teaching; much of it is hard to describe, but it had to do largely with increasing my capacity to observe."[19] And Richardson recognized that Peterson never stopped being a teacher:

> Roger Tory Peterson taught an ever-expanding classroom about much more than birds. He has made his fellow human beings aware of the ecosystem that we and other creatures inhabit together—and of the mutual dependency we and they share. What he has also taught us about the use of our senses, the role of our imaginations, and the love of beauty in all its forms will long be at the heart of his reverberating influence.[20]

In his remarks to the American Association of School Administrators, Richardson said,

> So I thank him for gifts to the eye, to the ear, and because of what he taught me about drawing and painting, to the hand. All of these are things that I have brought with me all my life, and I suppose it is fair to say that one of the things that has made it possible for me rather easily to adjust to pressures and changes in circumstances and the stresses of responsibility has been the fact that I have had the resources of a wider sense of my surroundings, and of the presence of nature that he gave me.[21]

During those teaching years, Peterson was on his way to becoming a professional gallery painter. Within a few years he would sign a contract with *Life* magazine for a ten-part series, including reproductions of his bird portraits. He was also climbing among the ranks of amateur ornithologists—already a respected member of the Linnaean Society in New York and soon to be elected to the prestigious Nuttall Ornithological Club in Boston. In the introduction to the *Life* series, the editors called him "one of America's most brilliant young ornithologists and bird painters." More importantly, he was pulling all of his training and knowledge together. He tells it this way: "I left New York in 1931 packing all the ingredients of my new synthesis: Seton's boy protagonist sketching stuffed ducks; Reed's rustic book; Forbush's felicitous paragraph heading [that is, 'field marks']; Griscom's attention to the unique combinations of features which identify almost every species at a distance."[1] Part of Peterson's creative gift was to call up the skills of synthesis he developed while growing up, skills that helped him recognize the possibility of these disparate elements taken together. To that he added his remarkable field skills and craftsmanship as a painter. All he needed was a push.

The push had come in December 1930. Peterson was returning from a Christmas Bird Count on the Hudson River with his friend William Vogt— a Bronx County Bird Club regular, a nature columnist, and the other person to whom the *Field Guide* is dedicated. Peterson had just identified an unseen flock of pine siskins overhead after having heard a tiny note barely audible to Vogt. The conversation turned to Peterson's dual talents—as an artist and as a birder—and Vogt suggested a book, a field guide. Peterson recalled, "As we walked back to the car we developed a plan. The illustrations would be simple and patternistic, rather like those sketches of ducks that Seton had drawn in *Two Little Savages*. It would concentrate on field marks, rather than full descriptions, and small arrows would indicate key points of identification."[2] It was an innovative system. Vogt guaranteed that he would find a publisher for the guide. Vogt tells the story this way:

> Roger Tory Peterson was, at that time, in his early twenties and, largely without teachers, had developed a skill in bird identification that was unmatched except among a few ornithologists twice his age. . . . On this particular December morning I was again impressed by his expertness. . . . 'Roger,' I said to him, 'you know more about identifying the birds of this region than almost anyone else, and you can paint. Why don't you pass on your knowledge to other people in a book?' . . . 'Nobody knows me,' he objected. 'Who'll buy the book if I write it?' I finally guaranteed him, with no justification whatever, that if he would do the book I would get it published.[3]

In 1931, Vogt took Peterson to his first speakeasy for a meeting he had arranged with Richard Westwood, then editor of *Nature*. Peterson had written a query letter to Westwood in which he proposed a series of three articles—about ducks, gulls and terns, and shorebirds—that would make long-range bird identification easier than ever before. He promised to outline and illustrate species "differentiations," some discovered by himself. To sell his idea, he told Westwood that copies of the magazine containing the articles "would be permanently preserved by bird students."[4] As references he listed Vogt and the bird painter Bruce Horsfall. The letter was quite accomplished for one so new at the game of publication, and Vogt's experienced hand is likely here. The letter and the meeting worked in that Peterson was contracted to do a piece on gull identification.

Nature published the article, titled "Half a Mile Away: Field Characteristics of Eastern Gulls," in February 1932. Peterson followed a brief introduction with descriptions of field marks of thirteen gull species, along with illustrations of ten of them. It was a dry run for the *Field Guide*—both the language and the plates were changed little for the first edition.

In the introduction to "Half A Mile Away," he set forward a premise that reflects his lifelong practice of emphasizing good news, especially as it concerned bird populations. For this particular piece, he wrote that gull populations were responding to "organized conservation" as "wild life is always quick to do."[5] As a result, bird observers "will accept the challenge of this increase in individuals and species"—and so the appropriateness of his article.

More importantly, he debuted the Peterson system, which makes gull identification easy even "half a mile away." He used Edward Forbush's "field mark" descriptions to call attention to a few definitive physical characteristics for each gull. The kittiwake, for example, has black legs, unlike other gulls with similar plumages. And the black wing tips are perpendicular to the axis of the wing, "as if they had been dipped in ink."[6] Remembering only these two field marks clinches identification. The "dipped in ink" simile serves as a mnemonic device, a technique that Peterson often found useful in his field guide texts. The black-and-white "diagrams" are abstracted—no attempt at realism such as feathers or shading—just indications of coloration that differentiate individual species. And the plates were patternistic, each species placed in the same posture to invite easy comparison.

At Vogt's suggestion, Peterson sent the pieces that Westwood didn't want to *Field and Stream,* which accepted all three in the series: how to identify bay ducks, marsh ducks, and sea ducks on the wing and at a distance. This was a different sort of venture in that Peterson's audience in *Nature* was already interested in bird study. All he had to do was convince them of the value of his system. Since *Field and Stream* was a sportsman's magazine, Peterson was faced with the task of making hunters eager to identify their game before they shot it.

In "Sea Ducks," he used carefully contrived persuasion. In his discussion of scoters—or, as they were known to hunters, "seacoots"—he derides their taste while he allows that they provide "a good deal of real sport." But if "as some folk think," waterfowl will eventually succumb to "the march of civilization and its destructive agencies," scoters will outlast all the other species. "Deliver us," he pleaded, "from the day when coot-hunting will be all that we have left!"[7] This hook in place, he went on to say that only time and observation will tell if present game laws will suffice to keep native game birds at the desired numbers. And observation won't mean much "unless we know our ducks." It was a pragmatic argument; Peterson was learning how to hold an audience for his message.

In "Marsh Ducks," the second of the series, he went a step further: he actually posed as a duck hunter. In an unpublished memo written in 1975, he wrote, "I myself have never been a duckhunter. I think ducks have enough problems without me." Yet there he was in October 1932 writing, "My old 12-gauge means about twice as much to me since I have learned to tell what I am shooting, and spotting a protected bird before I pulled the trigger has on several occasions saved me some awkward explanations to the game warden. Not so very long ago a wealthy New Englander paid more than $1,000 for some eiders he had taken!"[8]

Peterson showed in "Bay Ducks" that he could use flashy prose to sell a piece. The beginning is novelistic: "The northeaster had hammered every long line of rain into an icy blade of steel. Three pairs of socks, and rubber boots could scarcely fight off the chill that started at our raw noses and seeped downward. The bag had been fair, but nothing to boast about." He introduces his character, a "bayman without peer," and tries his hand at dialect as the bayman says, "Them's bluebills an' a few springs. An' that leetle feller skinnin' across in front of 'em—that's a greebee." Peterson eventually makes the point that the bayman's skills aren't that impressive; anyone can identify ducks at a distance because "every species carries its 'identification tag' on its wings."[9]

Whatever Peterson had to do to sell these pieces, he had a good reason: to keep protected and restricted species safe. And the essence of each article was Peterson's descriptions of the field marks of each species. He was clearly in the process of working out his method; some sentences would appear word for word in the 1934 edition of the guide, while others were amended. The illustrations carry the influence of Ernest Thompson Seton but look ahead to the small refinements that would be made in the next two years. As Peterson

ROGER TORY PETERSON

wrote later, "Although my drawings in *Field and Stream* were very archaic and crude, the idea was there."[10]

Like all really good ideas, it was simple, effective, and genuinely new. Of all his many friends, perhaps his oldest friend, Clarence Beal, knew Peterson best. From the beginning Peterson "had an active mind, frequently surprising me with the well planned thought which emerged while he was hiking," Beal wrote. "There is often a touch of the dramatic in his organization of facts; he senses truths which others may overlook."[11] This ability to think about factual things creatively, to combine his analytic and intuitive sides, made the *Field Guide* possible. As his old Bronx County friend Allen Thomas wrote, "Roger's invention is so well established that people writing field guides apparently think it always existed—they do not realize that it burst forth from the brain of one man."[12]

1934

The *Field Guide*, First Edition

Much has been written about the originality of the system that the *Field Guide* introduced to bird study, about its remarkable success and influence, and about how its publication changed Peterson's life so dramatically and thoroughly. But often ignored is the prodigious amount of work it took to finish it: three years of intense effort, often under circumstances that would have put off a less passionate and less focused writer. "It was a labor of love for the most part," Peterson would later write, "the kind of task anyone devoted to an esoteric calling might take on for his fraternity's sake."[1] Just how much love was involved can be gauged by the size of the undertaking.

The book describes nearly five hundred species of birds. Each description includes field marks of breeding plumages, winter or immature plumages, and often subspecies and color-phase plumages. It also describes characteristic behavior and concludes with ways to distinguish the bird from similar species. Only the field marks that can be seen at a distance (with field glasses) are given, and only those that are diagnostic. The result is a pared-down synthesis, pages of notes on each entry reduced to fewer than twenty lines. The first bird in the book, the common loon, gives a good sense of how each bird is treated:

> Size of a small Goose (28–36). *Breeding plumage:*—Head and neck glossy black with white collar; back checkered with black and white; under parts white. Adult in black and white plumage unmistakable. *Winter plumage:*—Mostly grayish; top of head, back of neck, and back dark gray; cheek, throat, and under parts white. In flight Loons appear like big Mergansers with legs trailing out behind but with much slower wing-beats than any Duck. On the water they appear to be long-bodied, low-lying birds. Sometimes they swim with only the head and neck above water. They somewhat resemble the Cormorants at a distance. A Cormorant would be much blacker than a Loon, especially in winter, and in flight the longer neck and tail and

faster wing-beats are quite evident. The cormorant swims with its bill pointed slightly upward at an angle.[2]

Having differentiated it from cormorants in the description, Peterson separates it from the less common red-throated loon at the end of that loon's description: "The bill of the Red-throat is more slender and seems to be slightly *upturned,* a character that is apparent at a considerable distance. The bill of the Common Loon is stouter and straighter. Another good point is the snaky profile of the present species."[3]

Of course Peterson knew much, if not all, of this already, but he also knew that his "fraternity" would closely scrutinize every word he wrote. The work entailed much more than "passing on your knowledge to other people in a book," as Vogt put it. Peterson conducted his research through four sources: museums, living birds, ornithology books, and other scientists.

He studied specimen skins. Luckily, he had close access to two fine collections near where he was living at Rivers School. And stories about his room, littered with notes and drawings and stuffed birds, indicate that he had borrowing privileges. But since these were "birds in the hand," most details wouldn't qualify as field marks. This made the second approach, ongoing fieldwork, a necessity. As much as possible, he had to observe each species carefully in the wild—to check his impressions and examine his conclusions.

His third approach entailed researching the literature. In his preface, he names fifteen sources, all of them systematic (bird-by-bird) discussions of either regional birdlife such as Chapman's *Handbook of Birds of Eastern North America* or bird groups such as Arthur Cleveland Bent's *Life Histories of North American Birds.* These were the classic works of ornithological study, whose information was invaluable but whose method Peterson wanted to avoid. The closest of them to Peterson's *Guide* was Ralph Hoffmann's *Guide to the Birds of New England and Eastern New York.* It was the first *field* guide. In addition to the usual descriptions, it had an identification system based on what Hoffmann called keys. These were a combination of field marks, behavior, and habitat that led to identification. The process was somewhat slow and cumbersome, but it was accurate. It paid more attention to field marks than the others, and Peterson relied on it heavily. His own copy of Hoffmann shows how

Peterson used these books. He underlined useful sentences, and his handwritten comments range from "cocking tail at an angle and dropping it" next to the hermit thrush entry, to "check museum" next to a swallow description, to a cryptic "?" beside the myrtle warbler. Each reference book, one assumes, was consulted in a similar way.

Finally, Peterson relied on the extensive network of fellow bird students that he had been building since his teenage years and his founding of the Nature Correspondence Association. Much of this was done informally with such important bird students as S. Gilbert Emilio, John Kuerzi, Joseph Hickey, and Alexander Sprunt. Formal examinations of the manuscript were provided by John May for hawks and owls, Charles Urner for waterbirds, Francis Allen, who was his general editor, and, of course, Ludlow Griscom.

All of this preparation applied to the illustrations as well. Each of the five hundred species is pictured, some in more than one plumage. The publishers wrote that the book "recognizes the fact that color-values rather than the actual colors are most important in identifying birds at a distance."[4] His black-and-white plates were drawn in a water-soluble medium, Chinese ink. The four color plates were painted with opaque watercolors. Then he hand-lettered the names of the birds and added another innovation: arrows that pointed to the most important diagnostic field marks mentioned in his descriptions of the passerine birds.

Peterson described his living quarters at Rivers as "cubbyhole size, about six by eight feet, with one window and two small lights."[5] Here he worked on the *Guide* for three years, except for occasional nights when Clarence Allen let him use the headmaster's office. The picture is compelling: Peterson as a young man in his early twenties returning every night from teaching and preparing the next day's classes to a tiny, cluttered room, then picking up where he left off the night before, working his way through the *AOU Check-list* species by species, synthesizing all that information and distilling it into a few sentences for each entry.

Peterson had prepared his duck descriptions for his 1932 *Field and Stream* series. But he continued to tinker with the text. As an example, the 1932 text for the American eider (now common eider) begins: "The eiders are among the most strictly maritime of all the ducks, rarely occurring far away from the rocky Northern coasts.

They are large and heavily built, and their flight, like that of the scoters, is sluggish and low over the water."[6] In 1934, he added: "The head is rather low-hung, and the birds often progress with alternate flapping and sailing. No other Duck flies like them."[7] The brief description of the male and female went unchanged except for the addition of his most useful word, "only," to the description of the male: "The only Duck with a black belly and a white back." In his closing observations, he deleted a comparison with the profiles of redheads and canvasbacks, saying that the eider had the canvasback profile. It is clear that a field guide is never finished. Peterson was able to add new observations, clarify passages, and remove unnecessary or confusing detail right up until press time. It was a process that would continue, unabated, through five editions and over six decades.

The illustrations were improved after the *Field and Stream* series as well. By 1934, Peterson had devised the now-familiar design of a male and female of a species flying in close formation, wings horizontal to suggest soaring. In 1932 he had drawn the ducks singly, with the wings beating—an awkward posture that gave the birds a hunched over and cramped appearance and obscured one of the wings. The new posture allowed him to repeat the wing patterns, which reinforced the field marks while giving a more satisfying, balanced appearance.

It was a labor of love indeed. That he was sustained by his passion for birds—and by his new passion for teaching about birds—is clear. But perhaps as much, he knew he had something extraordinary—a bird book, as the dust jacket declared "on a new plan." The "new plan," of course, comprised the descriptions of field marks, the schematic illustrations, the arrows—all intended to streamline identification.

In his "How to Use This Book" section, Peterson writes about what he calls "identification by elimination," reminding the reader that a given bird species is likely to be seen only during a particular season or in a particular region. Peterson applied this principle to his descriptions as well, where he makes effective use of the word "only." The magpie, he writes, is the "only large black and white bird with a long, sweeping tail." The yellow warbler is the "only small bird in the field that appears to be all yellow." The barn swallow is "the only native Swallow that is really 'Swallow-tailed.'" He makes good use of simile as well. The piping plover's back is pale, "like the sun-bleached, dry sand." The whip-poor-will "flits away like a large brown moth." And other times he is just plain terse. The robin is "the one bird that everyone knows," and the crow "needs no description."

This economy of language carries over to an economy of line in Peterson's illustrations—in spite of his training as a realist at the Art Students League and as a traditionalist at the National Academy of Design. The drawings "are calculated to simplify things a good deal," he wrote to Ludlow Griscom. "They are not pictures or portraits but pattern charts devoid of feathering and modeling, making possible quick easy comparison of the species that are most apt to be confused with each other."[8] Here the scientist in Peterson trumped the artist, although he would later claim to regret it: "I shudder every time I look at that first edition. The drawings are horrible—crowded, hunched-up little figures. I added plates in 1939 and spent a full year revising the *Guide* after the war, but I was never really satisfied."[9] The illustrations were never intended to be any more than teaching devices. Devoid of distractions such as modeling or settings, they were true to their source: Ernest Thompson Seton's schematic drawings of ducks, which Peterson remembered from his childhood. The twenty-six black-and-white plates, which Peterson often characterized as "simple-minded and crude," were, in reality, abstract and simple. His one concession to verisimilitude was to imply setting through posture: ducks float in midair, warblers perch on the idea of branches, hawks soar, herons stand. Yet even though these images represent birds more than they resemble them, the plumage patterns that distinguish each species are clear. The four color plates are, indeed, simple. Peterson painted them on a gray board with opaque watercolors so the gray wouldn't leak through into the plumage. The birds are tiny (the warblers are barely an inch from beak to tail), crowded (one warbler page has twenty-two species), and two-dimensional. But they are accurate; a careful observer with a pair of binoculars and those pages could identify any warbler in breeding plumage.

Finally came what was perhaps Peterson's most effective contribution to quick and simple field identification: the arrows. They direct the observer immediately to those distinctive field marks that clinch an identification. And each mark's label is hand-lettered

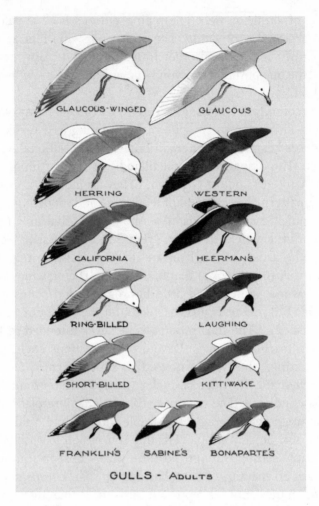

GLAUCOUS-WINGED   GLAUCOUS

HERRING   WESTERN

CALIFORNIA   HEERMAN'S

RING-BILLED   LAUGHING

SHORT-BILLED   KITTIWAKE

FRANKLIN'S   SABINE'S   BONAPARTE'S

GULLS - Adults

Gull plate from the first Western Guide, 1941.

on the plate. On the flycatcher plate, for example, the wood pewee gets two arrows—one for "wing bars" and one for "no eye ring." The phoebe next to it gets one labeled "no wing bars." No other information is necessary if you know that the bird in question is a flycatcher.

Beyond these innovations was the remarkable new balance that Peterson was attempting: between beginning and advanced bird students and, by extension, between the science of ornithology and the new sport of bird-watching.

10

William Vogt deserved receiving his dedication for more than merely urging the book on Peterson. He was a help throughout its writing as well. In a letter during the early stages of the *Guide*'s writing, he reminded Peterson of the nature of his audience:

> Remember, a great many of the people who will buy it will no[t] know a warbler from a sparrow or ducks from geese or coots. If you are going to have any sale for the book . . . you must make it valuable for beginners as well as for those who know a good deal. In other words, make it elementary—but also include such good material on difficult birds that no one in the East who seriously studies birds will be able to get along without it. . . . Don't write it only for Linnaean members. There are too few of them![1]

Peterson surely had this in mind in the four-page piece called "How to Use This Book." In it he refers to part of the book's new plan. Rather than describing and illustrating species in taxonomic order as all earlier bird books did, he grouped similar birds to simplify identification. He invites beginners to examine the illustrations generally:

> The briefest examination of the plates will be sufficient to give the beginner an idea of the shapes of our birds and the groups to which they belong. Birds of a kind—that is, birds that could be confused—are grouped together where easy comparison is possible. Thus, when a bird has been seen in the field, the observer can immediately turn to the picture most resembling it and feel confident that he has reduced the possibilities to a few species in its own group.[2]

A page of careful and basic instruction follows in which Peterson explains how to use the plates and the text. He then takes a beginner through a step-by-step identification of a red-breasted merganser to illustrate the Peterson system. That is followed, however, by a turn to his other audience: "Far from helping only the beginner who can scarcely tell a Gull from a Duck, it is hoped that the advanced student will find this guide comprehensive enough to be of service in recognizing those accidentals or rarities that sometimes appear in the territory he knows so thoroughly."[3] To this end Peterson turned to, among others, his friend and mentor Ludlow Griscom for a critique of the manuscript. Griscom gave his initial blessing, but a letter to Peterson as he was preparing for the second edition reveals what Peterson was up against among the scientists in his audience. After a couple complimentary paragraphs, Griscom added these three "general suggestions":

> 1. You are obviously weakest on those birds with which you have had inadequate personal experience in the field. You might even consider the possibility or advisability of having some experienced expert prepare the text for such groups. 2. You are exceedingly erratic and inconsistent in your treatment of immature plumages. If you reflect on it, you will find that quite a list of birds of eastern North America apparently don't have an immature plumage, according to your text. 3. The major fault of your guide is over-simplification of the identification of many difficult groups.[4]

What Griscom, as bird-watcher rather than professional ornithologist, thought of the book, however, is revealed in a story reported by William Davis in his biography of Ludlow Griscom: "Fred M. Packard, a protégé of Griscom, remembers the incident: 'I have a fond memory of a trip to Plum Island, shortly after Roger's first guide appeared, when he and Ludlow got into a hassle about the field marks of some bird before us. Finally, in fury, Ludlow reached in his pocket, handed Roger a copy of the guide, and snorted, 'Here, look it up for yourself.'"[5]

It should be pointed out, parenthetically, that Griscom had nothing but praise for the revised *Guide* that came out in 1947: "I am enormously impressed with the caliber of the new book. It will be immeasurably superior to the last one and commands my unbounded admiration and respect."[6] The point is, however, that Peterson's two sets of readers were so far apart that they seemed almost to ask the impossible—keep it simple; don't simplify. In a reflective piece from 1989, Peterson was perhaps responding to the difficulty and demands of this task when he wrote, "He [Griscom] was in the hallowed halls of academia at Harvard, while I was just a teacher who wanted to help neophytes."[7]

But Peterson considered himself an ornithologist as well as a teacher, and he clearly was struggling with how the recreational element of bird-watching related to serious bird study. Having chosen to create a new community of avid amateurs, what now?

His deferential apology to the scientists betrays a lack of confidence probably appropriate and certainly understandable for a twenty-five-year-old newcomer trying to break into the ranks of such a traditional and conservative field as ornithology. After all, he had recently been blackballed for membership in the prestigious Nuttall Ornithological Club because he was brash and cocky about his records. "Field birding," he wrote in the 1934 edition, "as most of us engage in it is a game—a most absorbing game. . . . Old-timers minimize the scientific value of this type of bird work. Truly, it is but little. Recognition is not the end and aim of ornithology, but is certainly a most fascinating diversion—and a stage through which the person who desires to contribute to our knowledge of ornithology might profitably pass."[8] This is clearly a sop to that group of scientists that he often referred to—with a purposeful edge—as the "old-timers."

However, this brief nod to the past didn't mean Peterson was backing away from his system or from the importance of fieldwork. Nor could he accept the frightening thought of the growing numbers of bird students all blazing away with shotguns just to satisfy old-time ornithology's need for certainty of identification: "Doubting Thomases need but take a few trips afield with some of our present-day experts in field identifications . . . to realize the possibility of quickly identifying almost any bird, with amazing certainty, at the snap of a finger. It is but a matter of seeing a bird often enough and knowing exactly what to look for, to be able to distinguish, with a very few exceptions, even the most confusing forms."[9] This doesn't imply that collection isn't an essential part of bird study. Peterson had collecting permits himself for several states, and in the second entry in the *Guide*, the Pacific loon, he inserts an admonition that he would use whenever necessary: "*Winter plumage*—As it is so similar to the other Loons at this season, it should be recorded only if collected." But for the most part, one must simply be cautious and highly skilled and follow the Peterson system. He wraps up the "How to Use This Book" essay on this note: "There is no reason why we should not trust our eyes—at least after we have acquired a good basic knowledge of the commoner species. Caution should be the keynote."[10]

11

William Vogt, as he promised, began to peddle Peterson's manuscript, but he was rebuffed. With all of its plates, the book would be expensive to produce; there was a depression on; and it probably wouldn't sell very well. In his *New York Times Book Review* article, Vogt said he took it to "virtually every well-known publisher in New York." In a letter to Peterson, Vogt told him that Putnam had turned them down and that he wanted a typed copy and some sample drawings to show other publishers. Then he heard from John B. May, state ornithologist of Massachusetts, that a Houghton Mifflin senior editor, Francis Allen, was an accomplished amateur ornithologist. Vogt sent Allen the manuscript, and according to Vogt, the acceptance came the next day by Western Union. It is doubtful that the manuscript was accepted overnight, but Paul Brooks, who was a junior editor at the time, points out two editorial reports that indicate that Houghton Mifflin was immediately interested. Brooks himself wrote, "I think I am in a fairly good position to look at this book from the point of view of a beginner. . . . It seems to me an excellent job." He anticipated "a moderately good sale." Francis Allen saw the book as "conceived on entirely new lines. . . . It is a book that would appeal not only to beginners but to the more advanced ornithologists and I think will prove practically indispensable to students of birds in the field."[1]

Peterson's version of the publication of the *Guide* is quite different—and more colorful. After four New York publishers turned the manuscript down, Peterson and May took it to Allen, believing that Vogt had written a letter of support. In fact, Peterson recalled, the letter hadn't arrived, but Allen liked the idea. To see if it worked, they brought in Ludlow Griscom, who was shown Peterson's plates from across the room. He identified the birds pictured with 100 percent accuracy, and the deal was sealed.

The deal was that Peterson got no royalties from the first thousand sold of a first run of two thousand copies. But he accepted gladly because, as he wrote later, "like many a teacher, I was enthralled at the prospect of becoming an author."² He remembered the joy of seeing a display of his new book in a bookstore window in Cambridge. Making money on the book was well beyond his dreams.

To everyone's amazement, all two thousand copies sold almost immediately, and the second printing continued to sell. Peterson can claim the greatest reason for this success: he had written a good book. Reviews were favorable and enthusiastic. The most important review for sales was in the *New York Herald Tribune*. In it, Lewis Gannett wrote:

> Of all the new books published to date this year the one I feel sure will be remembered a decade hence is Roger Tory Peterson's *A Field Guide to the Birds*. There are good new novels every year, every month, perhaps every week; a good bird book comes once in ten or twenty years. . . . It is a simple book, but far from an amateur job. . . . Mr. Peterson has had the aid of . . . experienced field observers. . . . He writes and draws not as one who has studied dead bird skins or mounted corpses, but as a watcher on the beach and in the field. . . . I predict a long life and many editions of this new book.³

Peterson was quick to express his appreciation in a letter to Gannett: "My *Field Guide to the Birds* is now in its second printing. The first was exhausted in a little over three weeks, due, I suspect, largely to your review!"⁴

Also important—to Peterson and to book sales—was the reaction of his peers. The book was as well-received in ornithological journals as in the popular press. The *Auk,* the journal of the American Ornithologists' Union and the most prestigious journal of the ornithological community, was properly restrained but laudatory:

> Many of our popular books have . . . added notes on 'field characters' to the time-honored detailed descriptions of specimens 'in the hand,' but the art of field identification which has been brought to such a high stage of perfection by our leading

field students has not been given the attention to which it is entitled. Mr. Peterson, in the little book before us, attempts to supply this lack and with notable success. . . . On the general conception of the work and its admirable consummation we heartily congratulate him. We feel sure that a proper use of the volume will make for more accurate identifications and the elimination of many errors that undoubtedly result today from the sight records of over zealous field ornithologists.[5]

In his capacity as chairman of the Massachusetts Audubon Society, Francis Allen reviewed the book in the *Massachusetts Audubon Bulletin*. He considered the *Guide* in terms of Frank M. Chapman's classic *Handbook of Birds:*

This book thus covers the same area as Chapman's famous "Handbook," and it makes an *indispensable* complement to the Handbook, or any other bird book, for any one who would learn in the shortest possible time how to identify our Eastern birds in the field. We have not the slightest hesitation in using that word "indispensable," for while many field ornithologists have become expert without it hitherto, it has been only by patient and long-continued observation on their own part, aided by scraps of information picked here and there from other observers and from printed sources. But here we have the combined knowledge of some of our best field men, who give unsparingly of their advice to the author-artist, himself an observer of experience and skill.[6]

As any invaluable reference tool does, the *Guide* provided a reliable shortcut for a knowledgeable reader, and, at the same time, it helped a beginner to begin. Recognizing this, Allen concluded by recommending the book to *all* bird students, beginners and experts alike.

In a review in *Bird-Lore*, Frank Chapman praised the book as well: "To produce a work of this kind requires keen discrimination and sympathetic observation, field experience with birds and birdmen, and exceptional skill as a draughtsman. These qualifications are all possessed by Mr. Peterson. He has done a fine job."[7] Chapman went on to say that "nowhere will the novice find better training or less sparing discipline" and goes on to point out how Peterson had identified and addressed a new *community* of bird students. Whereas shotgun ornithologists worked alone, field observers seek out companionship. *Bird-Lore* was aimed at that audience who understood that one element of birding could be what Peterson called "a most absorbing game." It promoted Christmas counts and encouraged competitions such as "big days," in which groups of bird listers vied to record the most species within a twenty-four-hour period. Chapman concluded, "If he goes no further he has made friends among both birds and men who will add endlessly to the joy of life. But he has gone further. He has contributed to a fund of information which becomes cumulatively more valuable."[8]

Thus a range of audiences, from tyro to master, was advised to buy the book. And they did. Peterson and his system had successfully achieved the desired balance that would ensure remarkable sales. However, to understand this success, the timing of the *Guide*'s publication must be viewed in the larger scope of its era.

More than satisfying a wide readership of bird-watchers, the *Field Guide* helped engender a shift in cultural paradigms. In the midst of a turn-of-the-century debate over the killing of birds for study, a noted ornithologist, P. M. Silloway, asserted, "It is the mission of lower animal life to minister to the gratification of the higher. This law of nature is enumerated in the Great Book and has ever been the basis of man's dealings with inferior creatures."[9] Eighty years later, Peterson offered the opposing view: "You come to see not only birds but also other animals and their patterns of life, not just as extensions of human existence but as individuals in their own right. . . . Each individual does its own unique thing, with a right to live, not because it fulfills some human purpose, but for itself alone."[10] Arguably, the bridge between these two statements, between shotgun ornithology and ecology, manifest destiny and environmentalism, conservation and preservation, was built by the 1934 publication of the *Field Guide*. The time was right. Shortly after the publication of the *Guide*, Chapman told Peterson that he had planned to do a pocket guide with Louis Agassiz Fuertes. And John Baker said he wanted to do one but didn't carry through because he wasn't an artist. "It was a refrain," wrote Peterson, "I was to hear several times from other top birders."[11]

The idea seemed to be in the air. As naturalist and author John Yrizarry pointed out, Henry Hill Collins had self-published a small pamphlet about pairs of birds whose identification was easily confused. Interestingly, the pamphlet, which appeared in 1931, used arrows to point to diagnostic field marks on its cover illustration.[12]

The two terms "conservationist" and "preservationist" are often interchanged, and both are often applied to Peterson. In the years just before 1934, they were politicized, black and white. It was a time of awakening to the unspeakable damage that had been done to the land in the name of progress and manifest destiny. Conservationists sought the most efficient use of the land; their motive was economic. Theodore Roosevelt's director of the United States Forest Service, Gifford Pinchot, pressed for a more scientific and less rapacious attitude toward the natural world. On the other hand, preservationists, led by John Muir, wanted wild America set aside and protected for its intangible values—as an antidote to the stress of the modern world. Regardless of the camp one chose, a new way of perceiving the environment was emerging: the environment mattered.

For the first time, Americans were beginning to realize, whether prompted by Pinchot's rationalism or Muir's emotion, a need to consider the nonhuman world. And the *Guide* would serve both sides—it was a book of science and methodology, while simultaneously reaching a less scientifically inclined audience that would enjoy what Peterson called a "most fascinating diversion." Looking back on the influence of his *Field Guide*, Peterson would say that it transformed bird study from "an arcane preoccupation of a few academics and wealthy eccentrics to the favorite pastime for millions."[13] His ability to synthesize the opposing attitudes of science and recreation in one book proved a major factor in its brilliant success. Another reason was his fortunate timing.

Americans in 1934 were, for the most part, broke and unhappy. In March 1933, President Roosevelt had closed the country's banks to clear the way for the Emergency Banking Act. The Federal Emergency Relief Administration had funded $500 million in relief in May of that year. To bridge the awful winter of 1933–1934, the Civil Works Administration provided jobs for more than four million people. It is difficult to imagine that *any* book would be successfully launched at such a time, to say nothing of a guide for an activity that Peterson, in his introduction, called a game.

On the other hand, that same year saw continued success of the new advertisement-laden and sumptuous *Fortune* magazine. Clearly the Depression was a capricious thing, as some sectors of the economy flourished while many suffered miserably. And even though the *Guide*'s first-edition audience was small, the quick sellout of the first run indicated an audience of more than "a few academics and wealthy eccentrics."

In a 1980 essay, Peterson reflected on his book's unlikely success: "Actually hard times may have helped sales to people who weren't completely strapped. Here was a book, priced at $2.75, which would serve the reader for more than a few leisure hours. It would be useful in the field for many days, maybe years, at no additional cost. People had time on their hands, and I think many of them turned to birding as a good way to spend it."[14]

Other factors may have weighed in also. For a group of people interested in the natural world (and who might be considered a bit genteel), financial poverty might not have been the only thing to escape. A cultural poverty grew up during the Depression as well. American radio, at first a boon to listeners, quickly turned to the lowest common denominator. Tasteless advertisements crowded out programming; on WJR in Detroit, for example, a forty-five-minute block of time might contain as many as thirty commercials. New programming, in the pursuit of listeners, abandoned the lofty standards of earlier radio.[15] The other major source of popular entertainment, talking movies, was no better, as films were mass-produced with little thought given to merit. The thirties were a decade when materialism and consumerism, in spite of the shaky economy, triumphed over taste, when technology replaced art as the highest form of expression. In fact, the age of Sinclair Lewis's Babbitt and H. L. Mencken's "booboisie" spawned a two-sided cultural revolution into which Peterson's *Guide* fit perfectly. On one hand, the revolution was a populist one: it rejected the notion of intellectual and cultural superiority. With the help of the new bird guide, all Americans could enjoy bird study, a pastime formerly reserved for wealthy white males. But technology's dominance also created a mass culture that quickly sank into a vulgarity, sameness, and triviality that didn't include those interested in a quiet and often meditative pastime such as observing birds. For this group, the *Guide* was a benign technology that became a gateway to an activity that was fun and satisfying without the shallow gratification of mass media and technological gadgetry. As Peterson put it, "Man lives in a kind of gadget world. . . . It confuses him. . . . Through the study of bird ecology man finds he has his own ecology and begins to recognize forces and influences that play upon him. Interest in wildlife may be the salvation of man in a world he fails to understand."[16]

The result of these many factors was an initial success of the *Guide* that provided the momentum that would carry it through five editions and sales of more than four million copies. It turned Peterson into an icon and gave him the world. He grew from a young man writing and drawing in a cubbyhole to a figure who was recognized wherever he went and who visited and worked on every continent during a twelve-month period in 1973–1974. His horizons were enlarged in the short term as well. In November 1934 he moved back to New York to start his first full-time job, as a member of the administrative staff of the National Audubon Society.

1934–1942

New York City

The events of Peterson's nonprofessional life seemed seldom to have an impact on his work. This is not to say that he was immune to the personal changes he went through, but it is difficult to see any effect on his writing or painting. He seemed to be able to live in two places at once, a skill he doubtless learned growing up, when he found that he could avoid the turmoil of his home life by entering the world of birds. But on his own, he became practical; he learned that from his father. The escape that bird-watching had provided as an adolescent grew into an escape into work. His ability to focus his field glasses on a bird is a good emblem for his single-minded approach. With the object of his passion centered and his mind organized, he could block out the rest of the world. Earning his livelihood in bird study enabled a similar escape. The years Peterson spent in New York were difficult enough to limit an ordinary person to satisfaction in doing his job, which he did with distinction. But what he accomplished after his hours at the office separated him from his peers.

A mere month after his *Field Guide* was published, on 1 November 1934, Peterson was offered a job at the National Association of Audubon Societies—on the same day that John Baker had been appointed president. As president of the Linnaean Society, Baker had known Peterson during Peterson's Bronx County days. And he showed particular interest in Peterson's color plates that he exhibited at the 1933 AOU convention. As Peterson said, Baker appreciated the field guide approach because "I was very systematic in my approach to teaching, because the Field Guide is a teaching medium really."[1] During its first five decades, Audubon had evolved into the perfect workplace for him. George Bird Grinnell, a paleontologist by education, a big-game hunter by avocation, and the editor of *Forest and Stream,* formed the first Audubon Society in 1886 for the protection of wild birds against market gunners, egg collectors, and milliners. To join the society, one had only to sign a pledge not to molest birds. Within a year, thirty-nine thousand persons had pledged, the society was incorporated, and a periodical, *The Audubon Magazine,* was launched. But the large response was wasted. By 1888, the idea expired, and the magazine folded; the society had attempted nothing concrete. It was merely language.

In 1896, however, Harriet Hemenway, a prominent Bostonian, founded the Massachusetts Audubon Society along with a group of like-minded friends and a number of nationally recognized naturalists. Its stated purpose was "to discourage the buying and wearing, for ornamental purposes, of the feathers of any wild birds, except ducks and game birds, and to otherwise further the protection of native birds."[2] As Massachusetts Audubon and other new state Audubon societies fought for their cause by lobbying and pamphleteering, William Dutcher, as head of the AOU's Bird Protection Committee, joined the battle. And when he was forced out of the AOU by scientists who feared that their bird-collecting rights were being threatened, he formed the National Committee of Audubon Societies of America, which was incorporated in 1905 as the National Association of Audubon Societies, a loose confederation of thirty-seven state societies, and which finally became the independent National Audubon Society in 1940. Dutcher and a few allies across the country continued the battle on three fronts: against the hunters who shot birds for their feathers, against the milliners who bought the feathers for hats, and against the women who wore them. The struggle lasted until 1913 when Congress passed a bill that ended the trade in wild birds—although illegal trade continued long after.

Dutcher led the association until 1910, when a stroke incapacitated him. Gilbert Pearson succeeded him and expanded Dutcher's work to include protection of all wildlife and the establishment of a nature education program. It was under Pearson's watch that the Junior Audubon Clubs began and the bird pamphlets, which had engaged Peterson so profoundly as a boy, were written—by Pearson himself. But Pearson came under attack in 1929 from a woman named Rosalie Edge, a bird protectionist with the soul of a partisan politician. She was indefatigable in her pursuit of issues, large or small, on which to attack Pearson publicly, in pamphlets, and at Audubon meetings. She accused him of being soft on hunting, misusing funds, mishandling sanctuaries; in general, she opposed everything he did. Finally John Baker, who had become head of the board of directors in 1933, persuaded the board that Pearson was losing effectiveness. The board agreed. Pearson stepped down, and Baker was appointed executive director of the association.

Baker cleaned house. He wanted the association to become a force in bird research and protection and in nature education. So he hired a staff of what Frank Graham called, in his history of the National Audubon Society, "the most extraordinary and idiosyncratic group of bird-conscious young men ever assembled under one roof."[3] The list reads like a who's who in twentieth-century ornithology: Robert Allen, Carl Buchheister, Allan Cruickshank, Richard Pough, Alexander Sprunt, William Vogt, and Roger Tory Peterson. They were tireless and idealistic, talented and mercurial. They were overworked and underpaid, and they didn't care. It was an office that believed fiercely in its common goals and that remained convivial during the long hours that Baker demanded (they worked even on Saturdays until 1:00 p.m.). Barbara Coulter Peterson, who worked there before she became Peterson's second wife, remembers tea breaks each afternoon that featured long, hilarious discussions about everything "from Gypsy Rose Lee to rodeo."[4] It was an environment that Peterson, alone and alienated from the world, needed and one that he was born for. Robert Allen offers a telling picture of Peterson living in Greenwich Village at the time: "Instead of going to bed he would hang around the greasy spoon on the corner playing the pinball machine for hours on end. Morosely he sent the little ball rolling across the intricate board, morosely watched the score fail to bring in the free games he was shooting for." But as Allen also observed, "He was being consciously anti-social, which meant that he was still maturing, still adjusting his originality and depth of thought to a world that seemed to him all wrong, a world that was unreal to his gentle, artistic senses. One forgets that Peterson, when he published his guide, was a young man of twenty-six, still emerging from an awful childhood and already on his own for ten years."[5] The association office was probably Peterson's first real home. Shortly after hiring Peterson, Baker named him director of education as well as art director of *Bird-Lore*, Frank Chapman's well-established magazine of bird study and protection, which Baker had bought to serve as a house organ.

More than an art director of a magazine, Peterson assumed the role of informal artist in residence. He not only provided illustrations, stand-alone art, and even bird portraits for Christmas cards but also designed the association's stationery; 1937 letters featured Peterson drawings of a robin, a bobwhite, and a canvasback in the left margin. His most visible task, however, was to vitalize *Bird-Lore*'s covers. William Vogt, the magazine's new editor, wanted something more dramatic than the cover he had inherited from the previous editor. The title appeared in red, Gothic letters above a black-and-white bird photograph, all boxed in by an elaborate frame. So Peterson designed a cover with art nouveau calligraphy and a different bird portrait for each issue. He was limited to two ink impressions: one black and one color of his choice. As a result, he had two options: either use his color of choice as a background for one of his black-and-white bird portraits or incorporate the color into the actual image of the bird. When he employed the latter option, the results were often ingenious and striking. He began experimenting in his second year with a red-winged blackbird with red epaulets. He followed that with appropriately colored redstarts. Color found its way into subsequent paintings — on a bobolink's yellow nape, a white ibis's red face and bill, a towhee's brown side. His first cover, a rough-legged hawk in winter, drew praise from no less than the renowned Arthur Cleveland Bent, who, Peterson later recalled, wrote to say it was one of the best bird paintings he had ever seen. Peterson modestly, and correctly, said that Bent's evaluation was an overstatement. The bird soaring high over a wintry landscape is dramatic, but the background and the subject never really connect; they appear to be two separate paintings. He second cover, which he later called a "disaster," depicted five shovelers springing up from a marsh. Here the birds are drawn without much feathering or shading and look too much like his field guide depictions. But the pieces quickly improved: the two willets in the July/August 1935 issue are well-drawn, and the canvasback cover in the January/February 1940 issue is superb, both in composition and use of color.

At first, Baker held off appointing Peterson to education director. As Peterson suggested, "I think he was going to see how things would work out in the office."[6] His first job was to reorganize the service department, a chaos of birdhouses, books, and other items for sale. Peterson put everything in order and created a catalog. Things worked well, indeed, and he was promoted. As education director, one of Peterson's early duties involved the establishment of the Audubon Nature Camp on Hog Island in Muscongus Bay, Maine. In the spring of 1935, he was sent to scout and take films of the property, which had been donated to the association. On the strength of his favorable report, plans went ahead to establish the camp. Peterson was the bird instructor during the summer of 1936, the camp's first year.

The announcement of the camp's opening in *Bird-Lore* emphasized that the camp was "primarily for teachers," and the program stressed the education of children: "A well-qualified staff of specialists, capable of imparting their own infectious enthusiasms, will concentrate instruction on field observation and on methods which they and others have found effective in imparting genuinely sustained interest to children."[7] This program contained two ideas for reform that would remain with Peterson and become the basis for the educational programs at the Roger Tory Peterson Institute fifty years later. They grew out of his own experiences at Camp Chewonki and the Rivers School and from discussions with John Baker and Carl Buchheister, the director of the Audubon camp. Essentially they called for two shifts in natural science instruction. The first would create a grassroots approach that involved "teaching the teachers." According to Peterson, Baker instructed him to prepare educational materials for both students and teachers: "However, this would only partially do the trick. . . . Wouldn't it be more effective to get to the teachers and youth leaders more directly? They would become the pupils, and we would be the teachers; thus the camp idea was conceived. The camp in Muscongus Bay in Maine was the first of several in various parts of the country."[8] The second was to get instruction away from the laboratory and into the outdoors. As Peterson later wrote, "Carl [Buchheister] shared my own views and those of John Baker, who felt that classroom biology and natural science were oriented too much in the Germanic tradition of the scalpel and the microscope. Young people and their teachers might know about the muscles in a frog's leg yet remain ignorant about the living animal, its habits, or even its name. The camp was designed to correct this, to take teachers outdoors and give them valid field experience."[9]

This latter idea Peterson knew instinctively, and his successful teaching at Chewonki and Rivers reinforced it. It led, in turn, to another anti-academic position that he summarized later in *Bird Watcher's Digest:* "In my opinion, kids, especially the younger ones, do not start with an ecological concept. They acquire one by using springboards such as birds, plants, or mammals. To expect youngsters to become 'instant environmentalists' is presumptuous. . . . [F]eelings must come first, then the names of wild things, then where they live, and what they do. Concepts follow. . . . There is no substitute for substance and passion."[10]

It would not be easy, however, for Peterson to implement his reforms. The official, educationist attitude of the time stressed the use of the scientific method in schools. Human culture, not human nature, was paramount in education, and Peterson's insistence on "feelings," passion for a subject, would have no place in serious scientific study. This attitude was coupled with the fact that the factory system of education continued throughout the twentieth century. Even now, it remains a system that resists change mightily, and the more radical the change, the greater the resistance. To change one facet—a biology class curriculum, for example—and not change the entire system would break down this carefully structured machine.

Peterson's failure to conform to the model student and the intractability of the educational system proved eventually to be a boon for nature education and ultimately for the conservation movement and the environment itself. He was by nature a teacher, yet he had been denied his calling through the traditional paths. The real solution came not in birding the littoral of Maine but in working behind a desk at the Audubon offices in New York. His charge as education director was, according to the announcement of his appointment in *Bird-Lore,* to "assist in the educational work of the Association with particular reference to the stimulation of interest and enthusiasm on the part of teachers and children."[11] In fact, he was hired to salvage a program that had fallen far behind in nature study in the schools. First he visited schools in New York, Massachusetts, and Connecticut that had Junior Audubon Clubs to talk with teachers to gather information about the impact of the Audubon educational program, and he traveled to children's museums as far away as Nashville, Tennessee. Armed with the information he gathered, he decided to approach the problem on two fronts: the extracurricular Junior Audubon Clubs and the integration of nature study into the classroom by teaching the teachers. Then he began to write.

13

During his time at Audubon, Peterson wrote to three separate and distinct audiences. His duties as education director included rewriting the Junior Audubon leaflets for schoolchildren as well as preparing the bulletins on nature studies for educators. Somehow he found time also to write articles of general interest that would establish a style and approach that changed little over the next four decades.

The Junior Audubon leaflets, which had inspired Peterson as a boy, were scientifically sound and straightforward descriptions of individual species and their behavior. They tended to be somber and somewhat pedantic studies; they were, in other words, perfect for a bird-obsessed boy who couldn't read enough about birds, but they were hardly a tool for introducing most schoolchildren to nature study. Peterson was well aware of this. He would later note, "The leaflets were written almost as though they expected their fellow ornithologists to pass judgment on them, rather than the school children for whom they were intended."[1] Peterson, on the other hand, crafted a style that was accessible but never condescending. Further, he realized the need for two sets of texts: one for fifth grade and younger and one for junior high and high school students. Unburdened as he was by pedagogical training, he was able to impart a remarkable amount of knowledge naturally, while still conveying his love and enthusiasm for birds.

In the leaflets, he shows a notable facility for adapting his style for young children. He keeps it light, as in this kingfisher description: "It is a fine-looking bird, larger than a Robin, gray above and white below. Notice the top-knot. When you wake up in the morning you sometimes look the same way. That is, before you comb your hair. Of course, your nose isn't so long."[2] But he manages to include a host of information about field marks and behavior without losing his young readers. His sentences are short and his diction conversational. He is always aware of his audience: baby loons are "as fuzzy as young kittens"; Canada geese feed by standing on their heads; wrens migrate south "when school begins in the fall."[3]

He tells a number of stories in the leaflets that would later appear in magazines and seemed as completely natural when written for children as for adults.

Leaflet number 56, "The Ruby-Throated Hummingbird," is a typical example. He begins by writing about hummingbird migration: "Think of it, from the land of the Parrots to the home of the winter-loving Crossbills—and the bird weighs less than two Audubon buttons." Describing hatchlings as looking "more like bugs than birds at first," he adds, "It would take a half-dozen such to fill the bowl of one ordinary teaspoon." And when they are fed: "How blood-curdling this feeding process is too!—a real sword-swallowing act! The mother thrusts her thin bill right down her youngsters' throats as if she would stab them to death. Really she is quite careful." He sprinkles personal anecdotes throughout, such as when he illustrates the hummingbird's preference for the color red by recalling a hummingbird feeding at some cut flowers he was holding or, while walking in town, seeing a migrating hummingbird trying to feed at a box of tomatoes in a storefront.[4] The tone never descends to an "Isn't this special, children?" level, but rather it carries Peterson's own childlike fascination with birds and their behavior.

Each leaflet concludes with activities—"Things to Think About" or "Things to Do"—and a list of further readings. And many teach a conservationist message also, as when, for example, he explains why kingfishers and herons are not responsible for game fish depletion and therefore should not be shot. In the upper-level leaflets, the connotation is sometimes dark: "If you were a Goose, southward-bound, perhaps you would feel uneasy too; uneasy not only because of the dreary prospect of winter—far below on the water would be flocks of Geese; perhaps real Geese, perhaps wooden. At a distance they all look alike. Chances cannot be taken, and anything that looks like a man or a blind in the marsh must be avoided."[5] And sometimes it is light: "The responsibilities of life seem to rest lightly on the Goldfinch's sunny shoulders. All year round it jaunts merrily over the countryside, sprinkling down its musical notes as it goes. No bird sings with greater ecstasy or abandon. . . . No bird seems to enjoy the sociability of the flock more."[6] Perhaps the grimmest is "The Snowy Egret," in which Peterson explains the prime cause behind the founding of the Audubon Society. The drawings in the margins set the tone: two plume hunters in a skiff, a dead egret,

egret chicks in a nest "left to starve," ladies in plumed hats, and an Audubon warden. The text is unflinching:

> It was only the [egret's] white spray, which attains its greatest perfection during the breeding season, that was wanted. This was ripped from the fallen bird's back and the broken body was left to float on the murky water of the swamp. . . . The death of the parents meant the death of the brood. Picture if you can, the orphan young, weakly imploring every passing Heron for food, until they lacked even strength enough to hold up their heads. . . . A scene of beauty was changed to one of dreary desolation. A stench arose from the swamp and the white bodies slowly sank into the mire.

But having upset his readers quite enough, Peterson turns to the happy ending—the story of sanctuaries, Audubon wardens, and the egret's comeback. The moral is clear: "The story of the Egret should give us courage to go ahead. We should remember that *conservation is not just a theory; it works.*"[7]

Even here, as in all the other leaflets, the importance of a child's ability to identify with birds is never forgotten. The leaflets were successful because of Peterson's versatility as a writer and because they convey one of his greatest gifts: his sense of wonder in the presence of birds. He understood and wrote for his audience.

As a final touch, Peterson returned to the magic of his childhood escape into books. "I have always been a visual person," he recalled in a 1975 interview. "I was very much taken with the work of Ernest Thompson Seton, and his use of . . . little margin drawings in all of his books. . . . So I thought this would be excellent for the leaflets—to put little margin drawings on the side to illustrate points."[8] Once more he was able to recreate his own childlike response.

When he was well into the task of rewriting the leaflets, he began a series of bulletins, essays that would serve to instruct teachers in the presentation of various issues of nature study and conservation. In addition to their publication in *Bird-Lore,* they were distributed to teachers. These were informational and, for the most part, written in straightforward prose.

In a 1938 essay that introduced the series—"How Should Nature Be Taught?"—he summarized his attitude toward teaching. The purpose of the forthcoming articles, Peterson explained, was to ad-

SACRIFICED

AND
LEFT TO STARVE

··· FOR
FASHION

*Peterson's illustrations for his Junior Audubon
Society leaflet "Snowy Egrets," mid-1930s.*

dress a basic problem with nature study in schools. Identifying that problem as "science teachers who are unable to vitalize the study of living things because of the inadequacy of their own backgrounds," Peterson added, "They are well grounded in a knowledge of broad physical principles, but are unable to associate them with the everyday forms of life that surround them."[9] He wrote that the aim of nature education should be based on an absolute premise: "Proper land-use requires a knowledge of biological laws, a knowledge of the interdependence of all forms of life, the plants, the birds, mammals, insects and all the rest."[10] According to Peterson, this premise is essential because wise or unwise use of the land is the prime determinant of our standard of living. The essay then lays out the approach that he held throughout his career: identification of species functions as an entrée to what he called "broader biological vistas." These vistas, he explained, achieve nature education's ultimate aim. "We should not content ourselves merely with taking a flower apart, recognizing its stamens, petals, and sepals, but should also find out what it means to the organic world and to us."[11] He concluded by advising on how nature study should be integrated into the curriculum—without turning the emphasis away from science to something the unprepared teacher is more comfortable with, such as creative projects in art or writing that merely employ a nature motif.

These pamphlets for teachers are a blend of information, practical advice, and a strong environmentalist message. In the most interesting, he experiments with a narrative form that centers on "the teacher" as a third-person character who guides a class through discussions and activities. Topics covered are generalized ecological systems such as grasslands, swamps and marshes, and forests. Other, more advice-centered pieces tell teachers how to plan and construct nature trails, build birdhouses, and create bird sanctuaries.

Peterson's environmentalism naturally took a pedagogical turn in his articles for *Bird-Lore*. No matter the topic, he always managed to find a place to teach a conservation or preservation lesson—often mildly stated by today's standards but, at the time, not a common practice. His piece on forests, for example, argues against clearcutting and woodlot grazing but emphasizes wise forestry practices that create more habitat for birds by opening up woodlands. Also, forest fires are seen as loss of habitat rather than as part of a natural cycle. About wilderness areas, he suggests, "A few untouched woodlands should be saved while it is still possible. These should stand as museum pieces to show people what the original forest was like."[12] Destroying habitat by draining swamps for development, farming, and mosquito control and overtaking grasslands for farming and grazing also receive notice. In each case, wildlife preservation is the primary issue, and bird populations the first concern.

In its May/June 1940 issue, *Bird-Lore* ran a photograph of the materials Peterson had assembled as yearly packets for the Junior Audubon Societies. They included a membership badge and six of Peterson's leaflets, each of which contained a full-page color bird portrait and an outline drawing for coloring. Additionally, there was a quarterly newsletter, *News on the Wing,* and a year's subscription to *Bird-Lore* for clubs with more than twenty-five members. For the teachers, sixteen *Nature Study for the Schools* pamphlets were included. It all cost each member ten cents a year.

The third type of article represented Peterson's first forays into essay types that he would return to throughout his writing career. "Down the Santee in a Folding Boat," which appeared in *Bird-Lore* in 1938, is in an early pastoral tradition of nature writing that is often called the ramble, in which a writer ventures into the landscape and returns with the material out of which an essay is made. Field notes and journals are considered along with research and other sources, and the essay emerges. For Peterson, there was never any doubt about the outcome; the essay would be about birds, their behavior, and their environment.

This essay describes a nine-day float down the Santee River in South Carolina "to settle rumors of the existence of certain extinct or near-extinct birds in the wilderness of the Santee Basin."[13] It is a typical nature-essay subject, but in Peterson's hands it becomes a bird essay. To evoke the mood of night on the river, he only mentions in passing the "sudden slap of an alligator's tail" but spends two paragraphs describing and discussing the night calls of white-throated sparrows, wood ducks, and barred owls. After Peterson and his companion, Lester Walsh, imagine a lightening of the eastern sky several times, dawn is finally announced by a cardinal's song: "We knew it was the real thing that time."[14] Birds are the reliable things, the things that really matter.

Although Peterson includes some interesting particulars about the setting, he marks the days by the species seen and detailed descriptions of their songs and behavior. He calls for a breeding-bird census of the area, and he is so enthralled with the birdlife that he barely mentions that he has been searching in vain for the ivory-billed woodpecker and Carolina paroquet. Eventually the essay closes with a brief plea for the preservation of such a spectacular bird habitat.

It is a well-written piece. The varied sentences flow smoothly; detail is fresh and precise; and the narrative never loses pace. And it is quintessential Peterson. Although he was a superb naturalist, all elements of the natural world were secondary to the birds in his writing. In total, "Down the Santee" marks Peterson's first attempt at an essay form that would be repeated in various settings around the world and that would define the body of Peterson's written work.

Another rhetorical mode to emerge from this remarkably productive period before the war can be seen in his 1941 essay "Symbols of Nature in Art." It is expository—loosely organized and lacking a clear thesis, but lucid and informative. Often overlooked in evaluations of Peterson's writing is his ability as a researcher, which is demonstrated here. One section of "Symbols of Nature in Art" comprises an encyclopedic survey of visual symbols derived from the natural world in both Eastern and Western art—with an emphasis on birds. Another section of the piece contains a general discussion of symbolism as it functions significantly in daily life. As a corollary, he writes, "It has seemed to me that our interest in birds actually springs from a symbolic source as does perhaps every major interest." That source, he suggests, is the "mobility of birds, their apparent freedom from earthly ties that appeals to many people."[15] Peterson never actually connects these two sections with any kind of thesis, and sustained exposition was clearly not his strong suit. But in this essay, and in others like it that followed, he proved that he could deliver large quantities of information in a comprehensible and readable manner.

Another example of Peterson's expository writing is a companion set from *Bird-Lore:* "Tricks of Bird Photography" and "Tricks of Nature Photography." Always a thoughtful writer, Peterson raises many more issues than his practical titles suggest. He reveals that, in spite of contrary statements elsewhere, bird photography was becoming, for him, more than merely a means of capturing a bird's image; it was a method of *engagement* with birds that inevitably had aesthetic and ethical elements. Therefore, before he offers up his photography "tricks," he reveals this other part of his agenda.[16]

His first point is a preservationist one. While bird photography may be a replacement for an atavistic need to hunt, it takes greater skill than hunting, has fewer restrictions, and doesn't destroy the object of the hunt. Besides, as Peterson mildly observes, "any earnest occupation could be regarded as a civilized substitute for hunting" (175). The point is that, unlike the hunter, the photographer doesn't establish dominance over his or her quarry but rather learns the pleasures of coexistence.

Peterson drew on his thinking about the visual arts for his second point, adapting his approaches to nature photography specifically to birds. Bird photography can be approached in two ways: "from the viewpoint which Fuertes used in his paintings—typical poses in direct lighting, with the details and geometry of feather pattern shown to advantage" or "with an eye for composition, values, and third dimensional activity" (175). Examination of his painting career shows that reconciling these two points of view was a lifelong project for Peterson. In the case of bird photography, he suggests that however one engages the subject, the rewards are worthy: "Thus the scientist and artist both find expression through the impersonal eye of the lens" (175). In his case, in photography as in painting, scientist and artist were eventually one.

His third point was to establish guidelines for a relationship of respect and mutuality between photographer and subject. Peterson once told an interviewer that his first exposure with his Premo was of a screech owl that some friends had caught and tied to a branch. He also asserted that it was the last and only time he faked a photograph. Birds are lured to feeders, ducks and geese are fed, baby birds are perched on branches so parent birds feeding them can be photographed—all these techniques allow the birds to act on their own "free will." Restraining birds, moving nests, doing anything that endangers the lives of birds or their eggs, is unacceptable. Peterson vowed that "in over fifteen years of photography, the writer [himself] has never, to his knowledge, been responsible for the premature injury or death of any of the birds he has photographed" (178). Behind that affirmation is his fundamental belief, often stated, that humans share the planet with other living things that have every right to live their lives, undisturbed and free. What follows in the essay are "tricks" that can be described as gentle and respectful, such as construction of simple decoys and blinds or information about where birds are likely to be photographed most easily. For Peterson, bird photography began with an understanding and promoted a deepening of that understanding.

In addition to all his other successes, and in spite of his shyness and inexperience, Peterson was a regular on WOR radio in New York City and became a popular and effective lecturer to a range of audiences from youths to ornithological societies. And he was a busy one as well: during one stretch between 28 December 1935 and 4 January 1936, he gave six lectures on a tour of bird societies that ranged from Erie, Pennsylvania, to St. Louis. And he occasionally gave as many as three lectures in one day in the New York area. It didn't start off well, as Frank Graham's recounting of his first lecture indicates. Allan Cruickshank had scheduled him to lecture just before a Douglas Fairbanks movie at the Brooklyn Academy of Music, and Peterson had hand-colored his glass slides for presentation. But he talked too long about the first slide. As Peterson, in one of the versions he recalled, described the day to Graham:

> Pretty soon I could hear the kids in the audience giggling. . . . While I was up there talking, the slide was melting in the hot projector because I hadn't used heat-resistant paint to color it. Somehow I got through my slides until the climax of the program, which was a demonstration of bird calls. I was to imitate a bird and Cruickshank, planted in the balcony, would call back to me. We began with a screech owl. [In another version, Peterson remembered that he was telling a ghost story about a screech owl appearing in a cemetery in Jamestown.] Suddenly all the kids began to whistle and yodel too, and the lecture ended in an uproar.[17]

But subsequent lectures got better, until Peterson learned to win audiences over with the same skill that made the leaflets so effective: his gift of imparting his love and enthusiasm for birds. John Devlin and Grace Naismith, who wrote a biographical book about Peterson in 1977, quote Carl Buchheister on watching Peterson at work with children:

> And how he held the attention of those children! Completely natural, unpedagogic, just acting as if he were a boy with his own interest in nature, talking to fellow boys and girls. A marvelous presentation, just coming out as natural as a boy in a meadow who had found a screech owl in a tree hole and was talking to his friends. At lectures he projected that he was feeling it all—how a bird lives, what kind of head it has, what kind of feet. What happened was that every single kid sitting on the floor had his mouth open, because here was somebody who was feeling it all. He could tell little stories and examples of his own adventures. It was as if the youngsters were out there in the woods together.[18]

Meanwhile, Peterson was gaining in confidence, getting more comfortable with himself. Robert Allen got him an apartment in Greenwich Village, and he happily entered an eclectic social circle there. Saturday night parties at the Allens included different views and lifestyles; regulars included actor Van Heflin, producer Vincent Minnelli, writer James Agee, band leader Jimmy Dorsey, and *Life* editor Joseph Kastner, who gave Peterson his first *Life* assignment during one memorable party. And he remained close with his Bronx County Bird Club and Linnaean friends, especially Allan Cruick-shank and Joseph Hickey. The bird club had not lost its youthful enthusiasm for birding, but the boys were obviously entering a less innocent world, as evidenced by the club's tenth anniversary party at William Vogt's house, recalled in Hickey's best Robert Benchley style:

> The club provided beer. Mr. Vogt provided cocktails, and
> Charles Urner, Willie Edwards and J. Fletcher Street took mat-
> ters into their own hands, arriving at the lodge in an advanced
> state of intoxication. The great part of the evening was spent in
> a spirited discussion of who was the best all-around field natu-
> ralist in New Jersey. Urner maintained that it was Lee Edwards,
> who had already passed out on a couch. Fletcher Street, with
> becoming modesty, maintained that it was Fletcher Street.
> This went on until about four in the morning, when half of the
> party collapsed, and the other half drove to Montauk.[19]

Peterson, for whom birds meant more than partying, would have been the leader of the early-morning field trip. Fun was okay, but ultimately it was birds that mattered. Even at the parties in the Village, according to Robert Allen, Peterson would sometimes "slump in his chair and sit there with glazed eyes while the rest us talked [about] the usual things young people talked of" until the talk turned to natural history and he would "sit up, more alert than anybody, and talk wonderfully."[20] This preoccupation can be seen in a story Peterson told on himself about a trip to Jones Beach for shorebirds. He had taken off his shoes to follow some sanderlings and, return-ing, couldn't remember where he had left them. There was nothing left to do but face "the embarrassment of getting off the Long Island train and walking through Grand Central Station to make my con-nection to Scarsdale in my bare feet!"[21]

Along with finding his emerging personality, Peterson began to find joy and pride in his work. In one letter to his mother from this time, he enthused about his work: "The job is more fun than ever—There are so many interesting things to do—prepare radio broadcasts—news releases—painting—lecturing—writing—photography—etc. All the diverse things I've done in the past are being put to good use in this job and best of all there are so many interesting and exciting people to meet daily."[22] And in another he wrote,

> Hardly a day passes but I meet someone who owns a copy of my book—When I lecture in some town . . . there are always several people present who want their copy autographed. This year it is being used in at least two universities as the standard text in Ornithology—at Harvard and Brown. One current radio contest is offering copies of my book as a prize. The three years of laborious preparation were certainly worth it![23]

Clarence Allen wrote of him, "I have watched him like a father watching his own son and have had the great satisfaction of seeing all these factors blend into this outstanding young man. The distance he has come from those early days when many of us despaired of getting him to complete his work or to be on time for anything to his recent industrious habits is, of course, a delight to me and to all his friends."[24] It should be pointed out, parenthetically, that Peterson still had trouble being on time in the mornings. Joseph Hickey wrote that in order to wake up for his Saturday morning radio show, Peterson would send himself a telegram every Friday night: "He was living in a small room in Greenwich Village, and the telegram boy would knock at the door at the designated hour, enter, sit down, and not leave the room until Roger was dressed."[25] But in spite of problems awakening, which stayed with him throughout his life, Peterson was already impressing people with his diligence and vitality, which Clarence Allen described as "deep and spiritual," adding, "With Roger it is a drive of great power and purpose. If life is kind to him, it will grow as he gets older rather than diminish."[26]

Peterson's time at the Audubon Society eclipsed Baker's expectations. In a 1938 report, Peterson recounted his accomplishments during his first four years.[27] It is an impressive account. He lists 100 lectures in eighteen states and seventy-five radio broadcasts. He wrote sixty-two new leaflets, with 3,800,000 copies printed, as well as nine teacher guides with a printing of 87,500. Junior Audubon Society enrollment grew from 120,000 in 1934 to 164,000 in 1938. He established and judged an annual essay contest. Nine million students had joined the Junior Audubon Clubs by the time he left in 1942. Thirty-three pieces appeared under his byline in *Bird-Lore,* as well as an illustrated calendar, *Learn a Bird a Week,* which appeared in each issue during 1937 and 1938. And, in addition to his cover art, he made over 480 paintings, drawings, and illustrations for *Bird-Lore.* He also painted four bird portraits—a blue jay, a red-winged blackbird, a cardinal, and a rose-breasted grosbeak—for lithographic prints to be sold by the society. And he fielded thousands of letters, ranging, as he recalled later, from "flowery requests from humble Hindus for numerous free books and field-glasses [and] requests from prison inmates for complete lists of birds so that they [could] bestow a sort of ornithological nomenclature on their fellow inmates," to serious and technical ornithological queries. Other queries made up his "dickey-bird mail." Responding to "everything from bird identification to the many problems that beset the window watchers who do not do their own research," he noted, "To facilitate answering, I devised about 20 basic letters covering the most frequently asked questions about cats, squirrels, starlings, bird boxes, feeders, birds fighting their reflections, birds hitting windows, etc."[28] These queries followed him throughout his life, and so great was his desire to teach people about birds, he would answer them all—with the help of his wife, Barbara, or through dictated responses that his secretaries would type. Peterson's stint at Audubon House was a busy and exhausting job, but the large volume of writing and painting he produced on his own, after his workdays were finished, was even more remarkable.

14

First, as always, came his field guides, which prevented him from following up on the success of his paintings at the 1933 AOU Convention. As he wrote later, "Ironically at that promising point, I dropped my 'painterly' painting. I was trapped by the field guides, which demanded a great deal of time and discipline."[1] In 1939 he published the first of four revisions of the eastern *Guide*. It wasn't a major overhaul, but in it he added entries for voice and range for each species, as well as editing for clarity and sometimes amending the descriptions for each species. Additionally, he painted four completely new black-and-white plates.

Reviews were favorable again. Frank Chapman begins his review in *Bird-Lore* with warm praise: "When, at the age of five years, a book graduates into a 'completely revised edition,' one concludes that it was well born and has passed a distinguished youth." He concludes by addressing Peterson's observation in the book's front matter that "recognition is not the end and aim of ornithology." "No," Chapman writes, "but it is a beginning, and a beginning is an essential part of any undertaking." He suggests that Peterson undervalued his contribution by minimizing the importance of "bird-naming." Every ornithologist has started at that point, Chapman says, and for future ornithologists, "we can suggest no better guide for this fascinating journey than the one for which we have to thank Mr. Peterson."[2] A review in the *Auk*, written by G. M. Allen, calls the new edition "a decided improvement over the first" and goes on to discuss the changes Peterson made. Allen's conclusion, though less effusive than Chapman's, is positive as well: "The small size of the volume, with its abundance of illustration and its condensed statement of differential points makes it a thoroughly practical field book and companion, which cannot fail to be of value to the amateur as well as to the more experienced field naturalist."[3]

The western *Guide*, published in 1941, was a more significant project. It was a logical next step, but one that Peterson was reluctant at first to undertake. Not only was the West larger and far more ecologically diverse than the area covered in the eastern *Guide*, but the western region also posed terrific challenges in dealing with the identification and naming of subspecies. In the end, however, Peterson trusted that the premise of the eastern *Guide* would work anywhere. He avoided the problems posed by the West's great ecological diversity by simply indicating the range of each bird, omitting any type of habitat descriptions. The subspecies problem, though, was tougher.

Not all bird species are uniform in appearance across their entire range. Some, in fact, vary consistently by geography, making it possible—in the museum, at least—to identify and name distinct subspecies, or geographic races. Nearly four hundred such subspecies had been described as western birds, many of them identifiable only in the hand; and many of them, as Peterson correctly predicted, would turn out to be not valid subspecies at all, but simply random or individual variations. To make matters worse, many of the western subspecies had been given names not immediately referable to the larger species to which they belonged. The western downy woodpecker, for example, had been divided into subspecies with such inscrutable names as "Batchelder's woodpecker," "Gairdner's woodpecker," and "willow woodpecker," none of them indicating to the reader that these birds were in fact simply geographic races of the familiar downy woodpecker.

In an addendum dealing with this problem, Peterson pointed out that his was a guide "primarily for the amateur who merely wishes to attach a name or a 'handle' to the creature before him." For this audience, and for field study in general, Peterson had to solve the problem of subspecies. He did so by applying a familiar solution: he combined the visual and the scientific. In the text, Peterson treated the subspecies that could be identified in the field, and then he laboriously listed the hundreds of subspecies and their ranges in the addendum. Thus both the ornithologist and the amateur were accommodated.

With the plan set, he faced drawing the forty cuts, painting the forty black-and-white and six color plates, and writing descriptions, range, and voice for each species. When he could use material from the eastern *Guide,* he did. But for the birds occurring only in the West, new entries had to be written. Additionally, the first western *Guide* was more instructional than any of his guides before or since. Perhaps because of a mind-set necessary for a director of education, Peterson included a great deal of text on the plates themselves, naming the field marks that his arrows pointed to and repeating key differences already mentioned in the descriptions. He also included a graphic analysis of adult gulls that simplified gull identification and an illustrative study of song variations of white-crowned sparrows. In all, it was a truly monumental task, made more difficult because it required extensive travel to observe western birds and because it was all done in addition to his heavy workload at the association.

But the hard work paid off. Reviews on both coasts praised the

Guide's plan and execution. The *Condor: A Magazine of Western Ornithology* said, in part, "Peterson has done a great service to active and prospective bird students in a large section of the country by working up this guide. Also, he has taken an important stand in favor of less emphasis on subspecies on the part of the field amateur, which attitude expressed in a book of this kind we may expect will have a distinctly beneficial effect."[4] In the *Auk*, G. M. Allen also praised Peterson's handling of the subspecies issue. And in *Bird Lore*, Ludlow Griscom summarized his review by writing, "Every person interested in 'western' birds should own and study this 'Guide,' and only a handful of field workers in any one generation will ever outgrow it. The reviewer, most emphatically, will never be one of them."[5] Another review, a chatty piece by Donald Culross Peattie, declared that "the famed Peterson rapid-identification system works in the West with the same *Blitzkrieg* efficiency as in the East." Peattie followed up that unfortunate choice of words with another in a discussion of the duck and geese illustrations that Peterson found dismissive: "Peterson's nifty little drawings, looking much like wooden decoys, give the camouflage pattern of these wary little navies." Peterson would refer to the "wooden decoys" often in later articles and interviews, considering it an insult to his painting skills. But Peattie meant it in a positive way. He was merely trying to point out that the abstracted, diagrammatic images were, in fact, the way ducks appeared to the observer: without discernable color and as "outlines only of the upper two-thirds of the bird, the lower part, of course, being submerged."[6] And the validation Peterson sought came in 1944 when he was awarded the Brewster Memorial Award for Nature Writing.

In addition to the guides, two more books appeared: *The Junior Book of Birds* (1938) and *The Audubon Guide to Attracting Birds* (1941). When Peterson rewrote the Junior Audubon leaflets, he made separate versions for older and younger children. *The Junior Book of Birds* is a collection of twenty-four of the leaflets written for children ages nine and under. *The Audubon Guide to Attracting Birds*, edited by John Baker, is a collection of twelve practical pieces that addressed a need created by the new interest in birds that had been sparked by the 1934 *Guide*. In addition to a full-canvas painting of two great blue herons in flight that was used as a frontispiece, Peterson contributed seven articles, three of which were slightly revised *Bird-Lore* pieces. The subjects range from the building of birdhouses and feeders to landscaping and photography. They are thorough and written in his "teacherly" manner—with one exception, an eighteen-page primer on bird-watching called "How, When and Where to Look and Listen." In it, Peterson was able, for the first time, to gather all the hints and tips that he had learned about the pastime he loved. The tone is relaxed, the instruction is easy to understand, and humorous anecdotes enliven the article. Clearly Peterson's intention was to welcome the growing number of new converts to bird-watching.

15

In spite of field guide pressures, Peterson was evolving the painting style that would make him the best-known twentieth-century painter of birds. He did full-canvas paintings for *Bird-Lore:* a great blue heron, reddish egrets, black ducks rising from a marsh, and others. And for a 1935 series of children's books called *The Nature Hour,* he painted a number of full-page illustrations, including a monarch butterfly, chickadees, a well-composed scene of juncos and grasses in the snow, and two striking treatments that combined a full painting and an inset: a screech owl hunting over a moonlit field with a close-up inset of the owl; and a luna moth, both in close-up and floating over a lake in moonlight. But these paintings, charming as they are, don't represent Peterson the artist. Although well-delineated, they are quite ordinary and predictable potboilers. Other work at this time, however, began to show the depth of his skill and training.

In an article written just before he died, he listed, outside his formal art training, three artists whose work influenced him: Audubon, Fuertes, and Aubrey Beardsley.[1] Those familiar with Peterson's work would readily accept the first two. Early evidence can be seen in paintings that he did for a 1939 series of postcards published by the National Wildlife Publishing Corporation, which show both the "feather maps" of Fuertes and the dynamics of Audubon. Pairs of birds are depicted in active postures in natural settings, that is, perched on branches appropriate to their regions and habitats. The

At his first job, painting "Chinese" designs at the Union Furniture Company, Jamestown, New York, 1925.

feather detail stands out, in clear contrast to field guide illustration. Peterson's naming of Beardsley, often popularly associated with decadence and exoticism, would be a surprise, however. But the design of many of the 1939 postcards does disclose an Oriental influence, perhaps by way of Beardsley.

If it can be suggested that the lessons of youth are the most profound, the case for Beardsley is a strong one. Before he saw an actual, full-size Audubon or Fuertes original, Peterson was painting in a style reminiscent of Beardsley's. When he began decorating furniture after his high school graduation, Peterson came under the influence of his boss, Willem Dieperink von Langereis. Oriental designs, derived from the late nineteenth-century European infatuation with "japonisme," were in vogue at the time, and Langereis studied the "Japanesque" work of Beardsley as he developed his own designs. Beardsley himself was a sickly and self-absorbed illustrator whose drawings are best known for their symbolism, eroticism, and ornamentation—not a likely prospect for an influence on a young painter of the natural world. But it was his design and line that captured Langereis and Peterson.

It is possible, too, that Peterson was exposed directly to Oriental design through Langereis or, later, in New York. Inexpensive ukiyo-e prints, the woodcut prints that carried japonisme to the West, were exported from Japan by the millions. Of special interest to Peterson would have been the landscapes of Hokusai and Hiroshige, the two most popular print masters. Whether Peterson was responding directly to their work is debatable; he never mentioned them, and he referred to his Oriental influences as "Chinese." But enough elements of the work of Hokusai and Hiroshige appear in Peterson's painting to indicate that he was at least reacting to their influence. The 1939 postcards established the design prototype for Peterson's songbird illustrations: a bird pair forms diagonals that interact with the strong diagonal of the branch they perch on. It is the design foundation of one type of ukiyo-e, the bird-and-flower prints, or kacho-e, popularized by Hiroshige.

The art nouveau period, with which Beardsley is associated, drew heavily on natural forms. The arabesque, that graceful curvilinear line that figures so prominently in Beardsley's most notorious work—his illustrations for Oscar Wilde's translation of *Salome*—describes equally well the neck of a great egret and Salome's belly. Beardsley's Japanesque designs—with their overlapping contour lines, backgrounds, graceful silhouettes, and other Oriental attributes—are repeated in Peterson's early painting as well as in his bird prints and in the illustrations for *Wild America*. In fact, in an article written just before his death, Peterson wrote that his bird prints "really owe their basics to Aubrey Beardsley via Langereis."[2] Peterson maintained his debt to Langereis throughout his life, and the appreciation was mutual; Langereis closed an effusive letter to Peterson written in the 1950s by saying, "Within you glows a spark of the divine."[3]

A striking example of the early Oriental influence on Peterson can be found today in an unlikely place: the dining hall wall at Camp Chewonki in Maine. There, sometime during his teaching stint in the early 1930s, Peterson painted four vertical panels, each about 1.5 by 4 feet. Rather than birds along the Maine coast, he depicted fish in a tropical sea: dolphins, bonitos, angelfish, and a swordfish. The panels are filled with motion. Graceful swirls of blue and green water and fantastically shaped clouds repeat the lines of the fish that jump and arch, dive and twist. Peterson's wave crests suggest the most popular of all the ukiyo-e prints: Hokusai's *The Great Wave*. And the four-panel design is an obvious invocation of Japanese screen paintings. The overall effect is of a furniture decorator set free; the lines and design are derivative, the setting and subject personalized.

Echoes of Beardsley can also be seen in Peterson's cover art for *Bird-Lore*. One brilliant example is his great egrets for the March/April issue in 1939. Peterson used the one color allowed him, yellow, only on the bills and eyes of the two birds. The rest is a satisfying white and black composition of arabesques—the curve of egrets' necks and sparse branches. Finely delineated Spanish moss provides ornamentation much in the way that Beardsley's vines grew along the borders of his drawings. The feeling is haunting—magnificent white birds in a darkened swamp, a sense of great space and detachment.

While remnants of Beardsley remained as the basis of Peterson's prints and in the design of some of his field guide plates, the influences of Audubon and Fuertes became increasingly evident as well. Peterson's style was, as he put it, "somewhere between Audubon and Fuertes; from Audubon a sense of design and space; and from Fuertes knowledge of how a bird is put together—the personality of a species."[4] Put another way, the dynamics and motion of a Peterson print drew on Audubon; the subtle essence and character of each bird were a Fuertes trait.

The roots of the art prints that Peterson produced for Mill Pond Press in the 1970s and 1980s can be seen in the series of paintings he made for *Life* magazine from 1938 to 1948. Although primarily educational in tone and concept—each spread contains instructional text such as field marks or behavior traits—the series produced some fine work that reveals, at once, the influence of Fuertes and Audubon, Oriental design elements, and an emerging Peterson style. The result has three principal characteristics: a plain background, bold design, and carefully delineated settings and birds. A good example can be found in the 1 June 1942 issue, a full-page painting of three blue jays tormenting a screech owl in a red pine. The design is active, with zigzagging branches creating a pattern that is repeated by the white breasts of the blue jays. The jays' postures are dramatic in the Audubon manner, but natural and realistic. The owl is imperious, a brown and round-eyed center of power with chaos radiating. The personalities of the birds are apparent, and the physical portrayal is precise. In total, the painting is a blend of the best of the two masters.

In 1939, one of Peterson's best prewar bird portraits appeared in the *Life* series. It depicts an osprey landing on a pitch pine branch, wings outspread and tail fanned. Even given the poor magazine reproduction of the time, the details, especially the eyes and beak, are vivid. The crest and neck feathers are swept back with quick, bold brushstrokes. And the feather molding throughout is precise in the Fuertes manner. The overall plan of the painting enhances the three-dimensional movement. The bird's posture is nearly horizontal, rather than the customary upright portraits of birds of prey. The angle of the body intersects that of the wings, which is reflected in the position of the branch. This results in a painting that is alive on the canvas. Even the clusters of pine needles shimmer with action. At Camp Chewonki in the early 1930s, Peterson had painted another osprey, at its nest. And although it's an attractive effort, it is somewhat static. Comparing the two paintings, one is startled at the development of Peterson's bird portraiture. Equally impressive is how, as in the blue jay and screech owl painting, he combined the analytical representation of Fuertes and the emotion of Audubon.

16

The 25 September 1939 issue of *Life* in which Peterson's osprey painting appeared was a special issue devoted to the War World. The painting stood alone among such martial features as "The Theater of War: A Pin Map" and "War Materials: A Dictionary of Modern Warfare." The lead story, "German Bombers Rain Death and Destruction on Warsaw," preceded a close-up profile of Hitler. Peterson's spread, "Birds of Prey," followed a pictorial story on bombers and bombing tactics. The irony of this lone nonmilitary feature among stories prompted by Germany's invasion of Poland two weeks earlier and England's subsequent entrance into the war suggests something about birds and bird study that Peterson would write of repeatedly

in his career—that birds were an escape, not from reality but into a different reality, more pleasant and eternal.

Another feature article that emphasized this perspective, this one on migrating birds, appeared in an issue of *Life* that was buried in a time capsule at the New York World's Fair in 1938. There—among stories of a battle between China and Japan over a village called Taierhchwang, "God Save the King" being played after a performance of *The Magic Flute* in Covent Garden, and pictures of Hitler, Mussolini, and Franco—were Peterson's illustrations of twenty-two migratory songbirds, portraits of six marsh birds, and a North America map depicting migratory flyways. As Peterson said later, "The historian who studies this issue in 2938 will learn not only about a world and its leaders edging toward World War II, but will also learn that the spring migration of birds was a week early in the year of 1938. Wars and their leaders come and go, but the birds will probably be performing their yearly ritual more or less on schedule."[1] Throughout his life, and especially during difficult times, Peterson drew comfort from this truth of the continuity of the natural world, especially as it manifested itself in the world of birds. And in the decade of the thirties, the times were difficult indeed.

In his late twenties, good-looking, and becoming successful, Peterson would have been considered a good catch. And stories indicate that in spite of his shyness and absorption in bird study, he tried for an active social life—within the parameters prescribed by the bird world. For example, Frank Graham writes of Peterson's time at the Audubon Nature Camp in the summer of 1936: "At one point Peterson asked for and was granted permission to keep 'some campers' out past ten o'clock at night to go 'owling.' The exemption lasted until Buchheister discovered that Peterson always limited those expeditions to a party of himself and the comeliest lass in camp."[2]

Peterson's playful version, which he wrote many years later, pretends innocence. His friend Allan Cruickshank announced that Peterson would take the young ladies on an after-hours owl walk if they did their work well—"typical Cruickshank banter," Peterson wrote. But one bold student took him up on the offer. "Obviously she was serious about the owls," so they met after lights out and walked "down the path that wound around the perimeter of the island through the spruce and balsam forest, and it *was* an owl walk, just that," he wrote. "I hooted like a barred owl on my cupped hands, but no answer. I intoned like a great horned. We listened. The owls didn't give a hoot." But John Baker had arrived from New York that night and happened on Peterson's "innocent" field trip, and the owl walks ended, as did, coincidentally or not, Peterson's camp days and nights. As he said later, "I have often wondered whether that was why John Baker assigned me to other duties in the New York office the following summer."[3]

One of the young women Peterson met at camp that summer of 1936 and, presumably, took "owling" was Mildred Washington, an attractive young socialite. Whatever form their courtship took, it was brief; they were married in December of that same year. Perhaps Peterson was lonely, or afraid of being lonely. He had always had people living around him—too many when he was a child, Nathan's crowded home when he moved to New York, roommates at the YMCA, DoRio's family. Even when he took his apartment in the Village, he ate all his meals with the Allens, and later he moved in with them when they moved to Scarsdale. But more likely, especially if the passion with which he encountered luna moths and flickers as a child carried over to women as an adult, he was smitten. The marriage proved to be unpleasant and short; Mildred Peterson filed for divorce in Las Vegas on 23 April 1942, charging mental cruelty. Friends indicated that the couple argued violently and often, that Peterson asked for a separation, and that Mildred Peterson finally agreed to divorce. Bias, the vagaries of memory, and Peterson's reticence to talk about his personal life obscure whatever fault may be laid. One fact can be inferred, however: Peterson's ability to go on with his work in the face of what appears to have been near-constant personal turmoil indicates either an extraordinary ability to focus, a desperate need to escape, or both.

Now his lifestyle, which could almost be called peripatetic, took hold. He discovered the pleasure of travel: new birds to study, contact with fellow ornithologists, and escape. He traveled extensively in the American West, working on the western *Guide;* went to Florida, Key West, and the Dry Tortugas; and took a pelagic trip out of San Francisco with Guy Emerson to photograph the Laysan albatross for *Life.*

Then current events finally caught up with Peterson in full

force, and at about the same time that events in his personal life did, in fact, affect his work. On 16 February 1943 he was inducted into the army, and in July 1943 he married Barbara Coulter. After he completed his six weeks of basic training, Peterson wrote John Baker playfully: "As you perhaps know, I am now a free man. . . . So far, I guess the girls haven't heard about it, for there has been no stampede in my direction yet."[4] But he wasn't telling the whole story, and in June he wrote Baker in an entirely different tone:

> This note is to let you in on the hopes and plans that concern my heart. These four months in the army have given me much time to think, and in that time I have enormously increased my fondness and affection for Barbara Coulter. I am sure no one would make a better wife—and I hope I can give her the happiness she deserves. She is a completely nice person. My approach to marriage will be different this time, for I believe I have learned my lesson the hard way.[5]

Whereas Peterson's first wife had been mercurial and difficult, Barbara Coulter was independent and competent. When she graduated from high school in Seattle, she wanted to be a veterinarian but knew she needed to find a "woman's trade." So in 1938 she moved to New York, where she took one year at Columbia, then one year at Katherine Gibbs Secretarial School. Through Gibbs, she was placed at Audubon to work as a typist for Robert Allen. Soon she was put in charge of the film and photography department. Her collegial friendship with Peterson became romantic when he and Mildred separated, and Roger and Barbara saw each other secretly while the divorce was being worked out. They became engaged when Peterson received his draft notice, but they concealed the engagement until June because the separation wasn't generally known.

Even such a practiced deflector of bad news as Peterson could not ignore the imminent world war entirely. In a letter to his mother he wrote that married men would soon be called up. He worried that he wouldn't get the western *Guide* done. Even though he had finished six large bird prints, he had more to do, and *Life* wanted more articles—all outside his work at Audubon. In 1942, he published "Birds and Floating Oil" in *Audubon Magazine*, which had changed its name from *Bird-Lore* to reflect its expanding interests.[6] The tone throughout is dark and reflects well Peterson's state of mind at the time. It begins, "A torpedoed tanker going down, a submarine mortally blasted by a depth change, or a ship simply discharging its ballast water forms a great oily slick on the choppy surface of the sea. The waters are quieted, and the glistening patch, spreading for acres, must seem to a sea bird, a pleasant respite from the ceaselessly moving waves. Instead of an oasis of rest, it proves to be a place of death" (217). Here was a force that was going to touch *every* facet of Peterson's life. On his headstone, an inscription reads: "Birds cannot speak for themselves. I must speak for them." He did exactly that in "Birds and Floating Oil." It is a bitter plea to the world's politicians to be aware that the world is inhabited by other sentient beings besides people. And Peterson acknowledges the even more bitter reality that his words will not be heeded. He begins with a discussion of the practice of discharging oil into harbors, pointing out that the United States had banned the practice in 1924 and that the League of Nations was working on a global agreement. But nothing had come of it, and by 1935, "world politics had become so tangled, diplomacy so bogged down, that it was hopeless. The world was on the long road to war, and nothing could stop its precipitous rush" (219).

Dumping oil, however, is not Peterson's focus here: "Oily water, discharged from a home-bound ship is as nothing compared to a full-laden vessel destroyed by a mine" (219). In February 1942, "the expected began to happen." Ludlow Griscom reported that 25 percent of the 20,000 wintering birds wintering off Cape Cod had been badly oiled. Peterson continues with several pages of dismal recitation. At Cape Sable, 90 percent of the eider ducks and goldeneyes and 75 percent of the oldsquaws had died. Near Grand Manan, at least 13,500 seabirds washed up on the island's shores. On Cape Hatteras, one-fourth of the common loons were dead. Similar devastations were reported all up and down the east coast. And to emphasize the despair he felt, Peterson included information on the futility of treating oiled birds—or even in finding them: "From now on the seashore will get poor attention, as few people escape questioning when seen with glasses along the beach. Whether they will be there to see it or not, the dismal tragedy will probably be repeated next winter. While the war lasts, it seems totally improbable that we can prevent oil pollution at sea" (219). If the article was an attempt to deflect the hopeless anger and fear he felt in his personal situation, it can perhaps be described as a transparent one. Three *Audubon* issues later, the following note appeared: "Roger Peterson and Allan Cruickshank . . . have been reclassified in 1A. With physical examinations passed, they now await definite date of induction. . . . [A]ll of you will sincerely join their colleagues here at Audubon House in wishing them Godspeed."[7]

At this period of his life, and for the first and only time, Peterson couldn't find refuge in either the natural world or in his work. As he wrote to Baker of his intention to marry, "There is no telling how long I'll be in the country and we would like to take what little happiness we can, while we can—even if it is only a matter of seeing each other occasionally on week-ends."[8] Not only was he facing a complete change of life but also, more urgently, the uncertainty of his military assignment, most likely the Pacific. In the month Peterson was inducted, *Life* reported that the United States was losing the war; with the fall of Singapore, Japan had gained control of the Far Eastern front. News from the defense of Bataan—as an example of what a new recruit might read about his future—included frightening stories of operating tables filled twenty-four hours a day, operations interrupted by bombs, and hospitals without enough tents to cover the wounded. MacArthur's army there was outnumbered six to one. The failure of his marriage had driven Peterson into a period of angst that gradually became more general and profound as it was fed by dread and uncertainty. In his imagination, he looked ahead to a world of regimentation and war, without the comfort of paints and birds.

1942–1953

Washington, D.C.

Peterson slowly emerged from his disquiet for three reasons: his gradual adjustment to army life, a reprieve from being shipped overseas, and his marriage to Barbara Coulter, which lasted thirty-two years, until their divorce in 1975.

Toward the end of their marriage, Peterson told Barbara, "I couldn't have done it without you."[1] He was right. For more than thirty years, she did the things that had to be done and left Peterson free to work and travel. While he was moody, she was constant. In areas where he was incompetent, she excelled. He was totally dependent on her and trusted her completely to act as his link to the world outside the community of "bird people." It fell to her to handle the "home"—the physical house, the children, the details of daily life. She typed all of his manuscripts, clipped newspapers, arranged his speaking engagements, and helped answer the huge volume of letters and queries that he received daily—the "dicky-bird" mail that followed Peterson from his days at the National Audubon Society. And her life entailed endless accommodations. She routinely prepared meals when Peterson brought home carloads of birders. She adapted to his unorthodox working hours, often preparing breakfast at suppertime and dinner in the morning after he had painted through the night.

Paul Brooks, a longtime friend, told a story in 1985 that he felt epitomized Barbara Peterson. It happened on a trip to Baja, California. As Brooks recalled, "My wife and I were in a small boat with Roger and Barbara when the propeller of our outboard motor struck a snag, breaking the shear-pin. The boatman had no spare. 'If someone will go back to the motel,' said Barbara, 'and look in the upper left-hand drawer of my bureau, he will find my tool kit, with some shear-pins in it.'"[2]

Barbara was quite skilled mechanically and a good carpenter, capable of doing her own interior decoration projects. And somehow along the way, she worked hard for conservation and preservation causes. She was an active supporter of Planned Parenthood and carried a passion for the world's future that equaled her husband's: "We are living in a brutal age driven by greed. . . . Right now there seems to be a total lack of ethics at all levels."[3] A significant tribute to her is the Vera Award, which was given by the New York Zoological Society each year to a woman who had made outstanding contributions in the fields of ecology and natural history. Barbara Peterson received the award in 1976, recognized as "a woman who is known in her own right as a conservationist, wildlife photographer, and horsewoman." In her acceptance speech she said, in part, "I have long felt that every time an award was given to the husband a small replica should be made for the wife for her charm bracelet. More often than not the behind-the-scenes are a shared endeavor and we, as wives, more often than not just bask in reflected glory."[4] It was not a rancorous statement, just an honest appraisal of mid-twentieth-century women's roles and of her place in the Peterson household.

Taken in total, Peterson's army experience turned out to be not so bad as he expected. He enjoyed the novelty of Corps of Engineers training, entertaining John Baker with a letter that listed his activities with some relish: "We do a thousand things—build roads—lay out landing fields . . . and such ticklish jobs as removing booby traps." And he couldn't resist some bravado: "Of course, we have to know how to deal with the enemy when he objects—such tricks as flipping a man's eyeball out with our thumb etc. . . . We play with dynamite every day—build bridges in a matter of hours then blow hell out of them. Right now I'm getting so adept that I could tell to a stick just how much dynamite to use on Audubon House without damaging the houses on either side too much."[5]

After his six-month training period, he was assigned to Engineer School. His first task was to work on a camouflage manual; as his discharge papers noted, he "illustrated camouflage practices and mistakes, sample problems and other phases of camouflage." In Peterson's words, the manuals were about "simple camouflage where the individual soldier made use of cast shadows or simulated cast shadows." He also made color, black-and-white, and half-tone illustrations for bridge-building manuals and "graphic portfolios."[6] In a letter to Baker, he put a good light on it, saying that the experience would be invaluable for the Junior Audubon materials: "I've learned a lot already about black and whites that will come in handy on marginal drawing."[7] In a 1944 letter to friend and fellow bird painter George Sutton, he wrote about his army art department: "twenty enlisted men, all of them very accomplished and at least four of which made $20,000 a year or more as nationally known illustrators. . . . [T]hey are the privates and corporals. The captain is a youngster who ran a high school paper." This group of all-stars received a commendation by working overtime with his unit for technical illustrations "in connection with preparation of a technical bulletin on a new floating bridge."[8]

But in spite of his accomplishments and his innate ability to make the best of any situation, Peterson longed for his other world, as he indicated in his closing words to Sutton: "Some day this war will be over and then, by God, we will chase the birds again."[9] And as he wrote to Baker, "During wartime one must live always in the present and grasp at every precious opportunity. . . . I am now hoping that she [Barbara] can come down here to live and that I can get permission to live off the post."[10]

He got his wish and the couple's life together began in a tiny bed-and-bath off base. Early on, Peterson began to establish a working pattern that would, at once, make him remarkably productive and put a strain on his marriage. He left for the base at 5:30 a.m., often returning home as late as 7:00 in the evening. Then he would retire to the bathroom and paint far into the night. At one point, he wrote plaintively to Joseph Kastner at *Life*, "This army life is getting monotonous. I hope the next job I do for LIFE can be done in a more leisurely fashion—by daylight instead of the small, late hours of the evening."[11] In the bathroom, in the best light available because of the bright light bulbs and white tiles, he made a painting of two snowy egrets, one of a series of lithographic prints he did for the Quaker State Lithographing Company from 1942 to 1952. His first contract called for eight portraits: blue jay, cardinal, redwing, rose-breasted grosbeak, cedar waxwing, Baltimore oriole, "Sea Swallows," and bluebird. According to an advertising booklet from Quaker State, "Roger Tory Peterson is the staff artist and author associated with the National Audubon Society. Mr. Peterson is now in the Army but he expects to complete a portfolio of 50 paintings for reproduction purposes when he is released."[12] The paintings were mostly portraits, but a few, like the snowy egrets and a flamingo, were full-canvas paintings. The bulk of them were reproduced in two sizes—22 by 28 inches and 18 by 22 inches. About them, Peterson wrote "When I see one, I usually cringe, though two or three of them have stood the test of time."[13] He was probably being modest here. Although the feather detail and the careful modeling of the later Mill Pond Press prints was yet to emerge, these prints do stand up well. Besides the full-sized paintings, the others depict birds on a branch against a blank background in the Audubon manner. But the composition often reveals Peterson's interest in Oriental design, with the branches, and the birds on them, dividing the surfaces with diagonal lines like so much of the Japanesque art he would have seen while working with Langereis.

By Christmas of 1943, the couple had moved into a larger apartment where Peterson could paint in the bedroom. Here he continued to work on the Quaker State series and the *Life* series with Joseph Kastner. When he wasn't painting or at the base, he and Barbara would take a bus to the edge of town and walk in the woods all day, where Peterson sketched and photographed. When he needed an image of a snag and its reflection for the snowy egret painting, for example, they made frequent trips to the Potomac so he could make study sketches. In May 1944, they used a fourteen-day furlough to travel to Charleston, South Carolina, where Peterson painted the Cherokee roses for another Quaker State print: *Summer Tanager with Cherokee Roses.* Barbara's letters to her mother during this time contain the first mention of Peterson's occasional morose periods of self-doubt and gloom, periods that would plague him throughout his life. But most of the year, Barbara wrote, was "rather blissful."[14]

Much of the bliss of 1944 came about because Peterson learned in May that the army considered him to have "a rare skill so he would not be useful overseas."[15] That fear shunted aside, Peterson continued his painting at an even more ambitious pace. He had fulfilled his contract of eight paintings for Quaker State as well as two *Life* features—on winter birds and waterbird courtship. He planned several others and often had two paintings going at the same time.

Just before he was drafted, in those days of dread and uncertainty, Peterson and a Bronx County Bird Club friend, Irving Kassoy, had concocted a scheme that was pure escapism. Since pigeons had been used as message carriers in Europe in World War I, and since the Pacific was to be the focus of the war, why not use seabirds as carriers? As Peterson wrote, "We hoped we would be sent to some interesting tropical islands to investigate the use of shear-waters, petrels, and other oceanic birds to carry messages from ships to islands, etc. We carefully researched our material and drew up a plan that we sent to the Signal Corps. The answer from the Army was a polite, 'No.'"[16]

As it turned out, Peterson did achieve a pale imitation of that fantasy. His last months in the service became "literally one continuous birding trip." In July 1945 he was transferred to the Air Corps and assigned to Orlando, Florida. Barbara, by now pregnant with their first child, Tory, stayed behind. In Florida he and fellow naturalists—Alexander Klots, who would later write *A Field Guide to the Butterflies* for Peterson's Field Guide Series, and Earl Herald, who did the fish guide—were to study the effects of DDT on organisms other than mosquitoes. At the time, DDT was being hailed as yet another triumph of technology over nature. The wonder chemical had made the world safe from malaria, and Paul Müller, the Swiss chemist who discovered its insecticidal properties, was awarded a Nobel Prize in 1948. Five-acre plots were sprayed with varying strengths of DDT and compared with control plots. Peterson checked the bird populations, Herald surveyed the fish and amphibians, and Klots monitored the insects. They found that the light doses killed the mosquitoes but had no effect on birds or even bees, but Peterson noted that studies by the U.S. Fish and Wildlife Service had found that heavy concentrations were lethal. His conclusion, written in 1948, was both ambivalent and prophetic: "Such panaceas as DDT give us pause to ponder. . . . Some believe that small doses of DDT may even be a boon to wildlife as a substitute for marsh drainage in the control of mosquitoes. But by using this dangerous poison widely, before we know more about its properties, we run the risk of turning our world into a biological desert."[17] Later, he would admit that "at the time, we had no idea about the residual effects and that birds that were in long food chains, such as pelicans, peregrines, etc. would be so adversely affected."[18] Along with the rest of the scientific community, he was at the beginning of what would become one of the most important environmental struggles of the twentieth century. It was a cause that would engage him more deeply as he became friends with Rachel Carson when he returned home and, later, when he saw the effects of DDT on the ospreys of the Connecticut coastal area.

Peterson's discharge in October 1945 found the couple in a newly rented house in Glen Echo, Maryland, and, along with Carson, deeply involved in the Washington Audubon Society, where Peterson planned the programming. The house was an outbuilding on a large estate near the Potomac, and Peterson found its wooded location perfect. As he wrote to Clarence Beal, "I can see pileated woodpeckers from my window; barred owls hoot at night; both scarlet and summer tanagers live in the huge oaks over the roof; Louisiana water-thrushes, Kentuckys, etc., nest in the back of the house, and even bald eagles fly over—saw two yesterday. Also osprey."[19] Because of his growing renown and the easing of both national and international travel restrictions after the war, the house was filled with visitors from the community of naturalists and became a focal point for gatherings that centered on natural history and, particularly, bird study. He had declared to Baker in 1944 that his "chief hope for the next ten years is to make myself into a first-rate painter, for I have decided that at the age of 36 I am by no means as far along as I should be, chiefly because I have not painted enough birds. If, by the age of 45, I find myself a disappointment and a fizzle, I will quietly relax into the less strenuous life of a vegetable."[20] But free now to work full-time, he went back to the pattern that had started in the thirties and would continue throughout his life: he would declare a desire to paint but end up working on his field guides. He immediately set to completing two major projects: a revision of the eastern *Guide* and his first major prose collection, *Birds over America*. He had developed the habit of nonstop work; when he tired of painting, he turned to writing until he was blocked. Then he would return to his worktable to paint and draw some more. This approach fit the task of field guide revision well, a project that fully engaged his skill with both images and words.

18

From the start, Peterson had a plan for his language in the field guides: to share the experience of field identification with his readers. This is best seen in the pre-1980 editions, which offered him the space to develop and practice a distinctive style. In these books—the 1934, 1939, and 1947 eastern *Guides* and the 1941 and 1961 western *Guides*—the text took precedence; the plates, located in separate sections of the book, served as illustration. After 1980, identification became more visual, with a condensed text across the page from each plate. Because the resulting descriptions served more as captions, much of Peterson's earlier style was lost and, with it, the personal relationship that bird students had with their "petersons."

In his field guides before 1980, Peterson personalizes most often by using direct address, speaking to his reader in the second person. The effect gained is a sort of master bird walk with gentle admonitions that aid in identification and warn of errors. The following examples are found in the 1947 eastern *Guide,* the best source for Peterson's bird guide prose. Golden eagle—"If you lack experience, be very careful. The adult resembles the immature Bald Eagle, but is darker." Fish crow—"Along tidewater listen for this small Crow. Go by voice, not by size, unless both Crows are together." American pipit—"Learn the note—you will hear many more Pipits flying over than you will see on the ground." On occasion, Peterson enhances this intimate connection with his readers by using the first person. In the royal tern description, he writes, parenthetically, "Although I have found bill color reliable, some observers have not." Finally, like any good teacher, Peterson allows his students to fall short occasionally. The entry for the parasitic jaeger contains sympathetic advice to bird students trying to separate the jaeger species: "Jaegers are very, very confusing. You will have to let many of them go by as 'just Jaegers.' Even experts do."

A second device Peterson employs is to create a short experiential narrative as part of the description. For example, the field marks of the meadowlark are introduced in this way: "As we cross an extensive field or meadow this chunky brown bird flashes from the grass, showing a conspicuous patch of white on each side of the short, wide tail." The ruddy turnstone description conveys the actual experience of observation: "In breeding plumage . . . it is handsome enough, but when the bird flies the real revelation occurs." This technique also enables Peterson to internalize the experience, as he does when describing the drumming of a male ruffed grouse: "At a distance the muffled thumping is so hollow that sometimes it hardly registers as an exterior sound, but seems rather to be a disturbing series of vibrations within the ear itself." Arguably, Peterson never wrote a better sentence.

This stylistic approach was made possible because Peterson was willing to break away from the diction and structure of traditional bird guide prose. Typically, as Nathan Copple points out in "A Field Guide to the Words . . . of Roger Tory Peterson," a field description begins with a template: "Recognized as [group name] by its _____; known as this species by _____."[1] Peterson, however, engages his readers by varying his opening sentences, often to superb effect: "Very dingy looking" [seaside sparrow]; "Purple is hardly the word; raspberry or old-rose is more like it" [purple finch]; "A voice in the woods" [ovenbird], "Dark and bizarre" [harlequin duck]. Other first sentences provide clinching keys to identification: "The only American Duck with entirely black plumage" [American scoter]. Still others are straightforward description: "Olive above, yellow below, with a gray hood completely encircling the head and neck" [mourning warbler]. And some are downright elegant, such as the carefully crafted kingfisher entry: "Hovering on rapidly beating wings in one spot above the water in readiness for the plunge, or flying with peculiar uneven wing-beats, rattling as it goes, the Kingfisher is easily learned by the novice."[2]

Unlike other guide writers, Peterson created a *voice*. Birdwatchers brought more than a book with them in the field; they felt the presence of another person when they read their Peterson guides. That person was authoritative, helpful, engaging, and personal. He kept them entertained and sometimes amused, and he taught them to *know* the birds, to both identify them and to identify *with* them. Any observer schooled by the early Peterson field guides, when identifying a Henslow's sparrow for the first time, would immediately remember Peterson's description of the bird's song: "The Henslow's perches atop a weed, from which it utters one of the poorest vocal efforts of any bird; throwing back its head, it ejects a hiccoughing *tsi-lick*. As if to practice this 'song' so that it might not always remain at the bottom of the list, it often hiccoughs all night long."[3] In the 1980 edition, this passage was slashed to "Song, a poor vocal effort; a hiccupping *tsi-lick*. May sing on quiet nights." For a while at least, bird identification, as a result of Peterson's unique language and style, had become bird recognition.

Peterson owed much to Joseph Kastner, his good friend from his New York days, who was a senior editor at *Life* magazine. It was Kastner who got Peterson the contract for the *Life* series, and it was the *Life* series that got him the Quaker State contract. In his own book, *A World of Watchers*, Kastner was the first to point out how Peterson's "laconic" writing style matched his illustrations: "His training in art, both as a modern realist and as an old-fashioned academic, had taught him how to draw with finicky accuracy, to match colors, to use shadings for small or broad effect. His mental discipline enabled him to ignore unneeded detail, and a stubborn confidence in his own system . . . enabled him to eliminate what other guides had always put in. He was not concerned with being complete, just comprehensible."[4]

Essentially, Peterson progressed through three painting styles in his American field guide illustrations. His first approach, which can be seen in the 1934 and 1939 editions of the eastern *Guide* as well as their 1941 western counterpart, was purely to illustrate the text. The 1947 eastern and 1961 western editions are examples of a middle period that revealed the beginnings of more interest in texture and design. Peterson's field guide style reached its peak in the 1980 eastern and 1990 western editions.

Little changed visually between the 1934 and 1939 editions; the first real change in his illustration work was seen in the 1947 edition. It was a complete overhaul—all new plates, sixty in all, with thirty-six in color. His publisher not only added more color plates and gave Peterson more space but also improved the production values a bit for the 1947 eastern *Guide*, which was stylistically repeated in the 1961 western *Guide*. The 1934 work was cheap; the Depression and Peterson's obscurity forced a business decision that resulted in a poorly produced book. Good book sales of the earlier editions and the competition from the new *Audubon Bird Guide*, written by Richard Pough, freed up some money to make the books from Peterson's middle period more attractive, but the end result does little to reflect the effort he put into his paintings. Furthermore, the addition of more color didn't signify a complete change in approach. As Peterson recalled, "Still, in 1947 I remained wedded to practicality and leaned toward the schematic rather than traditional portraiture for the field user."[5] And whatever portraiture technique he applied was lost in production, as a side-by-side comparison between the original plates and the book reproductions reveals. The original plates show a fair amount of modeling that is lost with the disappearance of brush strokes, sharpness of line, and entire washes of paint in the reproduced images. Color values are lost as well: whites are dull (the eye ring on the Connecticut warbler becomes indistinct, for example). Sometimes the colors are changed entirely, as is the case of the painted redstart, whose reds in the original are bright and highlighted only to turn nearly orange in the book. Certain detail disappears as well, such as the hint in the original of how feathers lay or the ridges and lines that separate upper and lower mandibles in some warblers. The overall result is a book of flat and lifeless birds reproduced from bird paintings that were alive and alert.

Practically speaking, there was no need for more color than he used; the birds illustrated by black-and-white plates were birds—ducks, gulls, and hawks in flight—that are most often identified at a distance by their overall patterns rather than color. And the ink plates, especially the gulls, show a marked improvement over their somewhat cartoonish predecessors. Aesthetically speaking, however, the color plates are disappointing—and not only because of poor production values. Although the illustrations are more detailed and larger by about 50 percent than those in the 1934 and 1939 editions, they remain two-dimensional: silhouettes with plumage patterns that are colored in. They line up in tidy rows on the page, like stuffed birds in a specimen drawer. Basically, Peterson's approach in 1947 remained aimed toward its original target: the mind rather than the eye. It was a device to teach the identification of birds; a reader is invited to browse and learn, not to browse and enjoy.

The reviews were of the sort that Peterson was getting accustomed to. In the *New York Post*, Devin Garrity wrote, "It is not often that a book appears which sets out to perform a specific function and accomplishes it so well that imitation seems unnecessary. But such a one is Roger Peterson's 'Field Guide to the Birds,' now published in a new and revised edition with sixty pages of splendid color plates added."[6] And Leonard Dubkin pointed out in the *Chicago Tribune* that the few "holdouts" who still felt Chapman's handbook was the definitive source would realize that "now, with the publication of this third edition, there is no longer any doubt as to which field guide is the better."[7] But the response that must have gratified Peterson the most came in a letter from his old mentor Ludlow Griscom, which read in part, "The new field guide, if anything, exceeds my fondest hopes. It seems to me as nearly peerless in its field as one could possibly reasonably expect of a human being. So strongly do I feel this to be the case that I feel genuinely proud of having been one of the many who gave you some small assistance."[8]

19

In the years following his army discharge, Peterson battled with a huge decision. John Baker wanted him back at the National Audubon Society; in September 1944, nearly a year before his discharge, Baker wrote to say, "I hope you won't get mixed up in any commitments to do this or that outside job until you are in a position to know what it is that the Society would particularly like to have you tackle."[1] A regular job would offer security for his new family. But with that security came restrictions, especially on his personal work schedule, which often had begun at noon and lasted until four in the morning. And he wanted to travel, at any time and for as long as he desired. In other words, he wanted the freedom that freelancing offered, but like most people who had battled through the Great Depression, he was fearful. Tory was soon joined by a brother, Lee, and Peterson, remembering his own childhood, was determined to provide for his family. He decided on a three-month trial period, which was extended, then extended again. And he gave himself a safety net of sorts, agreeing to be considered "on leave" from the society until he finished the revisions of his field guides. Part of the "leave" agreement included doing two paintings for *Audubon Magazine*, writing new texts for twelve Junior Audubon leaflets, and painting a series of common Pacific Coast birds for reproduction as bird cards. It was a time, Barbara remembered, punctuated by brooding, self-doubt, and anxiety.

The uncertain situation was compounded by the society's plans to publish a book—*Audubon Bird Guide*—to replace the outdated Chester Reed guide. This would not compete with Peterson's guide but rather would be handbook-type descriptions accompanied by a painting of each bird. Richard Pough was assigned the job, and he chose Don Eckelberry to do the paintings. When Peterson learned of this, he fired off a bitter letter to Baker that laid out his "resentments." He was upset first because he had turned down three offers to do a guide to replace Reed's, since he knew that the society was planning one and he had assumed that he would do the paintings for it. And he was hurt that Eckelberry, a good bird painter but new to the society, would get on-the-job practice whereas Peterson had been with the society for nine years with almost no chance to paint. As he put it,

> My chief discontent concerning my work with the Society has been that I was unable to pursue my chief aim—that of developing myself into a first-rate bird artist—except piecemeal evenings when I was tired. A large number of small portraits [for the Audubon guide] done day after day on schedule would improve my work no end. . . . I am getting no younger. . . . The chance to do some honest to God bird portraits, that will be distributed widely for the next 40 years [is] the opportunity of a lifetime.[2]

The two men exchanged somewhat surly letters, with Baker accusing Peterson of exhibiting "some indications of 'The Great I am,'" and suggesting that Peterson take a more conciliatory attitude and show some humility.[3] Seeing a larger issue, Peterson fired back in anger: "I assure you that I am not lacking in humility. If I had exercised less humility I would probably be an officer in the army instead of a corporal. This lesson has been rather a bitter one and has brought me to the realization that I must fight for what I want and not underestimate my own capabilities."[4] Baker eventually deflected Peterson's anxiety as they had some time to think: "I have a hunch that the new Audubon Bird Guide will be a stimulant to sales of your revised field guide. . . . [C]heer up, my lad. You sound positively Norwegian!"[5] And Peterson, indeed, did come back around, writing to Baker, "With all respect to the new Audubon Guide, which is excellent, I do believe I will still have the more practical Field Guide, and the one which will continue to be the standard."[6]

Peterson's association with *Life* was winding down; the magazine had turned to more diorama-type painting, which Peterson found "too finicky." In a letter to Joseph Kastner written in 1956, he reflected on his *Life* series:

> When I look over the twelve stories I did under your direction, I find them quite interesting in retrospect. The first one on migrations causes me to cringe—the birds are so stiff and static. However, I find I can still be quite proud of two or three of the last ones which dealt with behavior studies and life histories. To my knowledge no other mass publication has ever shown series on bird behavior illustrated by color drawings. It was quite an achievement, and I still get comments on them.[7]

However, the continuing success of the Quaker State series and the good sales of the field guides allowed Peterson to continue to put off a final decision about freelancing. Another financial backup was provided by the Audubon Screen Tours. The tour series was begun by Wayne Short, who had been running a model operation in St. Louis. He would bring in speakers to his local club and arrange for several other engagements nearby, making a trip to St. Louis financially feasible. The society asked Short, a superb organizer, to expand his concept to a national level, which he did with outstanding success. In 1946, Baker asked—begged—Peterson to join: "We need you desperately, Roger, and I certainly hope that you will see fit to participate."[8] Peterson was not a filmmaker at the time, so, much to his displeasure, he was provided with heavily spliced footage that other lecturers didn't want. With this he cobbled together "The Riddle of Migration," preparing a script that discussed each bird as it appeared on the screen. The result was a well-presented and informative evening that began with a general discussion of theories of migration followed by specific examples. Peterson would complain to Baker about the film, writing once that the tour was a waste of time for him and that it was "high time I tried to be a decent bird painter."[9] But he would continue to present "The Riddle of Migration" each tour season until 1954, when he was able to use his own film, *Wild America*. He preferred to travel from venue to venue by car. Barbara Peterson was enormously helpful here. She worked out his tour dates with Short and often went along, always as the driver because she couldn't stand to ride with him, citing his poor concentration and his cavalier attitude toward the rules of the road: at intersections, "he felt that red lights meant to approach with caution but to continue on if he deemed it safe," Barbara recalled.[10] The tours, the couple believed, made good business sense: they sold books. But they also provided an outlet for Peterson's increasing awareness of environmental issues as well as another small, but steady, source of income. The publication of *Birds over America* in 1948, however, made Peterson's future clear.

On more than one occasion, he declared an ambition to write more like the nature writer and novelist Peter Matthiessen, acknowledging an awareness of a side of himself, an expressive side, that he would never seem able to unblock completely. He called it a desire to "shed some of this brevity and objectivity, and let my inner feelings [about birds and nature] come through" and added, "I think they don't always, despite my deep feelings in these matters."[11] When he asked Paul Brooks, his editor at Houghton Mifflin, how he could emulate Matthiessen, Brooks reportedly said, "If you don't know, it would take too long to tell you."[12] Brooks knew Peterson well; he was his editor and friend for sixty years. The remark was probably the best way to let Peterson know that he would never be emotionally or psychologically capable of approaching writing as Matthiessen does. Consider Peterson's statement about "avant-garde" art in a *Bird Watcher's Digest* article about wildlife art: He approved of abstraction and geometrics, but "as for 'subconscious comment,' I would rather reveal it to an analyst."[13] Consider as well his writing technique as he explained it in a memo to Devlin and Naismith: "[I] work out a kind of structure. . . . I might readjust. I think we all do that. But I tend to write fairly close to length."[14] Then contrast Matthiessen—a writer variously characterized as lyrical, introspective, mystical, political, obscure—who described his nature-writing technique as filling notepads indiscriminately with notes during the day and, while typing them at night, allowing a rough draft to emerge. Two writers, both passionate about their subject, but poles apart temperamentally.

That Peterson deserves the sobriquet "writer" is beyond question. He worked hard at his craft, particularly at the sentence level. And his publication record—more than two dozen books and hundreds of individual pieces—is notable. But he wouldn't be considered by some to be a writer in a literary sense, eschewing as he did such literary devices as ornamentation, irony, indirection, and the "subconscious comment" mentioned earlier. Fortunately for Peterson and his readers, he apparently didn't waste time trying to write in a way that he couldn't. He wrote clearly and well, and *Birds over America* is the best example of this.

Comprising twenty-four essays on nearly every subject imaginable concerning bird study, *Birds over America* was Peterson's first "real" book in the sense that the collection contained extended pieces in the style and content of his choice. In his foreword he sets out his threefold purpose: to consider bird study as a "sport" rather than as a science, to examine the lives of birds beyond mere identification, and to present an environmentalist message with a "biological basis." Although those elements are present throughout, the book is essentially about bird-watching. But *Birds over America* was not merely about this new pastime, and it was the best book written on the subject at the time. Not surprisingly, it was well received by his professional colleagues—reviewer John Terres called it "one of the best bird books to appear in a long time."[15] And it received the John Burroughs Medal for nature writing in 1950.

An introductory chapter supports, enlarges, and personalizes one of the ideas from "Symbols of Nature in Art": that the appeal of birds is the freedom they embody. Here Peterson applies the theory to his own life and adds an observation that he would often repeat— namely, that with experience comes the knowledge that birds are as restricted genetically as humans are socially. This uneasy balance between emotion and reason, between intuition and scientific knowledge, is central to that part of *Birds over America* that presents the "sport" of bird study.[16]

In separate chapters, Peterson describes the three main competitive elements of bird study: listing—individuals recording the numbers of birds they have seen in a year, a country, a state, a lifetime; big days—teams trying to identify as many birds as possible during a twenty-four-hour period; and Christmas Bird Counts— groups identifying birds in one day within a prescribed area. In each chapter, the purpose is to entertain with stories and anecdotes. For example, in "Deceiving the Experts," he retells a story about a Christmas Count hoax that became legendary in New York City bird circles—so legendary, in fact, that in Frank Graham's 1982 piece about the Bronx County Bird Club, the story appears as alive as it had been nearly fifty years earlier. Toward the end of the 1937

Christmas Count, Peterson was checking Lake Agassiz in the Bronx for a gadwall that was wintering there. To his astonishment, he spotted a dovekie in the middle of the lake. Dovekies are birds of the Arctic that winter offshore; an inland record would have been the first for the region. But despite this and the fact that the bird listed slightly, Peterson and other observers decided to claim the sighting. What they actually saw through their 1930s-vintage binoculars was a wooden decoy, planted to embarrass another Bronx County Bird Club member, not Peterson himself. As Peterson relates the story's still-mortifying conclusion,

> At the long table that evening, we saved the dovekie till last. It was to be the *piece de resistance*. We had carefully guarded our secret from the others. They, in turn, gave us no hint that they already knew about it. When the dovekie was announced, one after another of us was asked to stand and give the details. Were we sure the bird moved? We said we were. Then, at a signal from the chairman, the plotters roared in derision and the hoax was laid bare. In our chagrin we consoled ourselves with the thought that we had identified the bird correctly, even though it wasn't alive. (49)

He also deals with the question of the "value" of these sporting activities. The Christmas census is a case in point. He suggests that the data from the counts have scientific importance, but "although the census taker thinks vaguely of these things while rushing about, it is not science he is espousing, but the fun of the chase" (37). In the end, Peterson comes down on the side of fun: "The Christmas Bird Count will continue to give us clues [to understanding shifting bird populations]. But even though there are many nuggets that ornithologists can mine from this rich lode of bird information, to me and to my friends it is our way of celebrating the holidays, an ornithological ritual that has come to represent Yuletide more than Santa Claus or the Christmas tree" (19). On the other hand, he notes, "There is a point of transferal that bridges the gap from the bird lister to the bird watcher." He then introduces examples of sport-birders who went on to make significant scientific contributions to the field of bird study.

The pieces that follow emphasize the pleasure, as opposed to the competition, of bird study. They include profiles of intriguing men whose hobby turned to scientific pursuits; these are the men who "bridged the gap" between listing and observation. Discussions of such topics as the introduction of exotic species and the adaptability of birds occupy several chapters. However, Peterson devotes the bulk of the book to recollections of his pursuit of birds; with chapters devoted to bird families—shorebirds, warblers, raptors, for example—and to habitats such as deserts, mountains, and marshes.

Birds over America also contains a fair picture of Peterson's rather optimistic attitude at the time toward humans' relationship with the land. It is, in fairness, a book about birds, so much of the environmental message is expressed in terms of birds and especially their adaptability. The point, however, is clear: what is good for bird numbers can't be bad for the environment. In "Long after Columbus," he writes about a dam project in western Pennsylvania that flooded valuable habitat but that ultimately brought in more bird species because of the large lake that was formed. He mentions such habitats as airports, golf courses, and other human interventions that birds have adapted to. He writes honestly what every bird student knows: "Some of the best shore-bird areas I have known have been not on the clean beaches but along the water front at the edge of some city where sewage and other organic waste pollutes the mud. Even pollution, provided it is not chemical waste, can at times be attractive to wildlife" (86). Although he writes about the effect of habitat loss—especially on larger birds—and about human blunders that damaged ecological balances, he also says, "Because of a fundamental decency in [man's] make-up, he seems to sober up at the eleventh hour, so we have ethics, sanctuaries and wildlife refuges. It is a man's better self trying to rebuild what he has destroyed, to safeguard for his sons what is left of his inheritance" (77). A similar conciliatory attitude can be found in "The Sky Is Their Highway," a piece about hawk migration. In 1935, while watching the sharp-shinned hawk migration for the first time in Cape May, New Jersey, he witnessed the yearly hawk slaughter that took place on a highway that bisected the birds' route: "I watched 800 sharp-shins try to cross the firing line [the highway where gunners lined up]. Each time a 'sharpy' sailed over the treetops it was met by a pattern of lead. Some folded up silently; others, with head wounds, flopped to the ground, chattering shrilly. By noon 254 birds lay on the pavement" (163). He continues the story with remarkable equanimity:

That evening, in a Cape May home, I sat down to a meal of hawks—twenty sharp-shins, boiled like squabs, for a family of six. I tasted the birds, found them good, and wondered what my friends would say if they could see me. Like a spy breaking bread with the enemy, I felt uneasy. I could not tell my hosts I disapproved, for their consciences were clear—weren't they killing the hawks as edible game and at the same time saving all the little song birds? It would have done no good to explain predation, ecology and the natural balance to these folk. (163)

He concludes by relating that a newly created sanctuary had taken care of the problem by 1948: "As at Hawk Mountain [Pennsylvania], the binocular has replaced the gun and hawks now enjoy a relatively safe passage" (164).

"Trailing America's Rarest Bird" illustrates Peterson's skill at assembling an essay, carefully putting together narrative sections to achieve a successful whole. He begins with a brief and inconclusive encounter with an Eskimo curlew, a bird thought by many at the time to be extinct. He sees a suspicious curlew in the distance, but he can't be sure: "Silhouetted against the low sunlight, it showed no color, nor did it call. It kept right on traveling until it was out of sight, and I had the uneasy feeling that I had muffed the chance of a lifetime" (202). The scientific rigor that Peterson brought to his field study prevented him from claiming the record. And one can feel his frustration; he might have been the last human to knowingly see an individual of a species about to vanish.

After more stories about other threatened species—California condor, trumpeter swan, whooping crane—he inserts an expanded version of his earlier essay "Down the Santee in a Folding Boat," adding more detail of the trip and ending with a dramatic scene in a backwoods cabin, with Peterson listening to an old hunter talking in his sleep about ivory-billed woodpeckers. But all of this is introductory. The real story is of Peterson's sighting of an ivorybill, one of the last documented records before the alleged reappearance of the bird in Arkansas in April 2005.

Devlin and Naismith record a version of that sighting that was told to them by Mildred Washington Peterson. She, Peterson, and his friend Bayard Christy traveled to the Singer Tract in Louisiana, the one remaining place in North America where the woodpecker had been reliably reported. They searched the swamp in vain, with Peterson becoming more and more irritated, grumbling that they were wasting time. An argument ensued, with Mildred insisting that they keep trying and Peterson wanting to give up. In the midst of their bickering, Peterson heard the bird and they spotted it, along with a second individual. Whatever happened that day can't be known for sure, but it is clear that if Mildred was there, she was "edited out," as she claimed, from the written version. Peterson never mentioned her. He dated his sighting as "May of 1942"; the announcement of his divorce appeared in the *New York Times* on 23 April 1942.

More important than the peripheral truths of the event is that Peterson took on the writerly task of consciously creating the most effective narrative for publication. His setting of the drama is detailed and evocative: "The trees whose massive crowns towered 150 feet or more above our heads were sweet gums, Nuttall's oaks and ash, while the lesser trees were mostly hackberries and pecans. In the lower parts of the swamp grew the pale green cypresses, their knobby 'knees' emerging from the dark coffee-colored water" (212). And ornithological detail focuses the reader on the purpose of the quest: "Seldom have I heard more bird song than filled the air in the Singer Tract that May morning. Cardinals, chats, white-eyed vireos, hooded warblers and Carolina wrens sang from the low tangles; Acadian flycatchers, gnatcatchers, redstarts and yellow-throated, parula and cerulean warblers poured their contributions into the cauldron of song from higher perches" (212).

He builds the tension by describing the first day's unsuccessful search with Christy and a guide. They return the second day, without their guide, to more frustration. And then, in the afternoon,

> We would make another sortie before throwing in the sponge. Hardly had we gone a hundred yards when a startling new sound came from our right—an indescribable tooting note, musical in a staccato sort of way. For a moment it did not click, but then I knew—*it was the ivory-bill!* . . .
>
> Breathlessly we stalked the insistent toots, stepping carefully, stealthily, so that no twig would crack. With our hearts pounding we tried to keep cool, hardly daring to believe that this was it—that this was what we had come fifteen hun-

dred miles to see. We were dead certain this was no squirrel or lesser woodpecker, for an occasional blow would land— *whop!*—like the sound of an axe. Straining our eyes, we discovered the first bird, half hidden by the leafage, and in a moment it leaped upward into the full sunlight. (214)

He goes on to capture the wonder, clearly amazed. But still a scientist, he includes enough field marks to convince any doubting ornithologist: "This was no puny pileated; this was a whacking big bird, with great white patches on its wings and a gleaming white bill. By its long recurved crest of blackish jet we knew it was a female. We were even close enough to see its pale yellow eyes. . . . We had a feeling of unreality as we watched them [two females]. They looked downright archaic, completely unlike any other birds" (214).

Peterson's concluding paragraph is a reminder to his readers that this is more than an essay about seeing a rare bird; it is about extinction, the terrible finality of the death of a species: "Unlike the last passenger pigeon, which officially expired at the Cincinnati Zoo at 1:00 p.m. Central Standard Time, September 1, 1914, no one will know the exact time of the ivory-bill's passing" (215). As all good conclusions do, this one gathers all the disparate parts of the essay and points them toward a larger central concern.

Most of the essays in the collection are not as tightly composed as "Trailing America's Rarest Bird." Peterson preferred the freedom of a meandering form that allowed him to center on a special characteristic of a region or a special circumstance and to fill in all the detail of bird life and habitat as he wanted. "Rain Shadows of the Mexican Border," which describes the mountain and desert areas around Tucson, is a typical example.

His first view is a landscape that reveals his painter's eye:

As our horses come to a halt on the crest of one of the desert ranges, the insatiate eye commands a great domain. . . . Range upon range of mountains fall away into the blue distance. Their summits are dark with evergreens, while lower down, the sparse brown oaks straggle to the desert's edge. Purple-blue shadows on the steep slopes mark the gorges where the water from bursting clouds plunges down during the rainy season, taking much of the mountain along, to be piled in a fan of boulders and gravel at the canyon's mouth. (247)

The next image is more detailed: ragged mountains whose lack of patterns leaves Peterson "puzzled and a little disturbed," where pine siskins fly and where white-throated swifts "slit the rarefied air with their scimitar-like wings and hurtle past the crags." Then, in a remarkable passage, he leads his readers down the mountain:

> So let's go down, down through the yellow pines where the red-faced western tanager sings its husky phrases, the big Steller's jay cries *shook shook shook* and pygmy nuthatches swarm over the rough branches; down into the steep-banked canyon where those two unbelievable warblers live—the painted redstart and the red-faced warbler—the only warblers north of the Mexican border that are decorated with intense rosy red; down still further where the oaks take over and a new jay, one without a crest, the Arizona jay, dominates the scene, and where lives the bridled titmouse with a harlequin pattern upon its face, and the little olivaceous flycatcher, the saddest voice in the Arizona woods; down past all of these to where the big sycamores shade the widening streambed, where big sulphur-bellied flycatchers creak like unoiled wheelbarrows in excited duet; and on down through the rocky gap at the canyon's mouth where the last few sycamores trail out across the flats. (250–251)

This kind of stylistic risk—a sentence of more than 150 words coordinated by its syntax—places Peterson above the level of a mere chronicler of bird records and field trips; it aligns him, rhetorically at least, with the more literary nature writers of his generation such as Edwin Way Teale and Sigurd Olson.

The fine writing continues when he contrasts the two faces of the desert. Most of the year,

> the desert has the look of hunger upon it and everything suggests a slender margin of survival and a fierce defense of the right to live. From the windows of a passenger plane the pattern of the plant life below is that of dark specks, clusters and polka dots on the bare desert pavement. Each plant keeps its distance, drawing the precious moisture from whatever radius it can command. (252)

On the other hand, the desert turns in spring:

The parched soil, rich in nutriment, requires only a good drenching to bring to life seeds that have lain dormant for years. These ephemeral plants waste little on stems and stalks but spend everything on showy blossoms. Soon they wither and die, their brief but gaudy show over, but in that short span the cycle is completed and new seeds have been produced, to lie waiting in the naked sands while the sun burns down. It is a story of resurrection. (252)

It can be argued that Peterson never reached this level of writing again. As the books and articles grew more numerous, his style became more workmanlike and his intent less literary. It may have been the audience he was writing for; it may have been a lack of confidence in a self-taught skill; or it may have simply been a predisposition toward a direct and unadorned style. Whatever the cause, while Peterson worked hard to grow artistically as a painter and photographer, his writing never advanced in a similar way, leaving *Birds over America* as the best example of his strongest prose.

As a bonus, the 105 photographs Peterson published in *Birds over America* make up the best source of his early black-and-white work. These pieces vary greatly. Some, such as shots of feeder birds that have apparently hopped up onto a prop of some sort, hearken back to his "capture" days. Others are in the Fuertes tradition, careful studies that emphasize details. Still others attempt to capture the mood of a scene, or a bird grouping, or birds in action. This last group is the most successful by his own stated standards. In a "Photographic Postscript" to the book, he wrote that "the important thing to me is not simply to record a bird on film, but to be an artist about it, to achieve good composition and proper balance of values, and, if possible, to catch a bit of the emotional quality that is essential to a good picture" (330).

Peterson made the *Birds over America* photographs with his second camera, a 4×5 revolving-back Auto Graflex, a bulky contraption that chiding friends claimed was big enough to serve as a darkroom. And it *is* huge. The basic box is a rectangle approximately ten by eight by eight inches and weighs around ten pounds. A focusing hood on top expands upward nine more inches, and the lens bellows expands forward after the front door of the camera is opened—truly an ungainly thing. But Peterson swore by it. A shutter gave him ex-

Early 1930s studio shot of Peterson with his Graflex.

posures up to one-thousandth of a second, essential for photograph-ing birds in flight. The reflex focusing system previewed the exact, erect image with the same depth of field—or area in focus—as on the film, and the hood allowed him to see it clearly. As a result, he was able to compose a shot precisely before he exposed it. Another aid to composition was the revolving back, which enabled him to select a vertical or horizontal format without turning the camera on its side. It also had an automatic flash attachment that he used to great advantage when shooting close-ups of songbirds. Finally, with what must have seemed a real luxury after the Premo's glass plates, the Graflex was equipped to handle either twelve sheet films at one loading or a six-exposure roll.

The most striking photographs in the book reflect Peterson's training and skill at composition and his deft handling of tonal values. These pieces become emotionally powerful images that go well beyond bird portraiture. For example, a great egret is photo-graphed from above, framed by overhanging branches. In raking light, its back shines so brilliantly that it seems luminescent. The arabesque of the egret's neck is reflected in water so still that it is disturbed only by the delicate hint of a current deflected by the bird's legs. The effect, in the abstract, is a field of gray tones dominated by a curvilinear white line. The emotional effect is one of elegant repose, a tribute to the evocative power of a natural form.

Again, from those whose opinions mattered most to Peterson, there was high praise for *Birds over America*. Arthur Allen of the Cornell Ornithological Lab wrote, "Roger handles his phrases with the same conviction and naturalness and artistry that he employs with his brush, and he has produced the epic of twentieth century bird study."[17] And Ludlow Griscom was equally impressed: "In *Birds over America*, Peterson adds new laurels to an already great reputation. The gifted artist and Field Guide author takes front rank as a bird portrait photographer. He writes with charm and humor of his wide experience over North America after birds. New facts, pungent comment and sound reflection show the scientific spirit of a true ornithologist as well as lover of birds."[18] Thus both men captured Peterson's versatility: equally at home with images and words, science and art.

20

In spite of praise for his writing in *Birds over America*, Peterson afterward settled into a style that was direct and instructive, while remaining informal and anecdotal. His subsequent writing featured clear analysis aided by copious detail that was both illustrative and evocative, but touches of the "literary" were sparse and unforced when they did occur. In other words, he taught and entertained.

Peterson followed up *Birds over America* with two other books in quick succession. Both are educational in intent and are books that *he* would have cherished when he was an adolescent as his reading was advancing to *Bird-Lore* and ornithological journals. The first, *How to Know the Birds* (1949), is a basic introduction to bird identification. Although the preface seems to include adult readers, the diction and syntax indicates an audience of young beginners. Yet it never connects with its young audience the way the Junior Audubon leaflets do. The fascination and delight that pervade the leaflets are absent here, and only the short sentences and "teacherly" tone remain. Except for a ten-page section called "What to Look For," which provides a masterful distillation of field identification techniques, the book often appears merely a simplified version of the field guides.

Wildlife in Color (1951), however, was an enormous project. It was, on one hand, a vehicle for publication of more than 450 wildlife portraits, which had been produced for the National Wildlife Federation's stamp series. Peterson had been making paintings for the NWF stamps since he painted sixteen birds for the series in 1939, and the book grew out of that involvement. On the other hand, Peterson saw the project as a platform to present his ideas and knowledge about wildlife and nature study. As his son, Lee, said, Peterson was "shy, but aggressive." When he saw an opportunity, he seized it. The scope of his text is no less than the flora and fauna of America north of Mexico, presented as wildlife communities and organized by habitat. It is, in this way, a preparation for an ecological understanding of the natural world, identifying eleven different geographical and biological life zones—such as swamps and marshes, prairies, deciduous woodlands—and discussing the trees, flowers, and animals that live therein. And it carries a consistent environmentalist message, woven into the text and introduced in an uncharacteristically strident preface:

> Man, contemplating the stars, gropes for a phrase to express his awe. He contends, somewhat tritely, that he feels "very puny." However, when he turns his thoughts upon his own planet he feels, by contrast, almost like a God. . . . [M]any men go through life as though they wore horse blinders or were sleepwalking. . . . They know business trends, or politics, yet haven't the faintest idea of "what makes the world go round."[1]

The tone changes as Peterson explains the purpose of the book. The following excerpts constitute his first complete statement of the steps to environmental awareness. One: "There is always life, new discoveries to be made. If [man] can attach names to the things he sees, so much the better" (9). Two: "Then, if a person is thoughtful, he may become interested in the way things live, their habits, their ecology, populations, migrations, and cycles" (9). Three: "One cannot reflect on the forces which make the outdoor world tick without becoming somewhat of a conservationist" (9–10). Knowledge, understanding, wisdom—it was a theme Peterson returned to for the rest of his life and is one of his most powerful legacies. "To sum it up," he wrote, "we are becoming aware that our world is 'one world,' where everything is interdependent—soil, robins, and hickory trees—brook trout, damsel flies, and mink—prairies, coyotes, rivers—and men" (11).

The popularity of *Wildlife in Color* represented only one of a number of triumphs and accomplishments that made Peterson's final years in Washington a landmark period. First, there were the publications: three books, plus the revised eastern *Guide* and a new work, *Field Guide to the Birds of Britain and Europe*—all within six years. Second, he reconnected with *Audubon Magazine*. Twelve new paintings of western birds were featured in the magazine in 1948, and two prepublication essays from *Birds over America* appeared the year before. Most important, he signed on to do a regular column, "Roger Peterson's Bird's-Eye View." Third, his work was receiving significant recognition. He won the 1950 Burroughs Prize for *Birds over America* and his field guides. That same year, he received, from Franklin and Marshall College, the first of his twenty-three honorary doctorates. *National Geographic* offered him a job as wildlife artist, which he turned down because he felt the magazine wanted too much control over his work. *Holiday* magazine made a similar offer. Then he accepted the position of art director for the National Wildlife Federation stamp program, where for years he planned the stamp sheets and albums, recruited artists and assigned subjects, wrote captions, and contributed numerous paintings. He managed to establish a reliable stable of painters, including Walter Weber and Don Eckelberry. Each sheet of stamps had to be carefully planned according to principles of design and tested audience preference. For example, the color balance of each sheet was of great importance as well as the movement—half the subjects faced roughly in one direction and the other half the opposite so that the action tended toward the sheet's center. The subjects were considered too: at least one red bird per sheet ("real juicy color for the kiddies," he wrote to Eckelberry), one duck, one trout every second year, and a careful balance—of large birds and game birds with small passerines, of saltwater and freshwater fish, and of regional and ecological groupings. Puzzling all this out was Peterson's task; he made it easier by keeping a large supply of paintings on hand and often added works of his own at the last minute.

As if all this weren't enough, he took on the Peterson Field Guide Series, an idea based on recognition as the first step in the three-part program that he had presented in *Wildlife in Color*. Back in 1941, he had written to Paul Brooks at Houghton Mifflin: "I have been giving considerable thought to the future extension of the series, and will be glad to discuss it more fully soon."[2] The foundation of the series was, of course, the bird guides. In his first editor's note (to *A Field Guide to the Shells of Our Atlantic Coast*), he stated the basis for the series: "Recognition, however, always comes first. That is why the Field Guide Series was launched — as a short cut to recognizing and naming the multitude of living things which populate America."[3] His preface to the second guide *(A Field Guide to the Butterflies)* told the field guide story:

> When the *Field Guide to the Birds* appeared in 1934, it met with instant approval. Intended as a short cut to recognition, its system, based on comparative patterns, field marks and distinctions between species, has proved to be very practical. It was inevitable that nature students everywhere should urge the author and the publisher to extend this plan to other fields of natural history. In as much as it would take a lifetime for one man to complete such a series, it was thought best to assign each subject to a specialist, while I acted as advisor and editor.[4]

Peterson, with Brooks's help as nature editor at Houghton Mifflin, was much more than a titular editor, and it turned out to be an enormous job — especially for a man who was already working impossible hours on his painting, writing, lecturing, and field guides. He did everything an editor does: he originated the subjects, recruited the writers and painters, edited the texts and illustrations, and handled all the personal issues that his horde of authors presented.

Some guides went smoothly, like the first one, Percy Morris's shell guide. Other early guides took huge amounts of time. He had to edit the formality out of Alexander Klots's butterfly guide. And he wrote to Brooks that he was doctoring the tree guide plates "4–5 hours a day" and rewriting George Petrides's text because it was

too academic. He counseled as well. In a letter to Richard Grossenheider, the illustrator for the mammal guide who was chronically
late with his work, he wrote,

> The way I keep on schedule best is to make myself a chart for
> the week, either so many hours per day or certain things to
> be accomplished within a day and hold myself to it. Have you
> tried this system? It works very well I think. If there is any-
> thing I can do to help you or make things run more smoothly,
> drop us a line or have Burt [his coauthor] drop me a line. Or if
> anything is troubling you, let me know.[5]

Peterson and Brooks would exchange hundreds of letters about the
series, letters that reveal a remarkable working relationship because
Peterson understood editing as well as Brooks understood writing.

At this time he also began in earnest to realize his dream of
a life of travel. He made his first international trip in 1950 as the
Audubon Society's delegate to the Tenth International Ornithological Congress in Sweden. The trip was typical of the hundreds he
would take over the years. As a delegate, he enjoyed extending his
network of ornithologists to an international level, and he noted the
cold-war boycott of the conference by the Russian delegates. But like
all trips, this was a bird trip—and a special one because of the new
birds he was able to study. He birded from France to Lapland, seeing, as *Audubon Magazine* reported, "everything from flamingoes
and bee-eaters to the nesting grounds of snow buntings and snowy
owls."[6] And he traveled by ship so he could watch the seabirds.
Like the others, this was a working trip too. He took thousands of
photographs as well as notes that would find their way into publication later. For example, in 1954 he would publish "Swifts—Voice
of Europe," a brief piece that contained an anecdote from the 1950
trip during which he and Barbara climbed into the tower of Oxford
University to view a large swift nesting colony.

Over the next four years, he would make four trips to Europe,
spending a total of about twelve months there. He was based in London but traveled extensively on the Continent. The project was the
British and European *Guide*, which he coauthored with Guy Mountfort and Phillip Hollom. Peterson had met Mountfort at Hawk
Mountain in Pennsylvania in October 1949, and the British ornithologist suggested a European bird guide. Mountfort would write

the text, Hollom would draw the distribution maps, and Peterson would paint the plates. To do so, Peterson logged over ten thousand miles of European travel, from the Arctic to the Mediterranean. Peter Farb would write later of the trip that Peterson's "thoroughness amazed the Europeans":

> He climbed every church belfry in Germany's Rhine Valley that contained a stork nest. To be certain of the wing length of one species of bird, he borrowed dozens of skins from museums to measure them. Many of the illustrations went through half a dozen revisions, always simplifying, always clarifying the field marks. By the time he sat down to illustrate the book, he had seen all except a handful of the 550 birds occurring west of the Iron Curtain.[7]

He found this a relatively easy accomplishment, as he explained in *Audubon Magazine:* "An experienced bird watcher, crossing the ocean for the first time, will not find identification as difficult as he might imagine." He used the figure of 450 birds and went on to say that roughly one-third are birds commonly seen in North America. Another third are European counterparts, easily recognizable. The remaining third take some work, especially the Old World warblers, which, he said, all looked "vaguely like Tennessee warblers in fall plumage."[8] And as always, he also made thousands of photographs for reference. The result was the best-selling bird guide in Europe in the twentieth century. But his best-known trip was in 1953, his journey with James Fisher around the perimeter of North America, which resulted in the best-selling book *Wild America*. All of this success must have come as a wonderful gift to a man who had been doubting his ability to make his avocation into his vocation. Filled with confidence, he and Barbara began to look for a place to live that was suitable and fitting for an artist and writer of his growing stature.

Yet his familiar self-doubt remained. He felt, in spite of all he had accomplished, that he wasn't doing enough to preserve and protect the natural world that he loved with such passion; he saw his field guides as failures. In short, he didn't trust his own happiness. He confided his feelings to his good friend Guy Emerson, a banker and birder whose depth of thought and concern would bolster Peterson often throughout their enduring relationship. Emerson composed a long and thoughtful letter in January 1950 that began with mild surprise, "Even the Nordics are swept now and then by waves of emotion!" Emerson's argument read, in part,

> It [the field guide] has been a clear and notable achievement, second to none in its field, in human history. But a field guide is not a panacea. It is not a do-all or cure-all even in bird iden-tification. . . . A wide, diverse, ingenious, and constant attack must be made on human ignorance and indifference in the field of outdoor life and conservation. But there are still some hundred and twenty-five million Americans who have not bought, seen, or heard of the Guide. . . . That is not a criticism of the book . . . But it is an obvious and undeniable fact, and I'm surprised, with all the glory you've achieved in the guides, that you feel the need to give them a job to do which they were neither intended to do, nor are capable of doing. . . . I've felt in the past few years you were gaining in balance, and a certain graciousness, and perhaps even in the pure joy of living. I have given Barbara much credit for this. Advancing years and solid achievement usually help also. But you've only one life to live, and no man can afford to let him[self] be torn open too easily.[9]

It was a logical argument, and Peterson's intellectual side had to accept it. But the artist in him sensed that something was wrong, something was missing. And it is one of the saddest facets of Peter-son's life that this doubt would resurface time and again and that he never identified what that "something" was.

1954–1974

Old Lyme, Connecticut

21

In 1952, *Audubon Magazine* announced the debut of "Roger Peterson's Bird's-Eye View," which was to appear in each issue. It would be an "informal column" in which Peterson would "tell of his experiences during his travels, and share with us his ideas and opinions on a variety of subjects."[1] The series ran until 1962, and although it appeared sporadically, it did amount to nearly forty articles—a sizable body of work. The pieces reflect Peterson's growing interest in travel and world conservation issues as well as his abiding interest in birds. He called on his bird adventures for many of the articles: flamingos in Nairobi, storks in Japan, cormorants in Patagonia, condors in Chile. He also included a few pieces from *Birds over America* and occasional opinion essays.

Peterson's first essay in the series, "A Night in a Channel Lighthouse," is typical of his "bird adventure" stories. He and other bird enthusiasts fly to a lighthouse on the Isle of Wight to observe a night migration, to see, as he put it, "the hordes of small travelers pouring out of the darkness into the dazzling beams."[2] The night proves magical: "Then we caught sight of our first real night migrant. Flickering and ghostly, it darted toward our high catwalk and swept over the top of the tower into the darkness. Soon another came in and another, like moths to a street lamp. During the next two hours there must have been hundreds."[3] Then there were thousands. Peterson and the others netted some of the birds (mostly whitethroats, a small European warbler) and banded them.

Here, and in other such adventures, Peterson was able to express his pure enjoyment and amazement at the experience and pass it on to readers who would never have the opportunities he did. This was one of his writing gifts from the beginning: to share, without artifice, his sense of wonder. *Audubon* readers who would never travel outside their own regions would come to rely on Peterson—quickly becoming famous and privileged—for a taste of the exotic, delivered in passages such as this:

> As they flew by, not a sound did they make. . . . I was deeply impressed with the silent drama that was taking place in this

world of blackness, revolving white light and rain. Weighing less than an ounce these tiny mites had crossed 60 to 80 miles of water by dead reckoning to be met by head winds, turbulence and rains. So tired were they when we scooped them from the air that they closed their eyes and fell asleep in our hands.[4]

In a different vein is "Reflections on Flowers," which Peterson recycled as the introduction to A Field Guide to Wildflowers. In it he first describes the task of making nearly 1,200 drawings for the wildflower Guide: creeping along backcountry roads in search of species in bloom, drawing specimens at night in motel rooms by the light of a 200-watt daylight bulb that he carried with him, and lying on the ground to draw flowers that couldn't be collected because of their rarity. He then moves to his observations on wildflowers—a meandering discussion of identification, propagation, and conservation.

Wildflowers presented a frustrating challenge to the Peterson system. As he put it, "Birds have wings; they can mix and standardize their populations. They usually look precisely the way they are supposed to look."[5] Flowers, on the other hand, were fixed in place, and developed individual peculiarities until, as he wrote, "I found, as I zigzagged from Minnesota to Maine and from Ontario to Virginia, that a flower I knew well could, at times, look strangely unfamiliar."[6] Also failing him was the methodology of science. He produces a wonderful list of specific terms that describe a leaf or stem that has "fuzz or hair of some sort." The list reads like a found poem of scientific terminology gone mad: "pubescent, puberulent, puberulous, downy, glandular, hairy, hispid, hispidulous, hirsute, hirsutulous, lanate, pilose, pilosulous, papillose, penicillate, scabrous, sericeous, setiferous, setose, setulose, strigose, strigulose, tomentose, tomentulose, villose, villous, villosulous, and wooly!"[7] For those lost in this confusion, Peterson offers his own unique approach: "Most of us belong to the picture-matching school. . . . Our system is based on the visual impressions: color first, then general shape, then the distinctions between similar species—the 'field marks.'"[8]

The essay continues to consider immigrant species, the loss of prairie species to agriculture, and, finally, the plight of rare wildflowers. Here, he returns to his point about the immobility of flowers. When a habitat is lost, flowers can't remove themselves to an alternate one; they simply perish. It is a thorough piece, as far as it goes, filled with information and some personal touches. But as Peterson, himself, admits, none of his inner feelings, no matter how deeply felt, come through. For example, a reader is left wondering what those lonely and exhausting nights drawing flowers in motel rooms were really like and what they meant to him. And he never mentions the fact that his son, Lee, went with him on one of the trips, much less how that might have changed the experience.

In 1962, shortly after "Bird's-Eye View" was discontinued, Peterson published "High Seas in a Rowboat" in *Audubon*. Here he perhaps was closer to writing the sort of essay he had declared that he wanted to write. A lengthy introduction places him in an open boat with a companion and a guide, rowing to an island off the Patagonian coast. He finds the bird photography on the island extraordinary: skuas, thousands of Magellanic penguins, blue-eyed shags and rock shags, sandpipers, two species of oystercatchers: "It was a three-ringed circus to try to document everything." Engrossed, Peterson and the others fail to notice a rising wind; the three-mile trip back to shore becomes a nightmare of several hours: "The big waves now were beginning to comb over the bow and there was no alternative but to hold our course and try to ride over them. It could be fatal to lose a stroke or two and get caught broadside." And here Peterson's view of nature changes to one of alienation: "The whole angry sea was moving upon us from the agonizing coast that seemed to remain forever distant. The spray that splashed our faces dried to form white patches of salt crystals. Swimming penguins outpaced us effortlessly, braying derisively." Then another new attitude enters, one slightly off-center and unpredictable—a rarity in Peterson's writing. We learn that he is actually relishing this brush with death. At one point, a black-browed albatross glides by, "reveling in the very wind that we dreaded." Peterson notes, "This was the first time Phil [Humphries] had ever seen an albatross. In fact, I can recommend no better way to see one's first albatross than from a rowboat in a high sea. He will never forget that bird." And his conclusion allows a subconscious feeling to come through: "Now that a year has passed, I realize that this experience, one of the most grueling in my life, and unpleasant at the time, was one that I wouldn't want to have missed. To take a chance once in a while and get away with it is to feel alive."[9]

While Peterson was meeting a decade of "Bird's-Eye View" deadlines and painting plates for field guides as well as regional bird books, he produced two more books. He edited *The Bird Watcher's Anthology* (1957), a representative collection from the body of bird study literature written in the previous one hundred years. It was a huge undertaking that involved an enormous amount of reading as he selected eighty-five pieces—a mix of essays and excerpts. As he wrote in his foreword, an anthology should reflect its compiler. To do this, Peterson organized the contents into what he often suggested was the "classic progress of the bird watcher." And he named three steps: "the first spark of interest through the discovery and listing stages to the thoughtful observations of the mature student."[10] The entire collection supports this thesis in a carefully organized way. And Peterson's introductions to each of the eight sections of the book represent a thoughtful summary of his ideas about bird study, a condensed version of the essays in *The Bird Watcher's Anthology*. His skillful editorship was noted by reviewers. Walter Harding wrote in the *Richmond News Leader* that Peterson had "chosen well and edited carefully,"[11] and the *Saturday Review* called the book "a creative work controlled and informed by the editor."[12] The other book to appear in the 1950s, *Wild America* (1955), was an even more extensive project.

22

Peterson first met James Fisher in 1950 during a field trip connected with the International Ornithological Congress in Sweden. His purpose for the meeting was to connect with Fisher in his capacity as an editor for Collins Publishers, the house where Peterson and Mountfort had submitted their *Field Guide to the Birds of Britain and Europe*. It was a stressful encounter for Peterson because Fisher, one of England's leading ornithologists, had the final word on the manuscript and also because he had heard that Fisher was "unpredictable and could be devastating if he thought you dull or did not like you."[1] But the two formed an immediate professional and personal bond; they shared many field trips in Europe, and Fisher taught Peterson the ecology of England. Three years after their original meeting, Peterson hatched a plan: he would meet Fisher, who had never been to North America, in Newfoundland and conduct him on a tour around the perimeter of the continent, ending up in the Pribilof Islands off the coast of Alaska. Fisher enthusiastically agreed. The trip lasted a hundred days, from 11 April to 12 July 1953; Fisher had covered thirty thousand miles before it was over. Peterson saw 531 species of birds, and Fisher 536. And together they would write a book for Houghton Mifflin about the experience.

The trip was a masterpiece of planning, as indicated by just one exchange of many between Peterson and Paul Brooks about the itinerary, which was planned to the hour, if not the minute. In this instance, Peterson was working on their stop at El Paso and train connections to Santa Fe so that they could spend two days with the Indians in New Mexico. Peterson wrote, "You spoke about getting La Farge to take us in hand for a couple of days. Could you follow up on this? If his tribe is Navaho I am afraid two days would not be enough to get to the reservations from Santa Fe and back. Two days is all we have. If his tribe is Pueblo they are close at hand."[2] Such remarkable foresight and attention to detail typified Peterson's planning. And Fisher eventually sensed it too, as he as wrote in Arizona, after about two months:

> Our stop [near the Canyon de Chelly] was indeed short, but in a quarter of an hour we had found what Roger was looking for, a short-tailed, sharp-billed bird, the gray-blue piñon jay—the 'little blue crow' of the piñon pines and junipers. Here we also made a much rarer find, the gray vireo, another juniper bird. I was gradually beginning to realize the planning and care and experience behind Roger's conducted tour of North America; scarcely a mile was wasted. Our apparently casual stop in these pinelands of northern Arizona had, I suspected, been contrived, quite deliberately, at Roger's desk in Maryland the previous winter.[3]

Peterson's remarkable scheduling was due in part to his legendary memory of his own bird sightings. Additionally, as Rick Wright points out in "Fifty Years Down a Long Road: On Re-reading *Wild*

America," it was Peterson's network of birding contacts, both amateur and professional, that led the pair to difficult species and regional sites of interest.[4]

The plan for *Wild America,* as Peterson presented it in the prologue, was simple: "After introducing each chapter, establishing the continuity and background, I usually turn the narrative over to James Fisher, who quotes directly from portions of his journal under the dateline."[5] Peterson deflected the credit a bit here; the amount of writing each did was nearly equal, and Peterson's contributions were much more than merely introductory. The book, in fact, is more like a duet with alternating voices responding to a common event. Further, each allowed the other to interrupt the narrative with occasional footnote comments. And further still, according to Barbara Peterson, Fisher tended to be a bit prolix, so Peterson took on the responsibility of editing the manuscript, which in draft form burgeoned to half a million words.

The two writers' styles are similar—not surprisingly, because the two men were so similar. Both were scientifically inclined, keen observers, and thoroughly knowledgeable. At the same time, they shared an emotional connection with the natural world that shines through the prose in their enthusiasm and sense of wonder—Fisher seeing things for the first time, and Peterson acting as the proud guide. What little difference there is occurs in Fisher's attempts to record his impressions and in his comparatively greater interest in style.

A good contrast can be found in their handling of the first scene of the book: Peterson on the ground at the Gander airport in Newfoundland and Fisher approaching from the air. Peterson writes:

> Stray wisps of fog were beginning to blow in; a plane should
> have no trouble landing, however. From overhead came the
> incisive lisps of unseen fox sparrows, the first migrants of the
> season. These large rusty-tailed sparrows had made their noc-
> turnal way across the Gulf of St. Lawrence and the width of
> Newfoundland, a distance of at least 300 miles, to this spot,
> their natal home, without benefit of complicated instrument
> panels. They seemed to be attracted by the airport lights. But
> where was the plane? (5)

Fisher records his approach this way:

My first sight of the New World, at daybreak this morning, was a brown-and-spruce landscape, a mosaic of brown bog, silver water, little rivers, great dark green stretches of spruce forest with brown, irregular, open patches between. Through parted clouds, more shining water, and snow patches, and an interminability of spruces, like Sweden. Then came a calm coast. It seemed almost beachless and tideless; peninsulas, lagoons, at last a little beach. And below, gleaming white with black wing-ends, flew my first New World bird. This is where you came in, I said to myself, for my last bird in Scotland had been the gannet, and here it was, my first in Newfoundland. (7–8)

Such contrasting passages, which illustrate an extreme difference that would imply set roles—Peterson as teacher/scientist driving home a lesson on avian versus human navigation and Fisher as aesthetic interpreter reaching toward the poetic—are uncommon, however. A reader can read long sections of the book and not be aware of who was authoring the words.

Yet differences do occur regularly, especially in descriptive passages. For example, Peterson's description of a predawn chorus on the Coronado Islands off California is evocative, but stylistically subdued:

Some time later, in the predawn I was aroused to consciousness by the sound of murrelets in the air. The eerie cries came from all around—the murrelets and the petrels, like the tortured demons and lost souls on Bald Mountain, were fleeing from their citadel of rocks with the first light of dawn. Then, in the increasing half light, another sound arose—the awakening chorus of the gulls, a most remarkable reveille. For some minutes every voice in the great colony seemed synchronized, beating out their yelping cries in perfect unison. (289)

Fisher's questioning of what he would remember from his trip, however, shows more willingness to take chances with language and word sounds as well as syntax:

Was it the searing vision of the Grand Canyon—the world's end, humbling, awful, serene? Or was it the other climaxes of scenic possibility: Yosemite, Crater Lake? Or the biggest and oldest living things—forests that shrank me to a tiny

monkey in an endless corridor of dim green light, mountains
that lifted white snow to white cloud, blue ice to blue sky; or
a child's dream of a million seals come true, among a million
seabirds; the great American desert, with its mountain-islands
and strange life; torrid Mexican heat; the California sun; coral
islands; goose-tundra? (417)

And on rare occasions, Fisher simply burst forth in a way that Peterson wouldn't or couldn't—as in this sentence about Miami Beach: "The place was a riot of parthenonian, byzantine, banker's gothic, broker's perpendicular, glasshouse, gashouse, bauhaus, bathhouse, and madhouse" (132–133).

But when they wrote about their observations and told their stories, they were nearly of one voice. The result is a remarkably entertaining and informative book, which improves as the trip goes on. Peterson's segues into Fisher's entries become less forced, as the two men become more comfortable with each other. They refer to each other more often and with genuine affection and respect, as well as with good humor. And, of course, the land that they are focusing on becomes more interesting as they move west, less dominated by humans—except for a brief visit to Los Angeles, which disgusted them both.

Wild America is often delightfully anecdotal, the best stories revealing two slightly offbeat and interesting characters. Absent-mindedness frequently plays a part; things are lost or left behind. For example, when someone forgets to remind the other to fill the gas tank before crossing the desert to Tombstone, Arizona, and the car coasts to a stop, the two scientists quickly realize they have a strong tailwind and, with both doors open, sail their car the four miles into town. And it was in the Southwest where they had their only tiff. A near accident on a switchback led to words, and Fisher called Peterson a "bloody bad driver." Peterson records the conversation "exactly as I remember it, because it was the only time in all the thousands of miles that tempers flared." He adds, "But I suspect James was not really too nervous [here Fisher inserts a terse footnote: "No comment"] about my driving because he dozed peacefully for hours on end when I took the wheel" (241). Peterson continues the story masterfully. They drive on through rugged and wild landscape: "Here on the plateau we found ourselves in an endless forest of piñon pines—a green land, for a change, instead of a brown land. Beyond lay the Painted Desert and the Petrified Forest National Monument. Night dropped its curtain of blackness while we were still far short of our day's destination, and we flew on and on" (242). And the tension is broken:

> Somewhere in the endless miles between the Petrified Forest and the boundary of New Mexico, while I was doggedly piloting the car through the empty dark, James suddenly burst into laughter. . . . All by itself, out in the middle of this infinite void, flamed a huge neon sign. Dwarfing the building which supported it, it was one of the biggest, most dazzling, most lurid neon beacons either of us had ever seen; it could have shouted down any of those in Times Square or Piccadilly Circus. All it said was: BAR. (242)

Many of the stories serve as reminders that although the trip was ostensibly about birds and the book is as well, *Wild America* is also about the natural world as reported by two scientists. In fact, long and notable discourses, written by both authors, dominate sections of the book, with bird sightings serving as occasional punctuation. They present Yosemite National Park at length, geologically and historically, as well as Native cultures—the Hopi and Navajo Indians in the Southwest and the Aleuts in Alaska, for example. Discussions of conservation issues dominate the other human parts of the book, in addition to sections about early explorers, the history of the national parks system, forest fire management, logging, and fur seal populations. Such digressions, especially those concerning the natural history of the continent, make *Wild America,* as Rick Wright asserts, "one of the last examples of a distinctive, and distinctively American, genre of popular natural history that incorporates 'hard science,' a type that thrived at the turn of the twentieth century in the writings of such literary explorers as William Beebe and Roy Chapman Andrews."[6]

Once the excitement of the trip was over, the real work began. In a letter to Paul Brooks, Peterson outlined the plan. The authors decided on a text that would be "more Fisher [than] Peterson"[7] in the proportion of about 70,000 words to 50,000 words. They planned thirty chapters, with Fisher sending his material to Peterson so that he could edit it and integrate his own contributions. On 2 April 1954, Peterson wrote out the method. Fisher had sent his first journal—on Newfoundland—which, like all of his contributions, was way too long. When Peterson had added his own 1,500 words, the total word count for the chapter came to 8,000 words. At that rate, as Peterson gently pointed out, the book would top 240,000 words. And Peterson wrote to Brooks in 1955 that he had to rewrite Fisher's last chapter from scratch—it was 10,000 words long; they had room for 4,000. The task involved a continuous cutting of Fisher's prose, which Peterson was able to do with surprising success—both in *Wild America* and in their other coauthored book, *World of Birds*. As Peterson later remembered, Fisher "furnished three times as much wordage as we could use and it fell to me to select out the material—ruthlessly."[8] But it took some maneuvering. When the two sat down to go over the editing, "I waited until he was relaxed after two or three martinis and this was good strategy. He glanced over what I had done, and his only comment was, 'wunnerful, wunnerful.' For some reason, he completely trusted me to do this surgery, although he disliked tampering by most other editors. I have seen him boil apoplectically when someone fiddled with his work."[9]

The organization was agreed on in the 1954 letter to Fisher:

> I will start each chapter, carry the continuity (our travel to the next spot), give some of the historic and research background of the new area we are about to visit, and then, as gracefully as I can, switch over to your journal under the date line. The latter requires a bit of ingenuity so that it is not done in the same way each time; it often requires just a bit of rewriting on my part, both of my closing remarks and the first paragraph of your journal (subject to your approval).[10]

Peterson then went on to comment on the general look of the book: "Paul [Brooks] would like the book to be not only factual, but also highly visual, and sensory, describing what we are seeing, what the birds are doing, also how hot we were and how the mosquitoes were biting, etc. This is essential if we wish to have a sale of 25,000 instead of 5,000." And Peterson cautioned that the book not turn into "one long bird list": "We should try not to have it become too completely birdy. Some chapters should concentrate more on the botany or the big trees (Yosemite, Great Smokies); mammals (Monterey peninsula, etc.); in Mexico the emphasis, in part, might be on the butterflies; geology, certainly at the Grand Canyon. In northern Arizona, the Indian part, it might be a good idea not to even mention a bird."[11]

As the work progressed, Peterson eventually outlined what he wanted from Fisher in each chapter: word length, slant, type of detail. And in some sections he actually interchanged authorship: "Because of some duplication in the parts we have already written I have appropriated certain passages from your material and have inserted them into my sections and in like manner, when the chapter switches over to your journal under the date line, I insert missing data which you have asked for, and occasional descriptions when necessary."[12]

The job of pulling it all together was as complex as it was daunting. Filling in factual blanks involved research and queries to friends met along the way. Inconsistencies in timing and the fiction of writing parts of a journal long after the fact threatened the spontaneity of the book. In all, it was a remarkable editing job by Peterson and a superb copyediting job by Paul Brooks and Helen Phillips of Houghton Mifflin. And not to be forgotten was Barbara Peterson's huge effort; she typed each draft of the manuscript.

If sales are a measure of whether it was all worthwhile, it was. *Wild America* made it to the best-seller list. If reviews are the measure, it succeeded as well. From England, Cyril Connolly's review in the *Sunday Times* was a bit prickly at the start: "It [the book] is a bit untidy and it credits us with an interest in birds, bird-watching and bird-name-dropping which we do not all possess. But even if I do not love birds, I happen to like the American Wilderness, and never have its various aspects been so refreshingly combined by two such experts about it." And he ends the review in enthusiastic praise that shows how well the authors avoided writing one long bird list: "Besides a succession of lovely places, of rare birds and animals, we meet with very pleasant people and escape to a community without sterility and cattiness. There are no cocktail parties, no smears, no politics, no anxiety, no resentment, only the changing aspects of the wilderness, the beauty of the birds and their names, the thrill of the chase under the tall shadow of Audubon, who first saw, loved and illustrated this Eden."[13] Edwin Way Teale, in the *New York Times*, called the book "a product of both wild America and civilized America": "Airliners and superhighways and aids to travel a quarter of a century ago made possible the volume which . . . adds the record and the viewpoint of the mid-twentieth century." He also commented on the coauthorship, noting that the two men, as superb generalists and naturalists, were well equipped to collaborate: "The result is smooth and integrated. . . . The reactions of visitor and native are nicely balanced. Neither dominates the book. This dual authorship, moreover, permits the gradual involvement of the personality of each man as illuminated by the reactions of the other[, providing] a kind of stereoscopic quality that gives added depth to the picture."[14] *Washington Post* writer Irston Barnes pointed to the stamina the journey demanded—the long days and short nights, the cameras, and the daily journals. And he echoed dozens of other reviewers who mentioned the book's overall and unique effect: "The fresh, spontaneous impressions of Fisher, combined with the sensitive perceptions of Peterson, create a vivid picture of a land of spectacular landscapes and of infinitely varied wildlife."[15] It recorded, as Teale wrote, the experiences of "two fortunate naturalists during great days of their lives."[16]

23

While Peterson and Fisher enjoyed their great adventure, Barbara scouted the Northeast for a new home. They wanted to be in a rich natural area, but with access to Peterson's publisher in Boston as well as the American Museum of Natural History and the National Audubon headquarters in New York. They also needed a big house, enough room for their two growing boys and frequent guests. And Peterson needed a place to work. The house they settled on, in Old Lyme, Connecticut, was a perfect match. It had ample room and a barn, which became Peterson's studio. The property, located where the Connecticut River empties into Long Island Sound and near the remarkable Great Island wetlands, provided Peterson with a list of more than 150 birds, including 60 nesting species. Called The Cedars, the estate would become the social center of bird study in

New England and the origination point for the Petersons' annual New Year's letters—a delightful source of news about Peterson's travels, world ornithology, and the Peterson household.

But the move provided an unexpected, and far-reaching, result. Peterson would later write that the first time he saw the house, two things "sold" him. One was a red-spotted purple, one of his favorite butterflies. The other represented an important turning point in his life. An active osprey nest stood in a large oak on the property. In fact, the area was loaded with ospreys—nearly 150 active nests within a ten-mile radius of the house. The fate of these ospreys at the hands of DDT contamination would involve Peterson in environmental issues more deeply than ever before, and in a significantly different way.

When he conducted his DDT studies in Florida in 1945, Peterson never imagined that he was dealing with a different sort of killer, one that, according to early DDT researcher Charles Wurster, could "wipe out an entire species of bird without killing even one individual."[1] Peterson observed this characteristic for the first time in 1957 near his home in Old Lyme:

> When Great Island should have been a scene of [osprey] activity, with young birds at the flying stage, I scanned the marsh through my telescope. I saw the usual number of adults about—but where were the young? The nesting season had obviously been a failure. The next year confirmed my suspicions. Although young osprey ordinarily pip the shell in about five weeks, many adults sat on unhatched eggs for 60 to 70 days. Other eggs mysteriously disappeared. One bird brought a rubber ball to the nest and faithfully sat on it for six weeks![2]

He, Barbara, and a Yale graduate student in ornithology, Peter Ames, began a recovery project with help from a grant from the National Geographic Society. Barbara and Ames put up twenty-one raccoon-proof nesting platforms, thinking that predation might have been the cause of hatching failures. But it wasn't the case. Each day during the nesting season, Barbara loaded a boat with a ladder and her springer spaniel, Dusky, and checked the nests. As she reported in her 1962 New Year's letter, "The ospreys quickly adopted the new sites. Each post was sheathed with a 3-foot section of metal; thereby we ruled out raccoon predation as a factor in the poor reproduction which has plagued the ospreys for several years. In spite of our efforts only 3 young were raised."[3] Among the first to do so, Ames and the Petersons had the eggs analyzed and found concentrations of DDT.

Others beside Peterson were becoming alarmed over pesticides as well. Edwin Way Teale saw the indiscriminate killing of insects as a threat to nature's ecological balance. Charles Broley, the country's most prolific bander of bald eagles and about whom Peterson had written in *Birds over America,* had suggested in the mid-fifties that pesticides were the cause of that species' dramatic population decline. Most notably, Rachel Carson, previously known for her entertaining and well-written books that illustrated interconnectedness in the marine and littoral world, spent four years researching the actual and potential effects of chemical pesticides on the natural world. When completed, her book was serialized in the *New Yorker* in June 1962 and published by Houghton Mifflin later that year. It would have been merely an important book if not for her brief opening chapter, "A Fable for Tomorrow." In four pages, she described a "silent spring" (the book title that Paul Brooks suggested), in which life in a fictional small town was dramatically altered by pesticides. Flowers withered, farms failed, people became ill and died, and no birds sang. Readers were immediately engaged, and the book quickly came to represent a major turning point in how humans viewed their relationship with nature.

Independently, and in light of the research by Peter Ames and Barbara, Peterson had become convinced of the connection between DDT and his disappearing osprey. Quickly, his passion for birdlife took hold and directed his actions. In August 1962, he wrote to Carl Buchheister:

> I realize that we have got to fight like hell in the years to come and that we have been playing at conservation most of us. I for one am going to become a very nasty fellow as the years go on because I see the disintegration in so many ways. . . . We have got to be far more militant, and I am afraid that biologists as a whole have got to be a bit more aggressive from now on. The bastards who are destroying America are very aggressive as you know.[4]

Later that year, he wrote to Allen Morgan of the Massachusetts Audubon Society, expanding his fears to include bald eagles on the Atlantic coast, peregrines in the Northeast, as well as bitterns and kingfishers in Connecticut. In researching peregrines, he had found that the bird had disappeared as a nesting species in the Northeast. British peregrines had been diminished by 90 percent. "I have tried," he wrote, "to get ornithologists worked up about this, but either they do not seem to comprehend the enormity of what is happening or they don't believe it."[5] And his frustration extended to his colleagues who were studying the problem. In a 1963 letter to Joseph Hickey, a peregrine authority, he complained, "I believe you stated that no species will become extinct because of pesticides. However, I do think that large populations in certain sections of the world may go out of the picture in certain species particularly species that are at the end of a long food chain and particularly certain fish-eating birds."[6] And in 1964 he took Alexander Sprunt to task over his cautious position on DDT and bald eagles. In a report published in *Audubon*, Sprunt had mentioned predation, human disturbance, and a "number of factors" for the abysmal (7.7 percent) nesting success for bald eagles. He emphasized the need for more field research. Peterson's response was not temporized:

> The obvious is not mentioned. This is pesticides in the food chain which I would have thought by now is the only economical hypothesis and has been more or less proven by [James B.] DeWitt's fine work. To ignore it is to be myopic and to refuse to face up to an admittedly overwhelming problem. . . . As an ecologist you must be aware that the birds at the ends of long food chains . . . would be the most vulnerable. . . . So many biologists say in their hyper-cautious way—'We need more field research.' Is this a way of insuring their jobs? . . . Peter Ames who expressed much the same view about ospreys in a hyper-cautious way, will now, when you pin him down, admit that pesticides are the only answer. The chemicals are in the eggs in very considerable amounts. And they are in the fish brought to the nests.[7]

Barbara Peterson echoed this sentiment in the Petersons' 1965 New Year's letter: "Even though many academic men and public servants alike are privately convinced that poisons are responsible for some of these disasters they are reluctant to say so publicly. Cynically, one of them commented that the price of speaking out comes too high."[8] And Peterson revealed his impatience with the scientific and academic community when he wrote to William Vogt: "Peter Ames, whom I know well and admire, went to his professors at Yale. . . . He asked to do this [an osprey/DDT study] for his doctorate. They said that the project was not worth a doctorate, and after putting a few facts in the computer (but not motivation) told him that he was to work instead on the syrinxes of thrushes."[9] Peterson was clearly flabbergasted that something so clear and obvious could be missed. Only the fear of authority could explain it. But he had no such fears.

In April 1964, at the invitation of Senator Abraham Ribicoff, he testified before a subcommittee of the U.S. Senate Committee on Government Operations. It was the opportunity he had been waiting for, and he made the most of it, pulling together all of his information into a superbly reasoned argument that insisted: "Aldrin, endrin, dieldrin and all compounds of the chlorinated hydrocarbon complex be banned. Permits to manufacture them should be withdrawn."[10] He began in almost the same way that Carson started her book, telling the committee members that he had heard that three hundred acres in Norfolk, Virginia, were to be sprayed with dieldrin the same night he was to speak there. He opened his remarks by saying it was good to hear mockingbirds again, then added, "You probably won't have them next week. . . . Rachel Carson's 'Silent Spring' was no fantasy." He went on to tell the subcommittee that more than 300 dead birds were picked up the next day in Norfolk. Applying that "yardstick" to the 100 to 150 million acres that are sprayed yearly, he suggested that more than 100 million birds were killed by pesticides each year in the United States. He went on to cite Joseph Hickey's estimate that half a million robins were killed when DDT was used on elm trees in the Midwest. But it wasn't the songbirds, whose populations could withstand such a slaughter, that worried him; it was the birds at the top of the food pyramid, "for they take poison biologically concentrated by their prey and their prey's prey."

He testified as a teacher rather than as a scientist, summarizing the causes and effects, explaining to the confused layman how a pesticide sprayed on a mosquito could end up threatening a hawk population:

> Traces of poisons ingested by little fish upriver—either in the runoff or through poisoned insects—make them easier prey for larger fish. Numbers of affected fingerlings compound their poisons in the predators, and it is the large fish that is wobbly, swimming near the surface, that is most likely to be caught by the osprey, which transfers the accumulated poisons to its own tissues. Natural selection becomes unnatural selection.

He saved his harshest criticism for the Department of Agriculture, saying that it "represents a special economic interest group." He went on to say that the department "has been almost arrogant in tending to ignore, even to scoff at, the proven damages to wildlife resources and the potential hazards to human health." And he suggested that since the department wouldn't act, Congress should amend the pesticide laws and create a control board with the "power to protect our environment."

Slowly the academics and researchers came around. For example, Joseph Hickey was a major witness in a 1969 Wisconsin hearing that legally established DDT as a threat to the environment. Hickey's conclusions were supported, in part, by results from the Old Lyme projects, which were continuing. From 1965 to 1971, Barbara Peterson monitored the yearly decline of the birds through their low point of only one young per year while other researchers conducted egg and hatchling trades with a healthy osprey colony to isolate the problem. And Peterson, for his part, and perhaps to his surprise, had become a spokesperson.

DDT was banned in 1972, and sixteen years later Peterson could report: "Things have been turned around, and almost as dependable as the tides, our Connecticut ospreys return to our estuary during the last 10 days in March. We now have perhaps 50 pairs nesting successfully in the lower valley, and given another 10 or 15 years the birds will probably be back to full strength."[11] The DDT success marked a turning point in Peterson's role as an environmentalist; he had seen his youthful optimism concerning population renewal rewarded and had discovered that his fame and reputation were becoming a useful, even powerful, tool. As a public figure, he had begun to extend his influence beyond struggles to preserve regional bird habitat (although that remained his first concern) to include a worldwide environmentalist perspective.

He had, as early as 1956, stepped out of the bird world into a larger arena. He joined Joseph Hickey in a mass mailing that began, "Will you—in the interest of preventing the loss of some of our irreplaceable wildlife resources—help us elect Adlai Stevenson to the Presidency? Our appeal is personal, not partisan, since both of us are Republicans who believe that the surest way to action lies in supporting candidates, regardless of party, on their conservation records. On these records, we support Stevenson."[12] The letter went on to attack the Eisenhower administration's conservation failures, which included oil leases on wildfowl refuges and patronage appointments to the Fish and Wildlife Service resulting in handing out "special favors in the name of the national interest." They concluded their evaluation by saying that "increasingly successful assaults upon our national parks, forests, and other public lands have been met by indifference or total unawareness on the President's part." Stevenson's record and potential as a conservationist president were presented in the letter as well, as in a three-page press release from Conservationists for Stevenson-Kefauver, a larger group that Peterson had joined.

As was the case with Carson's book, Peterson's involvement with the pesticide controversy led to a discussion of larger issues. The essential question for him was expressed in the title of a speech he delivered at the Advancing Science/Serving Society convention in San Francisco: "Man's Role in Nature." This and other speeches from his "activist" period (1960–1974) chronicled the appalling results of human interference with the natural world. As an appropriate emblem, he focused on threatened species and extinction. The speeches tended, naturally, to be somber in tone—his wife called them "voice of doom" speeches—while they became somewhat philosophical. And they represent, in their passion and intensity, some of Peterson's most eloquent prose.

In a 1964 speech in Andover, Massachusetts, he established his premises and his assessment of the world's state: "Man does not own the earth, or any part of it, save his home and tools: of nature he is but the inheritor, the central node of a transient web, alone capable of knowing what he is doing. There would be few problems if so many did not *want* to know, and cared not for the consequences."[13]

One of the "problems," of course, was the poisoning of the world's wildlife with chemicals—not just in America, where, he suggested "with usual American efficiency [we] even poison our environment faster." But other problems, he pointed out, such as overpopulation, pollution, and habitat destruction, compounded the issue and pointed to basic flaws in the human species: "Man has become the most dangerous, the most lethal animal upon the face of the earth. Poisonous, he can, through his endless proliferation of toxic chemicals, change his venom, a thing no snake can do. But he may not be immune to his own venom. He is also the filthiest animal that ever evolved and lived, polluting the streams, the sea and the air."

An extension of this idea, which also found its way into *World of Birds*, contains a dim hope for the future: "Now [that] man has the power to destroy nature and himself almost totally, he has been compelled to make a searing re-assessment of himself; of his own aggressiveness, greed, power and impact. Those who now face each other with machines of almost cosmic destruction and talk seriously of peaceful co-existence are preoccupied with political systems. But it is significant that healthy doubt is beginning to replace old, sick doctrine." He saw, in the Kennedy-Johnson years of global war averted, "a philosophical revolution":

> Inherent in [this] new philosophy is the assumption that the planet will *not* involve itself in an atomic holocaust. As a consequence of this assumption: the target is the re-naturalization of the world. A world at peace is still a world grossly disturbed ecologically, sadly and expensively damaged agriculturally; a world of insufficient and polluted water, vanished wetlands, slashed forests. Lost and poisonous soil, extractive farming, over-fishing: and semi-starvation for half its humans. This is a bad world; but it is not sick to death.

He went on to point hopefully at the contributions of science toward the reestablishment of "the great old philosophical concept of nature as a whole: Darwin's discovery of organic evolution, Haeckel's development of the concept of ecology, and Mendel's work with genetics." And he returned to one problem that is, in fact, a simple one— survival, particularly of species, and especially of bird species. Birds, as always, were the "litmus paper" of the environment for him. He pointed out that in the last three centuries seventy-six species of birds had become extinct, and another two thousand were endangered. "The majority of these are extinct or rare because of man, not nature," he warned.

He concluded the Andover speech with a quotation from *Paradise Lost:* "Accuse not Nature, she hath done her part; / Do thou but thine; and be not diffident / Of Wisdom; she deserts thee not, if thou / Dismiss not her." And he closed with his own admonition:

> Let us, on our way to paradise regained (in other words, peaceful co-existence), pause to learn lessons from the fate of birds. Birds are the most beautiful of all the animals, the flower garden of animal evolution. Evolution is a process, and in time each species must pass from the earth, and others (doubtless as beautiful) to come. To hasten this process by ignorance or foolishness is an outrage to nature, and an affront to human dignity.

Addressing a convention of scientists ten years later, he pointed out, as he had in "Man's Role in Nature," that the solution was not to impose rules and laws—an environmental dogma—but rather to help each individual define his or her own role: "The plain fact is that we cannot decide the role of man in nature for anyone but ourselves. To do otherwise is arrogance."[14] Humans differ from the other animals, he suggested, in two ways: they can limit their populations, and they have to teach their young. By employing these two differences, there is promise: "If . . . we can stop competing with nature—stop treating it as if it were something we had to defeat—something to pound into shape—something we had to subdue—if we saw ourselves as *part of nature,* instead of separate from it, we would have taken a giant step towards survival." Abandoning religions that

> have fostered the idea of the separateness of man, the individual can arrive at a new, and hopeful, relationship with his environment. . . . The *civilized* man, the *humane* man, readily accepts not only the humane ethic, as we think of it, but also the conservationist's philosophy as well as the environmentalist's point of view. They are overlapping and interlocking. All are essential to a better and more civilized world. It is a matter of attitudes—a reverence for life—all life.

Even though Peterson was often thrust into public view and spoke out forcefully and sometimes beautifully when the time and venue were right, he remained, by nature, reluctant. He saw his most effective environmental role as that of an educator. As he told William Zinsser in 1993, "I'm not an activist in the sense of bothering my congressman. I'm an opinion-maker in my writing and my painting. I'm a publicizer. I like to give people information, and over the years I've written a great many articles for magazines. Activists sometimes work on information that's not valid."[15] He learned during his DDT battles that if wildlife was to be protected, work had to be done in three arenas—in the field and laboratory, in print media, and in public forums—gathering information, synthesizing it, and presenting an argument.

Gathering information began with his field guides and the premise that individuals can't be effective by trying to save what they don't know. In fact, Peterson often said that the goal of his work was to "create naturalists." For him, knowledge was based on specific identification, which leads to an understanding of ecosystems. To be effective, conservation measures must also be based on empirical data. During a discussion about nongame wildlife programs, an important cause for Peterson, he pointed out, "We can't begin to help wildlife about which we know so little. Therefore, one of the first things we might do is create atlases of the species living within the various regions of the country."[16]

Peterson was best suited, by both temperament and talent, to synthesize knowledge and relay it to the public and to the activists who would bring the fight to the streets, the boardrooms, and the courts. He often described himself as an elucidator, a middleman who connected laypeople with scientists. He did this primarily through his articles, writing specifically, avoiding generalizations and platitudes, preferring to focus on one individual issue or locale at a time. Many such pieces appeared in his "Bird's-Eye View" column in *Audubon*. Three of them from the 1950s stand out and can be seen as patterns for the many that followed there and elsewhere.

In "Mexico, Exciting and Depressing," he employs a favored technique of describing in rich detail a birding or wildlife trip, filling his pages with information and wonderful sights. Then he juxtaposes it all with an environmental threat. In this case, he describes crisscrossing Mexico from north to south, learning new birdsongs.

But he pauses along the way to write about the destruction of a wet-land jungle for subsistence agriculture. Land for farming is cleared by burning, he explains, and the soil left behind is usually depleted after one season. So the farmer simply burns off more jungle the next year:

> We found the jungle reduced to gray pumice-like ashes except for a few blackened trunks, gaunt and devoid of limbs. From their eyrie on one of these tall stubs a pair of little bat falcons surveyed the wreckage which in places was still smoking. Par-rots and toucans traded back and forth across this bleak no-man's-land and momentarily a Guatemalan ivory-billed wood-pecker tested one of the charred stubs before moving on. These birds and many others had been dispossessed from one of the most bird-rich areas that probably existed anywhere.[17]

Describing an incident reminiscent of his saw-whet owl story of decades before, he tells of finding and photographing a colony of Montezuma oropendolas. When he went back to make more photo-graphs the next day, the tree that held the nest had been destroyed. "Mexico," he concludes, "may be the naturalists' paradise, but it is also the conservationists' despair."[18]

An untitled 1956 article about the need for hawk protection is a straightforward explication of the problem. He begins with some history, including his 1935 visit to Cape May to see the sharp-shinned hawk flight, which he wrote about in *Birds over America,* in "The Sky is Their Highway." He recalls the horror of watching one of every four hawks he saw being shot out of the sky: "I can still remember the shrill chattering screams of those sharp-shins which suffered head wounds."[19] He points out that the protective laws that have been put in place at Cape May have also been implemented in other hawk migration focal points such as Hawk Mountain, Penn-sylvania. But in a reversal of his earlier stance, he asserts that the laws have proven impossible to enforce. As a result, as many as one thousand hawks were killed on a strong flight day at Hawk Moun-tain. He concludes that even though some states have effective in-formation programs and strong and enforceable laws, the situation remains grim because hawks must pass through *other* states during migration: "Legislation and education—progress is being made. So it would seem. But let us look below the surface. To put it bluntly, the hawks are still going down, shot and trapped by the tens of thousands along every autumnal flyway."[20]

Peterson used a different technique when his writing turned to more exotic subjects, as it did in "Tragedy of the Albatross." He would often devote a considerable section of the article to educating his readers. Then, when the teaching was done, he would tell the environmental story. In "Tragedy of the Albatross," after a discussion of albatrosses in general, he takes on the United States Navy. As he relates the story, the problem began when the Navy built an airfield on a Pacific island as a staging area for radar reconnaissance planes. The island was also the nesting place for one-fourth of the world's population of the Laysan albatross. Planes and birds, inevitably, collided. But instead of leveling dunes near the runways that created the updrafts that carried the birds into the planes' paths, the navy chose to kill the birds—30,000 in 1958. Peterson lets the event speak for itself: "A crew of 15 enlisted men were assigned the disagreeable task of dispatching the birds, striking them with heavy wooden clubs at the base of the skull."[21] When this didn't reduce the number of collisions, the Navy decided to kill the remaining 100,000 birds. Peterson leaves his obvious conclusion unspoken, again letting stupidity and arrogance speak for themselves.

He wasn't always so reticent, as a 1968 *Audubon* article, "A Plea for a Magic Island," reveals. The piece begins calmly enough with a discussion of the unique "evolutionary treasures" found on Aldabra, an atoll in the Indian Ocean. The last home of giant land tortoises, a flightless rail, and several other endemic species, as well as a gathering place for thousands of frigatebirds and green turtles, Aldabra earns Peterson's praise as "a magic equatorial island, the last refuge of the Indian Ocean."[22] Peterson then shows how each of the species would be threatened or extirpated by the building of a British airfield. Having laid out the problem and offered alternatives, the article turns strident: "The Aldabra plan is, plainly enough, another blunder of that suave but shallow and quietly arrogant group that John Kenneth Galbraith has coined a name for—the technostructure, that small band of powerful men in government and big business who rule our lives by their closed committee decisions."[23] He asks if the plan isn't merely "U.S. policy under a temporary British cloak" or "simply that inexorability which characterized every project of the technostructure," a technique of committing to a project in stages until it becomes a fait accompli. Peterson closes with as powerful a call to action as he ever composed:

> The only defense . . . is to create such a public clamor that our elected representatives will override premature commitments and review the problem objectively. Indeed, quite aside from its great potential for scientific study, Aldabra's greatest contribution to civilization may be that of serving as the testing ground for our democratic way of life made dangerous by runaway technology. This debate over Aldabra's airfield may decide whether we can reverse dangerous commitments made on our behalf but without our consent, or whether we shall henceforth be the new slaves of a technostructure grown so unresponsive to our needs and its own limitations that it will drag us all to destruction through a series of technoscientific blunders.[24]

The struggle to keep the military base off Aldabra was fought alongside his longtime friend and fellow explorer-conservationist Lars-Eric Lindblad. Lindblad was on the forefront of the ecotourism industry, which became a principal vehicle for the worldwide extension of Peterson's influence. Peterson was already a seasoned world traveler, and his position as lecturer for Lindblad's wildlife travel tours aboard the ship *Explorer* afforded him the opportunity not only to do fieldwork in remote areas but also to teach environmental principles in Lindblad's floating classrooms. Each company of travelers became Peterson's students. In addition to explaining the natural history of whatever had been seen during each day's field trip, his lectures instilled the basis of environmentalist thought: not to be satisfied with merely observing an animal or bird or habitat but to develop a concern about its future. He and Lindblad, as Lindblad wrote in *Passport to Anywhere*, "contacted every opinion maker we knew to emphasize that Aldabra was one of the most important wildlife areas in the world."[25] It was an effort that illustrated how, as a public figure, Peterson took full advantage of his fame to preach his causes. It began when, as an Audubon lecturer, he would often check ahead to the next venue to learn of a regional environmental concern and then take time during his lecture to explain the issue and urge his audience to action. Numerous keynote addresses, dedications, acceptance speeches, and interviews carried his message as his fame grew.

Another lesson Peterson learned was that ideas, no matter how well-intentioned, are of no use unless they are implemented. As a planner in his capacity as a director on numerous boards—such as the National Audubon Society, the International Committee for Bird Protection, and the World Wildlife Fund—and with public appeals, he helped raise thousands of dollars. On the Lindblad trips alone, for example, nearly $20,000 was raised toward the purchase of Cousine Island in the Seychelles, thousands more for the Charles Darwin Research Station in the Galápagos. Often he helped by merely lending his name and reputation. For example, in 1972 he wrote in *Audubon* of just such a success:

> The visitor from another country can sometimes be the lever that starts a conservation project moving. Nakuru, the famous flamingo lake in East Africa, is a case in point. Upon my return from Kenya in 1957 I devoted my 'Birds-Eye View' column in *Audubon* to this extraordinary saline lake. I stated that it was the greatest ornithological spectacle in the world. . . . This article, reprinted in the Nakuru press, came to the attention of the town council, which then designated the entire lake a sanctuary.[26]

In all, it is hard to imagine a more potent and versatile advocate for environmental concerns.

Peterson received some criticism for being concerned only with birds and not the wider environmental issues. But as he put it, "We are too close to ourselves, much of the time, to see our proper relation to the natural world. . . . Watching birds and other animals seems to clarify my perspective." His fully developed ethic, then, evolved from bird protection to a planetwide perspective.

The *world's* mortality is what Peterson glimpsed when he learned about the widespread effects of DDT (which were indicated first by ospreys and peregrine falcons), the decimation of penguin populations from oil spills, threats to untamed systems like Aldabra, and the destruction of Central American rain forests. It led him to a more biocentric view of the planet. For centuries, humans had perceived the earth and its resources as merely a source for economic gain. But more than greed was at work; the relationship was skewed.

As Peterson said in 1983, he had "come to see not only birds but also other animals and their patterns of life, not just as extensions of human existence but as individuals in their own right."[27]

24

Although the Quaker State series ended in 1952, Peterson's painting remained in the public eye. He was, after all, a freelance painter and writer trying to make a living. He produced a number of prints and postcards for the Barton-Cotton Company, including proven sellers: birds and their babies. And in addition to birds, he expanded his audience by painting series of fish, shellfish, butterflies, and moths.

Even more visibility came from the Red Rose Tea cards. The cards were tiny (1 ½ by 2 ¾ inches) and came as free premiums with Red Rose tea and Blue Ribbon coffee. They were among the many reappearances of the National Wildlife Federation wildlife stamps, images that also appeared on such items as playing cards, paperweights, and postcards. Not only were many of Peterson's paintings reproduced, but he also wrote the text for the back of each bird card. He eagerly seized the opportunity to reach a new audience. Writing in an easy and readable style, he packed as much information as he could into the maximum of one hundred words allotted him. Arguably, the cards contained some of his most efficient teaching. He was even able to work in an occasional ecology and bird protection lesson, as he did in his goshawk description, which explains bird predation and ends with an admonition that "to shoot a goshawk does not increase the number of grouse."[1]

The Red Rose Tea cards were straightforward bird portraits that offered Peterson little room for expression. However, another premium, this one from the John Morrell meatpacking company, gave him a chance to represent his birds for a popular audience. For one dollar and three labels from Red Heart dog food, any American could own six Peterson bird prints. Two packages of six were offered, from a series of twelve that Peterson did for a 1954 John Morrell calendar.

Polyphemus moth and fern fiddleheads, published by
Barton-Cotton in the 1950s.

These were truly *popular* paintings, common birds presented with a common touch.

Peterson once told a story about a girl who came home from a Junior Audubon meeting and told her parents that she had joined the "Junior Atom Bomb Society."[2] He used the story to support his point that the world at midcentury had spun out of control. He went on to say that the natural world, and especially birds, provided a haven of sense and security. The twelve paintings were Peterson's offering to people weary of materialism and technology gone wild and frightened to death of the cold war. Instead of the usual "Birds of North America," the series was given the homey title "Birds of Our Land." The birds he chose were familiar, and many of the settings were domestic rather than natural: a wren flutters around its birdhouse; picturesque farmyards repose behind a kingfisher or a flock of barn swallows. For Quaker State, he had painted evening grosbeaks on a mountain ash; for the Morrell series, they appeared at a backyard feeder. He set his new robin portrait on a sidewalk rather than on a magnolia, as he had done for Quaker State. Two redheaded woodpeckers perch on a dead snag against a backdrop of the quintessential emblem of rural-America home life: a snowbound farmhouse, complete with a stone fence and human footprints leading to the front door. These pieces show clearly how well Peterson understood his audience and popular taste.

While these various enterprises were making Peterson a familiar name in many households, he continued to work on plates for field guides—*Mexican Birds*, *Birds of Texas*, *Birds of Britain and Europe*, and *Wildflowers*—as well as illustrations for *The World of Birds*, which he coauthored with James Fisher, and illustrations and vignettes for regional bird books of Newfoundland, South Carolina, New York, Colorado, and Washington State. In a foreword to Owen Gromme's *Birds of Wisconsin*, he wrote about Gromme's mastery of what Peterson called a vignette, an artistic response to the familiar composite plate, which represents several species of birds. A vignette, he wrote, places the birds in a realistic, full-canvas setting and gives the artist some small license for expression, and he painted many of his plates in this form. For example, in his plate of alcids in *Birds of Newfoundland*, he arranged puffins, murres, a guillemot, and a razorbill on a rocky ledge. The full-canvas background evokes the North Atlantic coast, and he was able to suggest a sense of the wildness of the place, a hint of cold winds. What stands out, however, is the design of the piece, with its careful use of white—on the wing bars of the guillemot and the bellies of the other birds. Yet in spite of this variation from the abstract design of the undecorated bird plate, Peterson would often express his frustration at the sameness of this work, "rarely allowing for more inventive expression."[3]

In addition, he hadn't completely abandoned his bird portraiture either. His eight plates for *Arizona and Its Bird Life*, by Herbert Brandt, fill their frames with a rich palette and active design. The phainopepla, for example, is a study in black and yellow. The birds

BIRDS OF OUR LAND · PAINTED BY ROGER TORY PETERSON

REDHEADED WOODPECKER

Red-headed woodpecker from the John Morrell calendar
"Birds of Our Land," 1955.

stand out in striking contrast to paloverde blossoms against a back-drop of adobe buildings and a distant mountain ridge. The painting captures well the crisp, dry desert air. In another painting that seems almost parenthetical to his other work of this period, he gave an early indication of the kind of work he would do in the late 1970s and early 1980s. For presentation to John Baker on the occasion of his retirement, Peterson produced a full-canvas painting of whooping cranes on their breeding ground. It is dramatic in scope, with its dried grasses in the foreground and gray lake reflecting distant firs. Five cranes dominate the work in a nicely balanced arrangement against the drab, sometimes gestural background. It is clear that

Alcid plate from Birds of Newfoundland, *1951*.

he drew on his formal art training for the work. And in a letter to Mrs. Baker, he mentions the self-imposed limits on his painting for the first time. "I'm afraid it is purely representational in treatment," he wrote, "and does not contain any subconscious comment as so much contemporary art is supposed to do."[4] Perhaps if he could have continued work of this sort, he might have been satisfied. But he was trapped by the necessity of making a living—and by his own success.

The black-and-white illustrations he made for *Wild America,* done either on scratchboard or as pen-and-ink drawings, stand as a release rather than an entrapment, however. Whatever Peterson thought of them at the time, they represent some of his most expressive work. Freed from color—and therefore a need to focus on field marks—Peterson could express the essence of his subjects, rather than delineate them as he would as an educator and ornithologist.

When working with scratchboard, an artist either draws on or covers a prepared white surface with India ink, then scrapes away the black layer. The result looks remarkably like a wood engraving, bold and black shapes that relate across white negative space, lines that stand out vibrantly, and compositions that rely on design for their movement and emotion. Many of Peterson's scratchboard images in *Wild America* are duets, pairs of birds or other animals that interact with one another, rather than with the viewer as in his paintings. One has the feeling that the birds in his paintings are on display; in the illustrations for *Wild America,* they exist informally in their environments as the viewer looks on. This freedom from formality allowed Peterson different perspectives as well: two sunning turtles are seen from water level; two avocets in flight are depicted from above, while a river meanders far below. And the setting often takes on an importance that it lacks in the paintings. The result is often more evocative. For example, the dark serenity of a coniferous forest becomes the central concern in an image that pictures a ruffed grouse tucked away in the lower left corner, gazing across a meadow toward the solid silhouettes of the trees. In another, a tassel-eared squirrel in a pine at the Grand Canyon's edge looks out over the chasm. It is the canyon's awesome size and scope that a viewer takes away from the piece.

Released from the restriction of a picture frame by the cut-in images and from the need for "field guide" accuracy by the absence of color, Peterson was able to focus on other issues. On page after page, the more than one hundred images remind the viewer of subtle things: the textures of a seal's fur, or the shapes of posturing gulls and feeding egrets, or the interplay of environmental elements such as water, rocks, grasses, and trees.

But more important, perhaps, is the sense of design that Peterson was allowed to exhibit in these works. A few are full-page

Snowy egrets, ink drawing produced for Wild America, *1955.*

scenes—such as a tern colony in the Dry Tortugas or thousands of alcids on an Aleutian Island—that are filled with activity and motion. Most, however, are merely quarter-page cut-ins. Black images appear to float on the white pages, unified by careful balance and motion: where a simple line becomes a suggestion of a shadow on water that defines the white space around it, or where the exchange of contour lines and negative space creates dynamic rhythms. Also noteworthy throughout are echoes of the Oriental design that he learned from "Beardsley via Langereis." Several songbird depictions bear a strong resemblance to the Japanesque images from the 1939 postcard series. And two avocets soar over a generalized background whose surface is divided by the sweeping arabesque of a river beneath. Peterson's treatment of the river, with sweeping parallel lines of varying thickness, also strikingly evokes the Japanese tradition. But as successful as *Wild America*'s illustrations were, to Peterson they remained illustrations, an impediment to his painting.

He revealed just how much time his illustration work occupied in a speech he made at the American Nature Study Society in 1951.[5] In the speech, he pointed out how different illustration jobs—such as magazine stories, magazine covers, and field guides—call for separate approaches. For example, the National Wildlife Federation stamps, which were painted on five-by-eight-inch board, demanded what he called a "semi-poster-like use of color and design." They demanded accuracy, but not too much detail, because they were reduced so dramatically. A magazine story, on the other hand, would emphasize pattern and page organization. He couldn't simply reuse bird paintings he had on hand from other projects. He went on to identify the composite plate, the form used in most bird guides, as the most difficult job of all, making use, as it does, "of everything an artist knows about painting and about birds, and every bit of past experience." He added, "The plate must hold together logically, and with some unity. Inasmuch as fresh specimens of most of the birds cannot be obtained at the time they are wanted for the plate, the artist must use study skins from the nearest museum. This means that he has to draw heavily on his previous knowledge of the birds and merely use the skins as points of reference." He illustrated the extent of his involvement with working on a regional guide by walking his audience through the preparation of the thirty-two color plates for the *Birds of Newfoundland:*

> I always like to see the area of the birds which I portray, however, so that my backgrounds and accessories will be convincing. The first thing I did, in July, 1948, was to fly to Newfoundland and cover the island from one end to the other: not watching birds so much as taking notes on the landscape and the vegetation. Also, I took hundreds of Kodachromes, for, while I rarely copy a Kodachrome, they are invaluable for reference.

Back in his studio, he would make his pencil sketches, design and compose the plate, finish the pencil work, and, finally, begin to paint. Each project plundered enormous amounts of Peterson's time, but none more than the plates for the Mexican bird guide. Not only was the project huge, but it also represented a significant change in his field guide painting, one brought about partly by his desire to return to more painterly work and partly by competition.

25

The 1966 publication by Golden Books of *Birds of America* marked the first challenge to Peterson's field guide supremacy. Peterson had gotten wind of the project in 1964, and he immediately wrote of his concern to Paul Brooks: "I just had a word with Arthur Singer who is doing the bird guide or field guide for Golden Books—Chan Robbins is the author and Singer is the artist, and that is why I am so concerned. Couldn't be a more high-powered team."[1] He was also worried about the number of color plates—115—whereas he had asked for only 48 plates for the western *Guide* revision. And he wondered if the new guide's range—all of North America—would cut into sales of his eastern and western guides. His overall response, however, was to move forward: "I must therefore get busy as soon as the flowers and Mexico are out of the way and do the eastern birds completely over. It should meet the standard of the Western Guide and be at least 30 per cent better."[2]

He was especially concerned that the Golden Guide would use "arrows, circles or tricks of that sort." He "spoke to them strongly" about that until he was reassured that his special innovation would not be co-opted. Throughout his career he had jealously guarded what he called the Peterson Field Guide System. On one occasion, he had written to Ohio field ornithologist Harold Mayfield: "My books are copyrighted . . . but I assure you that this has not stopped the Russians, the East Germans, the Thailanders and individuals in several other countries from employing that part of the system that is particularly my own—the schematic patterns with little diagnostic arrows (even overtly copying at times)."[3] In 1964 he wrote to Brooks about one such plagiarism:

> Send out for a copy of *Naming Birds at a Glance* by Blatchley and Jenks so that you can speak to Knopf about the blatant adaptation of the background material of our own book and lavish use of arrows, etc. The trouble with this book is that it now leaves the door open for the use of arrows by Putnam and

Golden Books, both of whom we had rather talked out of it. Now they will both have a precedent breaker in this book.[4]

And he wanted to sue an East German publisher who stole the "system," but the Western legal system could not breach the Iron Curtain at that time.

He was to have no such worries with the Golden Guide, due in part to the friendship and respect of the author, Chandler Robbins. In 1966 he sent Peterson a copy of the book along with a letter that put Peterson's mind to rest. "I can't help but feel," Robbins wrote, "that I am imposing in a field that is rightfully yours."[5] He went on to assure Peterson that the field guide system was inviolate as far as he was concerned:

> I've tried very seriously to depart from your excellent format and to introduce as many new ideas as possible. How well I have succeeded only time will tell; but I do hope that my guide will catch the eye of a lot of people who are not now active birders and that this in due time will increase the sale of Peterson guides. They [the publishers] even scrapped the gorgeous cover design Arthur [Singer] had painted while I was at Midway last March. It showed male tanagers, Scarlet, Summer and Western. I just about went through the roof when I saw it and wrote them a 2-page letter explaining why we couldn't possibly use it—it looked too much like your Western dust jacket.[6]

And Peterson responded warmly, "The new book is magnificent! . . . It is a book you must be very proud of, a fine contribution to popular bird study."[7]

The artwork was another matter for Peterson. The plates in the Golden Guide were painted by Arthur Singer, who was best known at the time for his illustrations for Golden Press's *Birds of the World* (1961). He followed up that huge task (750 plates) with the commission for *Birds of America*. Singer's birds are more lifelike than Peterson's 1947 efforts. Their feathering and shading give them a more three-dimensional appearance. Further, many of them assume more natural postures than Peterson's silhouettes. But it is the design of the individual plates that made the Golden Guide so appealing to the eye. Even though he had to crowd birds together to illustrate each of the more than 650 species, he added detail in setting and overall composition that aided in identification while producing pages with a more satisfying whole. Birds perch on identifiable trees indicative of their habitat: a cedar waxwing on a mountain ash, kinglets on a spruce. Sparrows cling to grasses, towhees scratch in dried leaves, and ducks cast reflections in the water they float on. Attempts are made at unnatural, but attractive, groupings such as four species (eight individuals) of woodpeckers working on the same red pine. Occasionally Singer tried a unified design; a full-page saguaro cactus dominates the plates of small owls, for example. All this was new to field guide art and drew more on the portraiture of Fuertes than Peterson's schematic work.

Peterson admired Singer as an illustrator. But Singer was competition, and Peterson was competitive. His ego, he admitted, was bruised: "Many people have judged me as an artist by the third edition's illustrations. Frankly, I'm a much better artist than that. I didn't want to go to my grave with the third edition as my artistic testament and be remembered primarily as a 'schematicist.' In fact, I might just as well admit that the matter of legacy cost me some sleep."[8]

Peterson dealt with the matter of legacy in two areas: in his approach to each individual bird painting and in his design of each plate. He *was*, of course, a far more skilled artist than his early illustrations showed. And he began to prove it in the plates he painted for the *Field Guide to Mexican Birds*. In the front matter of the book, he acknowledged that he had changed his approach. His paintings were "portraits and at the same time somewhat schematic." As a result of this lean toward portraiture, the Mexican *Guide* is a precursor of the 1980 eastern *Guide*. For the first time, Peterson permitted the artist into a field guide, and with a remarkable result. All forty-eight color plates are grouped in the middle of the book in a riot of color and motion. The plates are cramped and crowded—one thousand species are included in the book. Birds overlap, brilliant colors abound, and Peterson's diagnostic arrows seem to be flying everywhere. It is as if all the abandon and extravagance of the tropics had entered the bleak landscape of field guide painting. Concerns about legacy may have prompted the changes in Peterson's style, but perhaps the Mexican birds helped—with their bold patterns and uninhibited hues.

While the Mexican *Guide* plates are frantic and exuberant, the greatest change came in how Peterson painted the individual birds. All the plates show this; the first of two jay plates shows it dramatically. There is nothing "schematic" about the feather detail of these birds, especially the brown jay. Brilliant shades of blues and greens shimmer; posture and modeling are lifelike. In short, the birds come alive on the page.

26

Although illustration certainly inhibited Peterson's desire to paint, his lifestyle was a major contributor as well. He worked like a fiend when he was home: Barbara said that they worked eighty-hour weeks to finish the western *Guide*'s second edition. Home time was work time, but the actual time he spent at home was scant; by his own admission, he could tolerate only four months at a stretch before he had to travel again. His absence as a father and a husband was exacerbated, therefore. As his younger son, Lee, remembers, Peterson was someone who was "just passing through," either to his studio or off on another trip.[1] The pleasures and problems of raising two sons—good students, fine athletes, well-rounded young men—were left to Barbara. When his friend, Clarence Allen, suggested that Peterson try to connect with his sons before it was too late, Peterson responded that the time had already past. He appeared to be more concerned that his aversion to domestic life kept him on the road, away from his studios and the painting he wanted to do.

He took on numerous responsibilities for conservation work, attending board and committee meetings all around the country. And he was an active member and officer of a number of professional organizations, such as the American Ornithologists' Union and the Wilson Ornithological Society. Additionally, there were the yearly Audubon Screen Tours. But as Barbara wrote in 1959, Peterson defined staying at home as not leaving North America. In 1960, for example, he visited Bermuda, Japan, Midway Island, Hawaii, Buenos Aires, Patagonia, and Tierra del Fuego. And he was just getting started. The frequency of his overseas travel increased until, during

From left: *Helen Moe, Lorimer Moe, James Fisher, Peterson, and
Jack Livingston (coeditor of the American Naturalists Series)
on Mousa Island, off the coast of Scotland, 1961.*

a twelve-month period between August of 1973 and 1974, he traveled to all seven continents.[2] This is not to say that Peterson was a
tourist; most, if not all, of his trips were related to his work. Attending international conferences, lecturing on ecotours, researching
for his articles and illustrations, making wildlife films—all these
activities helped make his career his pleasure and his work his life.
Evidence for this is that more than half of his articles for *Audubon*
were travel pieces and that he developed a distinctive travel-writing
style.

In 1971 he published a travel piece, "How I Photographed All the
Flamingos of the World," in the first issue of *International Wildlife*.
Later that year, he was named "roving editor" for the new magazine
and eventually published six pieces between 1971 and 1974. The assignment was a perfect fit for someone whose passion had turned to
world travel; the settings ranged from the Falkland Islands to Aus-
tralia to the Galápagos.

The flamingo article is typical—a blend of exotic settings, travel
adventure, a conservationist message, and, of course, information

about birds. In it he tells of his quest to become the only naturalist to photograph all six species of flamingos, traveling to such far-flung spots as Kenya, the Galápagos, and the Bolivian Andes. But his lead—"Just getting back into their nesting places [in the Andes], so inaccessible to man, was one of the greatest physical challenges of my life"—promises more than he delivers.[3] All we hear of the challenge is rather general: the "deep, dangerous" mud on the lake where the birds nested, the altitude sickness at fourteen thousand feet, the potential threat (to Peterson and the flamingo population) from Native peoples who gathered the flamingos' eggs. Close detail of the adventure is left out. The emphasis here is on the "documentary" facet of writing; the piece is a thorough compendium of flamingo behavior, including this gem: "Flamingos are in possibly the shortest food chain in the world, an almost completely closed circuit. . . . In Kenya, at least a million birds eat their fill of blue-green algae, day after day, week after week, year after year, and the recycling process produces more algae as they defecate into the lake."[4]

Peterson's first piece as roving editor was a report on his sixth expedition to Antarctica. Here he hit his stride as a travel writer. His descriptions are clear and memorable, pictures sent home from an emissary to an exotic land. For example, he begins with a rather straightforward paragraph on icebergs: "Icebergs take many forms. Big or little, bergs can resemble whales, dragons, castles, ships, bridges, cathedrals, aircraft carriers. Those which break off the Ross Iceshelf in the New Zealand section of Antarctica are tabular, like huge flat sugarlumps. Many are large and flat enough to use as airfields: huge ones may occasionally be as much as 50 miles in length. A tabular berg the size of Connecticut was once reported."[5] Then when he describes a close-up tour of the ice field, he adds a sense of wonder: "Cathedral arches sculptured in ice loomed over us as [the captain] guided the rubber boat. Almost too breathless to shoot pictures, we were awed by dazzling grottos of green and blue crystal."[6] Peterson loved his Antarctic adventures for the inexpressible joy they gave him. He kept daily journals, which he often used for his evening lectures on the Lindblad tours. In a 1980 entry, one finds this revealing sentence: "Anytime we have whales I am in a state of emotional shock and I'm unable to really log in anything except that I am happy."[7]

The story of the expedition is told in narrative loops that always

Peterson and king penguins in Antarctica.

return to the chronology of the journey. They vary from a self-deprecating description of his training in Antarctic survival skills to a poignant recollection of joining his friend Peter Scott on a pilgrimage to the cross that honors Scott's father, the Antarctic explorer Robert Falcon Scott, who died on an Antarctic expedition years before. Skillfully woven into the narrative is a wealth of information about the human and natural history of the place, especially the penguins.

The piece concludes with a thoughtful examination of the effect of humans on the environment of Antarctica. Peterson begins in general terms: "Everything 'human' on this continent seems fleeting—an interruption: Ice is the environment; ice is the beginning and end."[8] He then examines the impact of this interruption: the early excesses of sealing and whaling, the disposal problems, the pervasive presence of DDT. But he ends on a positive note, first showing how bird and seal populations have renewed themselves, then envisioning the continent as a sort of Eden, the chance for a new beginning that drew him so powerfully to the place: "It is a continent for science, and for the free exchange of knowledge. There are rules of course; rules of conduct laid down when the Antarctic

Treaty was signed. Significantly, many of these rules relate to conservation—making Antarctica the only continent to have guidelines from the very beginning."[9]

Another example of the utility of travel was the opportunity it provided for making films for the Audubon Screen Tours. After its modest beginning in 1946 with "The Riddle of Migration," Peterson's career as an Audubon Screen Tour lecturer took off with the making of the film *Wild America* in 1955. By today's standards, it is little better than a home movie, but at the time, a full-color, ninety-minute nature film was groundbreaking. Its organization and content were provided by the book, and even though the pace is choppy and the scenes lacking in transition, the feeling for Fisher and Peterson's great journey comes through. And it's not merely a film of bird images spliced together; the many pans of scenery were composed with an artist's eye, and passages of Inuits interacting with the camera and Peterson create a good documentary effect. Peterson's commentary, which he delivered from a script but modified for each audience, is relaxed and often amusing. In all, it was a fine evening's entertainment with a conservationist message.

His next film, *Wild Europe* (1960), was also a silent film. It begins with typical tourist scenes that his audiences would perhaps expect: the Eiffel Tower and the Arc de Triomphe, London Bridge and the changing of the guard. But as he said in his commentary, "there are still wild places in Europe," and the film becomes a bird tour of the continent, recording birds seen on trips to the Irish Sea, the South of France, and Spain.

Wild Eden, his Galápagos film, was finished in 1967. About it, he wrote in his autobiography, "Inasmuch as my film on the Galapagos, *Wild Eden*, was really about Darwin and his philosophy, I was somewhat apprehensive whenever I spoke in a church auditorium as I sometimes did: wondering whether some in my audience might be creationists or fundamentalists. . . . But, I got my message across quite neatly. I simply avoided the dirty word 'evolution,' substituting 'adaptive radiation' and similar terms which seem quite acceptable."[10] In fact, the film is more cohesive than his earlier efforts, with a strong thesis—a clear explanation of the theory of evolution with a conservation subtext.

Wild Eden was the first of his films with sound, but *Wild Africa*

(1972) was the first to make effective use of exotic natural sounds that were recorded on location. In the introduction to his commentary, which he still delivered from a podium, he said, in part,

> Fifty years ago . . . relatively few Americans went to Africa, and when they did they brought back the heads of elephants and lions to put up on the library wall. . . . [Now] the long lens has replaced the rifle. I suspect color film has done more than anything else to change the pattern of African safaris—and tours. In fact, tourism of the right sort may be the no. 2 industry of East Africa, second only to agriculture.[11]

He went on to say that he didn't want audiences to infer from his film that Africa was "one endless parade of big animals": "Parks and reserves make up only one percent of the area of Africa but support 50 percent of the wild game. These parks are as precious as any great museum, perhaps more so"—because they could prevent possible extinction of some species. His conservation message is powerful, and it pervades the film: "A bird like the whooping crane is more divine than the most inspired work of art. Why? Because it is creation itself; unfiltered by human artifice." The film is made up of typical African footage, gathered over seven safaris, with one difference—it contains more feet of rare and exotic birds than any film made before or, likely, after.

Yet in spite of its utility, there was an urgency to Peterson's need to travel; in 1970, Barbara wrote to her mother that no matter where he was, he was "always wanting to be somewhere else."[12] His 1974 itinerary is a case in point. New Year's Day found him on a seven-thousand-mile circumnavigation of Antarctica on the *Explorer*. In March he was traveling along the Pacific coast of South America; then he flew to Addis Ababa to check on the feasibility of bird tours in Ethiopia. From Africa, he went to his hometown of Jamestown, New York, for the ceremonies announcing its designation as an All-America City. In July he was onboard the *Explorer* again, this time on a cruise to the Canadian Arctic and Greenland. Near Resolute, the ship became icebound, so he was taken by icebreaker and helicopter to the nearest airport in order to speak at the one-hundredth anniversary of the Chautauqua Institution in Chautauqua County, New York. In September he sailed to Sable Island, and in November he camped in Patagonia. This was followed by another month in Antarctica. On New Year's Day, 1975, he was back at Old Lyme. During his "downtime," he gave major addresses in eleven cities from San Francisco to Oklahoma City to New York. His travel had become a form of flight from the reality of home and a reaction, in part, to two life-changing events.

In 1964, Peterson had suffered a near-fatal automobile accident. As Barbara reported it,

> He was driving alone to Ithaca, New York, to attend a council meeting of the Laboratory of Ornithology. Just before reaching Ithaca at dusk he misjudged a curve, reacted too quickly with the brakes, and sent the car out of control. He took off three guard posts, plunged over an 18-foot embankment and went through the windshield. Fortunately, a farmer fixing his roof saw the accident and help was on its way within minutes. Otherwise Roger may well have bled to death unobserved. 210 stitches were required to piece together his face.[13]

Peterson's account, written to Fisher, added a few details. He had been drowsy, and he wasn't wearing his seat belt. As far as his injuries were concerned, "most of them [the stitches] are quite unnoticeable now, but I have a bad scar on my chin and a lump there," he wrote. "If it does not go down completely in another 6 months I shall have this fixed by a bit of plastic surgery. The inside of my mouth was all chewed up and for a week the stitches made it feel as though I were eating cactus. My wrist was broken and has been in a cast which will be removed in another week." Then the letter ended on a foreboding note. "Do promise me that you will not drive as fast as you do on some of your country roads. Both you and Guy Mountfort are excellent drivers, but I fear you both press your luck."[14]

Indeed, six years later, Fisher was not as lucky as Peterson. In September 1970 he died in an automobile accident near his home in Northampton. A month later, Peterson wrote a sad letter to his good friend and confidant Lorimer Moe:

> I had seen James just three weeks earlier in Holland and worried about him very much because though he had just had his hip operation giving him a new hip joint, he was still using his cane and was simply drinking too much—I presume to kill

some of the discomfort and he was also popping pills into his mouth for the same reason. He expected to discard the cane in about a month and told me that his doctor said that it was quite all right if he drank because it wouldn't hurt his hip. However, it did hurt him in other ways as was evident to everyone. He seemed bent on self-destruction.[15]

Fisher's life had become a series of crises, and his responses had become increasingly emotional. In fact, Peterson had written a long letter in 1966 consoling him over various perceived slights, insults, rejections, and general persecutions. Peterson, no stranger to bad stretches, tried to pull Fisher out:

> I detect a deep undercurrent of depression in your last two letters, and I wish I were there to cheer you up. I went through a similar—and terribly low—period last autumn and it has taken a complete change of scene on the other side of the world and an additional month after my return for me to pull out of it.
> ... In fact, I was so depressed after the 1964 A.O.U. meeting that I am sure that it contributed to my near-fatal accident a week later—literally a death wish, if you will.[16]

He followed that unfortunately prescient remark with six pages of advice, sympathy, and motivation.

At any rate, Peterson had lost his best personal and professional friend. Barbara was to say, in retrospect, that he was affected more than anyone knew by Fisher's death, the loss of his "most intimate friend in the ornithological world."[17] Two separate stories from earlier, happier times show the differences between the two friends' personalities. At a banquet during the 1954 International Ornithological Congress, the first one that Russian delegates attended, a Russian delegate was admiring Fisher's Royal Society for the Protection of Birds tie. Fisher, in his expansive way, immediately took off his tie and handed it to the Russian. The Russian returned the favor, and the banquet turned into a tipsy exchange of neckwear and goodwill. Peterson's story was told by Irston Barnes in the *Washington Post*. In a cabin at Hawk Mountain, the campers were awakened by a cave rat—a rodent twelve to fifteen inches in length with a long, furry tail: "Finally, after much effort, we awakened Roger. He rolled over and the rat turned; they regarded one another with calm understanding. 'Cave rat,' said Roger and settled back in his bunk."[18] These two men, one ebullient and emotional, the other introspective and often laconic, were the closest of friends because, as Peterson wrote, "We both built our lives on the love of nature, birds in particular."[19] The bond was deep and profound.

Shortly after Fisher's death, a fund was established by Barbara, Lars Lindblad, and others to buy a British seabird island in Fisher's memory. The result was the Copinsay Nature Reserve, administered by the Royal Society for the Protection of Birds, on Copinsay Island off the north coast of Scotland. It was a perfect choice: an uninhabited, craggy place that was home to Fisher's favorite bird, the fulmar, along with gannets, puffins, razorbills, and guillemots. In July 1973, Peterson delivered the eulogy at the dedication. Reading it, one can clearly see that those qualities he admired in Fisher were those he cultivated in himself. He spoke of Fisher's only fear concerning his own death—that he wouldn't have time to write all the books he wanted to. He called Fisher a scholar who realized that scholarship was "barren" unless it was communicated to the general public. And he called Fisher a "teacher of teachers," who "bridged the gap between the academic and the layman." Finally, he praised Fisher's role as a conservationist, especially through birds. It was Fisher, he said, who coined the phrase "ecological litmus paper," a description of birds that Peterson would use so often. It is no wonder that the two men were so close.

Two such assaults on mortality as his accident and his best friend's death would drive anyone to some form of escape. Barbara wrote that "Roger is taking a slightly more benign view of life after his accident, feeling that he is now on borrowed time."[20] And Peterson did step up the pace of his international travel. But more importantly, he remembered the lesson of his youth: that an escape *from* reality could become an escape *into* another reality, more meaningful and profound. He remembered his idol Louis Agassiz Fuertes, who died in a 1927 automobile accident in upstate New York, not far from the site of Peterson's accident thirty-seven years later. In an observation that would, ironically, describe his own painting future, Peterson wrote of Fuertes in 1942, "There is no telling how much farther he would have gone. He had always expressed a desire to get away from painting mere portraits of birds, such as those he did on commission, and hoped he would some day have time to make paintings that were more pictorial."[21] The recollection must have resonated deeply. Speaking of his own career, he said, "The Field Guides have undoubtedly been the most important contribution that I shall ever make, yet I have the nagging feeling that I have drifted away from my original goal."[22] He had been experiencing periods of angst, as he had indicated in his letter to Fisher. Most often, he was plagued with self-doubt over his reputation as an artist. And once more his friends came to his aid. Brooks, as he often did, tried to help Peterson put his career in perspective:

> I suppose it's almost a cliché to say that the most talented and successful persons are the very ones least likely to be satisfied with what they have accomplished; their divine discontent has made them what they are, and they are not likely to shed it short of senility. . . . All I'm trying to say is for God's sake don't underestimate what you *have* accomplished, don't forget that you are the leading figure in the world in the fields that you have chosen and that you're not riding a nine-day bicycle race with someone breathing down your neck.[23]

And Guy Emerson provided spiritual advice: "The danger of self-analysis is that it tends to become abstract and general—to never come to a point. . . . Mostly you must keep working happily, and not be torn by vain regrets over the fact you are not someone else in another time and place." He urged Peterson on to a "spiritual adjustment," to put material life in its own place and allow room for his soul. Only then, Emerson said, would he no longer be "subject to periodic moments of rudderless speculation and discouragement."[24] The two friends directed advice at Peterson's two conflicting sides. And there is no indication that Peterson made any progress toward a life along the lines that Emerson suggested; perhaps the practical and scientific side was too powerful. Rather, Peterson indicated to Brooks what his next direction would be: "Inasmuch as I seem to be going through the male equivalent of the menopause, I seem to be foundering a trifle in an identity crisis but it will take care of itself— Barbara assures me. I hope to be increasingly productive from this point on and not slip into self-destruction as did poor James. I am suddenly aware of the rapid passage of time and I don't like it."[25]

So he promised himself that he would paint again. He had a

In his studio at Old Lyme, Connecticut.

wing added to his studio, feeling, as Barbara said, that the old building, "though efficient and functional, just right for Field Guides, was not sympathetic enough for interpretive painting. Now he has an elegant place with picture windows, skylight, walnut panelling, etc."[26] It was waiting for the time when the field guides were done, all deadlines were met, and he was free.

1974–1980

Old Lyme

27

Peterson found field guide illustration onerous, but two guides in particular—*Wildflowers* and *Mexican Birds*—were nearly paralyzing. The wildflower guide was twenty years in the making. It had a routine beginning; Margaret McKenny, the director of the City Gardens Club of New York, was to write the text. Trouble began when Lovell Thompson, an editor at Houghton Mifflin, was not happy with the artist originally selected and suggested she submit some of her work for his approval as well as that of Brooks and Peterson. The situation was never resolved, and Peterson finally decided to do the illustrations himself. It turned out to be a monumental job—he made 1,500 illustrations, 1,344 of which were used in the book. The main problem lay in the nature of flower illustration. To be done properly, they had to be painted in the field. Therefore, an artist had only a small window of chance—each year's flowering season. Compounding the issue for Peterson was McKenny's text. It needed to be enlarged—her original 600 species were expanded to 1,300—and it badly needed to be edited. Peterson later wrote that he "left in some of her 'literary' touches" but had to edit down the entire book.[1]

The work dragged on. In 1956, Peterson reported to Brooks that he planned to finish the field drawings that summer and to start inking the hundreds of pencil drawings he had made. "It has been a far more extensive job than I bargained for," he said, understating the case considerably.[2] He hoped for a 1958 launch, but it was not to be. He didn't complete the color plates until 1965 and continued to submit the black-and-white work in installments. The delay became so blatant that the New Year's letter for 1967, when the work was finally done, began with an apology for not sending the previous year's letter because "we were ashamed to admit that the Field Guide to Wildflowers was not finished."[3] The book finally appeared in 1968. Peterson said he got walleyed from driving country roads looking for flowers, and he deeply regretted losing so much time that could have been spent painting. But, at the same time, he felt that what he learned was invaluable in his understanding of environmental issues.

The Mexican *Guide* fared even worse. In a 1943 letter, Guy Emerson planted the seed:

> I made the suggestion to a friend that it would be a very valuable contribution to ornithology if you could get out a field guide of the birds of Mexico. . . . And after the war I think that the Audubon Society could well afford to give you leave to do the ground work. I believe this would be the most practical way in which the Audubon Society could indicate its standing and competence in the field of Pan American bird protection and good relations.[4]

The next year, George Sutton, who had worked and painted extensively in Mexico, wrote to say he had talked to Emerson about the project and that he wouldn't take Peterson's working on a Mexican *Guide* as an infringement on his own work. In fact, he wrote, "You might think kindly on some sort of joint thing."[5] Peterson wrote back to express his interest because he knew from the beginning that the project was too large for one artist. Sutton, however, ultimately felt that he couldn't do the work, and Don Eckelberry, who had agreed briefly to take it on, dropped out too. Once more Peterson was stuck.

In the meantime, Edward Chalif had signed on to do the text but enlisted the help of Irby Davis, an authority on Central American birds. Davis turned in his work—a revision of Chalif's original text—in 1954, but problems developed. Davis wanted to expand the book to include all of Central America, and Peterson and Chalif could not come to an agreement with him concerning questions of taxonomy and the use of vernacular names. In 1967, Peterson wrote a letter to Davis that effectively ended Davis's involvement with the project. He said that the book wouldn't be expanded and that, as editor, he would make all the decisions concerning taxonomy and bird names. Davis's manuscript was returned, leaving Chalif and Peterson to write a new text from scratch—the fourth text that Barbara had to type. The project was moved along at last, thanks to Peterson's stint as Distinguished Scholar in Residence at Fallingwater, the Frank Lloyd Wright house at Bear Run, Pennsylvania, where he had uninterrupted time to complete the plates. And the guide was finally published in 1973, a better book because of the new information added over the years, but a tardy one indeed. Peterson was, in both cases, a victim of circumstance, but he had to accept some blame. As Barbara chided him in the New Year's letter of 1965, "The flower guide and the Mexican bird guide would both be closer to completion were it not for the tempting expeditions which Roger at his rapidly advancing age believes he should make."[6]

These two field guides were not the only impediments that stood in the way of Peterson's ambition to paint once more. Two other projects from the 1960s demanded a great deal of his time—and with mixed results. The first was a series of ecology books that came to be known as the Naturalist's America, books that Peterson and Brooks proposed would augment the field guides. More scientific in tone—Peterson wrote to Brooks that fine writing wasn't an issue—the books were to be in two categories: regional or zonal books and books about basic ecological concepts. The series announcement, which appeared in March 1963, read in part: "A principal objective of THE NATURALIST'S AMERICA is to combine scientific accuracy with readability, in order to provide the growing number of outdoor enthusiasts in America with a deeper understanding of the world they live in."[7] They represented, in other words, another attempt by Peterson to educate the readers whom he had brought to nature awareness with his guides.

As early as 1959 he was hard at work rounding up writers while engaging John Livingston, a Canadian Broadcasting Corporation producer, as coeditor. The first title, Maurice Brooks's *The Appalachians*, appeared in 1965. However, extensive correspondence and much hard work resulted in only one more title by 1970: *Sierra Nevada*, by Verna Johnston. And in a 1971 letter to Brooks, Peterson indicated that he was beginning to sour on the idea. He was worried about competition from Time-Life's American Wilderness Series and the lack of sales appeal of their books, "particularly the Sierra book which I would not have been tempted to buy unless I were acquiring every nature book that came out."[8] A total of four titles appeared before 1977, and the series expired.

The second—and even more time-consuming—project was *The World of Birds*, published by Doubleday in 1964. Flushed with the success of *Wild America*, Peterson and Fisher started planning a major text that would encompass all the birds of the world. It was to be, as Peterson wrote to his friend Francois Bourliere, "probably the most important book that either of us will ever do—in effect, the sum total of our life work in ornithology." Peterson painted hundreds of illustrations, and the text, mostly by Fisher in collaboration with Peterson, was to "interpret for the intelligent but uninformed audience . . . [to] bridge this gap between science and presentation."[9]

It was a monumental task. On the book's publication, Peterson wrote to John Terres that "neither James Fisher nor I will ever attempt anything quite as ambitious again. . . . In the future—once I finish the flower guide and the Mexican book (which are embarrassingly overdue)—I will attempt only 'fun' books."[10]

Most of the reviews were positive, but some pointed to the book's failure to deliver on its intent to "bridge the gap." A reviewer for the *Christian Science Monitor* praised Peterson's illustrations but criticized the text's failure to take its audience into account: "The book is really adequate neither for expert or layman. It uses too many unfamiliar concepts and terms without proper explanation to enlighten most readers, yet it is generally too superficial to be of much value to the experts."[11]

World of Birds did not sell well, and Peterson, in a 1966 letter to Fisher, provided the best explanation why. It was overpriced at $22.50; its large format suggested that it was a "cocktail table" book rather than a serious ornithological teaching tool; but ultimately, it failed because "we tried to be all things to all people."[12] This attempt resulted in the problems noted in the *Monitor* review. Compounding these issues were various promotional shortcomings and publication delays by the publisher. Fisher was understandably upset, but Peterson seemed to accept this rare setback. Perhaps he had no time to lick his wounds: the flower book and the Mexican *Guide* still hung over his head.

But finally all the impediments were out of the way after nearly three decades, and Peterson's spirit and imagination took wing. He was free, finally, to pursue his ambitions as a writer and painter. In a lengthy memorandum to Paul Brooks in March 1973, Peterson outlined an ambitious list of writing proposals. The first was a guide to the wildflowers of the Southeast. Three were *Wild America* spin-offs that would call for illustration and travel writing. *Wild Islands* would recount his "experiences in the wilder islands of the seven seas." A similar proposal, entitled *In Search of Eden*, would deal specifically with the islands of the Indian and Pacific Oceans. Both of these books would involve travel already done and some writing already completed. *The Atlantic Coast* was a completely original proposal. Peterson's description is an almost wistful fantasy, but one that seemed within reach: "During the last half dozen years I have had a dream of acquiring a Boston Whaler or perhaps a slightly fancier small boat that would sleep at least two people and start up the coast on the inland waterway from Florida to Maine, investigating every channel, every bird island, every bird marsh." Sadly, the trip was never made. For yet another title, *Long after Audubon*, Peterson would retrace Audubon's travels in the United States while commenting on changes in the natural world that had occurred. Finally, he proposed "an autobiographical book, not an autobiography," that would be not so much his life story as a recounting of his life's work. As early as 1964, he had discussed the idea with Brooks, and two biographers had asked permission to do a book on him, permission that was denied. Although none of these books was ever published, Peterson's papers at the Roger Tory Peterson Institute show evidence that he worked, sporadically, on all but the Southeast wildflower guide and the dream trip.[13]

It is in his painting, however, where Peterson's new attitude was best displayed. It involved a brand-new approach, which he expressed in numerous speeches at the time. He announced his intentions in his keynote address at the 1975 exhibition "Animals in Art," at the Royal Ontario Museum in Toronto, when he said, "For my own self-respect, I have had to free myself from this field guide type of drawing. I am not entirely free, but I will be."[14] At the 1979 meeting of the Society of Wildlife Artists in New York City, he expressed his desire in the language it usually took in interviews and in letters to his friends:

> As for my own painting—now that I am getting away from
> field guides—The recent things that I have done as limited edition prints are a transition stage—They fall into the category
> of decorative portraiture somewhat in the Audubon tradition. I
> fully intend to paint more expansively, to get back into oils and
> canvas again. To play with mood and color and light. To paint

more sensuously. And it remains to be seen how successful I will be in making the switch. I like to think that an artist can change direction if he chooses.[15]

The "transition stage" had already begun in 1973 with Peterson's association with Robert Lewin's newly founded Mill Pond Press. When Lewin worked for the printing company that produced the National Wildlife Federation wildlife stamps and Peterson was art director, the two men had become friends and correspondents. After his retirement, Lewin and his wife, Katherine, established the press and planned to produce a series of decorative china plates featuring Peterson's bird portraits. When the arrangement with the china company fell through, the Lewins decided to reproduce the portraits as signed and numbered limited-edition prints, and the profitable relationship was born. The Lewins became an important influence at this stage in Peterson's career—helping to manage his painting schedule, exhibits, and tours. Typical of their involvement, the Lewins or their son, Richard, delivered each press run to Peterson in Connecticut for signing. Typical of their forbearance was a dozen years of encouraging and cajoling.

By June of 1973, Peterson was well into the project, which called for two subjects a year until the series was completed with twelve paintings. Lewin was enthusiastic about Peterson's setting aside time from his field guide painting. He wrote in June, "Just can't tell you how happy I am that you are really painting now and even though the Eastern Field Guide should have a great deal of your time, it is absolutely wonderful that it would be boring to you to devote more than half your time to it."[16] In a return letter, Peterson wrote of how important the Lewins' support was to him: "Your own confidence and enthusiasm is infectious, and this is reassuring when one considers the debilitating effect of these summer days. . . . I appreciate all the loving care that you and Katie have lavished on the project." He went on to mention other series such as waterfowl, waders, and tropical "glamour" birds. He even enthused about taking "a crack at African wildlife."[17]

Peterson's first four subjects—Baltimore oriole, cardinal, flicker, and wood thrush—sold out quickly. His own assessment was upbeat, saying that although he knew his limits when it came to critical detail, his "actual drawing and feeling of the bird" might be better than that of the "super-realists."[18] By the end of 1974, he had painted four more: bald eagle, barn swallow, bobolink, and great horned owl. Peterson continued to produce more paintings; by 1975 he had done companion pieces: ruffed grouse and bobwhite. Prints from these two paintings were enormously popular, and the originals were priced at $18,000. Most important, he was excited and engaged in the work. In a 1975 memo to Lewin, he listed subjects for future work. The list mentioned no fewer than thirty-two larger species and nineteen species of songbirds. In another memo, he discussed "concepts": the head of a great horned owl or bald eagle, a saw-whet owl being pestered by kinglets. He could barely contain his enthusiasm: "The above subjects would be a cinch to do and I could knock them off in the months ahead in addition to several other smaller size songbird prints. In fact, I may eventually do more than six subjects this coming year if you can handle them."[19]

Peterson had evolved a long and complex technique for his paintings. He began with sketches on tracing paper, often as many as twenty to thirty tissues, taking the same care with detail. Then he began to work on composition by overlaying the tracings or cutting out the drawings and manipulating them while planning and sketching in the background. He would often work on two or three approaches to the same subject simultaneously before arriving at a concept that pleased him. The painting process was the same as well: a laying on of watercolor washes—transparent, then opaque, then adding acrylics toward the end for modeling.

Each print represented a single species, usually an individual or a pair. The visual approach was pure Audubon; Peterson presented birds and settings against a blank background with a careful eye to design. The early subjects, because they were intended for reproduction on plates, were tight compositions conceived with a circular format in mind. In fact, the first prints were mounted in round mats. But Peterson's birds were much better than those of the man he called his role model. Audubon was an obsessive gunner; he clearly preferred killing birds to studying them. His description of how he obtained "lifelike" poses for his bird paintings—he wired freshly shot birds into position on a gridded board before they stiffened from rigor mortis—is not surprising, therefore: "I shot the first kingfisher I met, pierced the body with wire, fixed it to the board, another wire held the head, smaller ones fixed the feet

. . . there stood before me the real kingfisher. I outlined the bird, colored it. This was my first drawing actually from nature."[20] The result was predictable: Audubon's birds often look like dead birds tortured into strange poses. Peterson's birds avoid the often grotesque contortions and artificial attitudes of Audubon's. Because of his years of careful observation—Peterson was as obsessive a bird-watcher as Audubon was a bird shooter—he was able to convey what he called the gestalt of a bird as well as its field marks. In a letter to Martha Hill of *Audubon Magazine* about his peregrine falcon, for example, he explains why he chose a "stark" approach of peregrine pair with bare branches on a white background:

> The peregrine is a bird that transcends its terrestrial environment. Its true environment is the open sky. It roams the world. I have watched them as they pursued shorebirds on the coasts of Greenland, and terns on the Strait of Magellan. I have observed them nesting in Moorish watchtowers in Spain, riding the updrafts in the high Andes, and consorting with various African fauna in the Rift Valley. It is a super-bird, the ultimate expression of a bird—*all bird*. And so I chose to portray it as the hard-muscled, hard-plumaged bird that it is—treating it almost as a bit of sculpture, using the sensuous, virile quality of the branches as an abstraction to further emphasize this quality.[21]

His *Barn Swallows on Phragmites* suggests the busy, fluttering grace of the species. Phragmites leaves taper away to the edge of the print and crisscross each other. The swallows' pointed wings and deeply forked tails take up the same rhythms. A story has it that Peterson waited until fall to make the painting so the efflorescence of the phragmites would have turned to russet. Presumably he wanted the double effect of the phragmites repeating the orange of the swallow's breast and the intensification of color achieved by juxtaposing the blue of the birds' backs with its orange complement. And even though he sacrifices some three-dimensionality by putting cool colors in the foreground and warm colors in the back, the swallows still stand out brilliantly against the white background.

He twisted one bird to show both the breast and forked tail, but the result is not a bird frozen in time and space, as one often finds in an Audubon print, but rather one in motion. Swallows are like that, and the next moment the wings might be folded and the tail straightened. The overall effect, as in most of the prints, is an image that serves to identify a barn swallow as well as to convey its essence—yet another example of Peterson the teacher, artist, and naturalist, and a spirit large enough to contain all three.

28

While he was in the process of changing his artistic direction, Peterson's personal life was changing direction as well. Those qualities that made him the success he was—his focus, diligence, and drive—put a heavy strain on his marriage. As early as 1954, Barbara complained that he was "remote" with his children. As his younger son, Lee, remembers, "Basically we saw him at meals."[1] But Lee also recalls that Peterson was not estranged from his family. Although his absence might have been physical and, perhaps, psychological, he involved himself with the general direction that decisions would take. A good example is the publication of Lee Peterson's *Field Guide to Edible Plants*. In an editorial meeting discussing future titles for the field guide series, Peterson mentioned Lee's interest in doing such a book. He stepped back and allowed Lee to make his own presentation to Houghton Mifflin. And after that meeting, Peterson wrote a long letter to Paul Brooks, defending, as any father would, Lee's answers to difficult questions that were posed. In addition, he wrote glowingly of the project, while removing any hints of nepotism: "Lee's determination to do such a book has been entirely self-generated. It was sparked two years ago when he helped teach at an environmental workshop in Maine; he had also led wilderness treks where he gave instruction in survival, cookery, woodcraft, etc. He discovered that books written about wild foods were almost useless as field manuals. Their weakness was field identification."[2] But when Peterson was at home, his enormous workload and frequent absences dictated that he focus on his work, usually at night and often through the night. In 1962, Barbara wrote a letter to James Fisher that captures the mood:

There have been times recently when I feared for Roger's health (this is between you and me) for I have never seen him work at such an intensive pace. Right now the schedule is from noon until I get dinner for him at breakfast—he works right through. He doesn't stir from the studio—I have been errand boy and get his bird skins, art supplies or whatever so that he doesn't lose a moment.[3]

The tension was compounded by what Barbara called his "dark moods." He had always been able to see his life in segments, with specific goals for each segment. A fear of not reaching these goals grew into a fear of aging that was made worse by occasional attacks of writer's and artist's block that he found agonizing and that filled him with self-doubt. As he confessed to an interviewer in 1983, "I'm fighting with concepts—that is the hardest part—and also what I feel are my own limitations. I might look at a canvas and have something in mind for weeks and just remain idle, not able to start it."[4]

For her part, Barbara must have felt a tremendous strain in trying to find an identity in a life that was devoted wholly to the career of another. Just one example can be seen in a letter she wrote to a photo researcher who was cataloging and selling her own photographs: "Dr. Peterson has returned home and now most of my efforts go in his direction—not my own so I do not have the peace of mind to worry about my efforts."[5] And in a thank-you note she showed how even small things that recognized *her* became important: "I am always tremendously pleased that you send your calendar to *me*. So much mail comes for Roger that I get a great lift to have a piece directed to me, personally."[6] Eventually the couple lived virtually apart except for meals. Barbara continued to do his typing, answer his letters, and plan his trips, and Peterson poured his energies into his studio work and travels. As a final irony, it was Barbara who understood Peterson's need to make the artistic changes that characterized his work in the 1970s and pushed him firmly in that direction. In March 1976, they divorced.

29

At this time, Peterson began to choose more subjects that were better suited to "full" paintings, paintings that incorporated a landscape background. These were subjects large enough—such as raptors—to fit their environments without distortion. As he had explained in an address he gave in the 1950s, a larger bird can be placed "at a great enough distance from the eye so that the horizon line, or things in the landscape, can be encompassed logically."[1] Songbirds, on the other hand, must be painted at close range, making a landscape illogical because of the limitations of the human eye's depth of focus. So in 1976 he painted a pair of snowy owls in an Arctic setting and a golden eagle in the American West. In these full paintings, which Peterson called gallery paintings, he also began to confront another issue that his illustration prohibited.

Missing in the early paintings that Peterson did for Mill Pond is what he often referred to as the "fall of light." His barn swallows, for example, take their shape from their contour lines; their color is "local color." They are not as the eye sees them, but rather a representation of how they *should* look. It was in his gallery paintings that Peterson finally felt free to explore fine art issues.

Every bird artist must confront the problem of the bird in relationship to its environment, whether to paint the subject *against* the landscape or *into* it. In discussions of this issue, Peterson used terms coined by his friend and fellow bird artist Don Eckelberry. For Peterson, given the necessity of realism in wildlife art, the artist still could choose to paint the subjects "impressionistically, as the eye sees them, bathed in light and shadow." Eckelberry called this "objective realism." Its counterpart, "intellectual realism," is described by Peterson as "detailed feather maps devoid of modifying atmosphere."[2] Privately, Peterson was more direct. In a 1962 letter to John Terres, he wrote, "What Don calls 'objective realism' would be called, in snide tones, by some contemporary critics—'photographic' or 'academic.' They tend to use the term 'academic' as a dirty word whereas Don actually feels (as I do) that this is perhaps the most desirable approach." In the same letter, he discusses Eckelberry's division of bird painting into "art" and "illustration," admitting that he is "never quite sure when to call a thing 'art' and when to call it 'illustration.'"[3]

Perhaps in self-defense, Peterson had trouble with the word "art" from the beginning. As he wrote to George Sutton in 1962, "I am a bit chary of using the word art for the simple reason that today art does not seem to embrace representational painting. It seems to be largely non-objective and for that reason birds find it difficult to fit into that definition."[4] He was well aware, when he enrolled in the academy in the 1920s, that the mainstream of art was moving in a direction inimical to him. His expressed view—even to Sutton, a fellow painter—was dismissive: "Actually most of them [modern artists] are a bunch of phonies, and this I think I can say with conviction inasmuch as I was exposed a bit to the non-academic tradition in painting awhile back."[5]

It was the issue of bird painting that remained at the core of his distrust of nonobjective art. In the letter to Terres, he mentions the work of Morris Graves as an example of bird art that critics tended to favor. Graves could best be called an abstract expressionist, whose paintings of birds and other nonhuman subjects became quite popular in the 1960s until his death in 2003. Graves' birds are easily recognizable as birds, and with a little effort, one can identify the species of most of them. His settings, however, are completely nonrepresentational and evocative, and his delineation is spontaneous rather than accurate. Peterson's take on Graves was that "he paints those curious birds that look as though they were wrapped up in tissue paper—plovers with shoebutton eyes and matchstick legs, etc." He has no problem with Graves painting "what he feels about what he sees," but for Peterson, it just doesn't work with birds: "The critic will ask 'isn't it just the very essence of ploverness?' My answer is 'hardly; I know too damn much about plovers.'" He closed his discussion with Terres, as he did with several other such discussions with other correspondents, with a vulgarism: "I avoid the word art like a plague. . . . Art rhymes with fart."[6]

He closes the letter to Sutton on a different note, however, one that he could take into his studio: "Probably the best thing for us to do in our own painting is to be true to ourselves and not worry too much about what other people think."[7] So he tried to find a way to live in two worlds: artist and bird-artist. But he did it in his own idiom. He remained the painter who came out of the traditions of Audubon and Fuertes, with an irritating desire to somehow break away kept in check.

Some of Peterson's paintings betray their Audubon roots more than others. His *Snowy Owls* (1976) is a good example of a beautiful, but static, bird grouping placed in front of a backdrop. Of the painting, Peterson wrote, "In this painting I have attempted an ecological composition involving not only the birds, but also a bit of glaciology (a distant glacier, an iceberg, brash ice, etc.), a bit of geology and a bit of Arctic botany represented by golden lichens and Arctic grasses."[8] In fact, in spite of the environmental detail, it is first and foremost a bird portrait. Peterson focused his detail on the feet, eyes, and beak of the owl. The leg feathers and the talons of the foreground owl are delineated with fine precision, but the rock the owl stands on and the adjacent lichens are treated with gestural brush strokes rather than fine lines. Since all these features are equidistant from the viewer, the effect is surreal; the owl seems to be floating just above the rock. The face, especially the beak and eyes, is equally precise, with the brilliant yellow eyes easily dominating the painting. The owl in the background is, properly, less detailed, but again, the eyes and beak receive the same delineation as the other owl's face. The somewhat unnatural result is a good example of Peterson's use of both "objective" and "intellectual" realism, an attempt to paint his subject as the eye sees it *and* as it really is. The "fall of light" is apparent, but it falls differently on the owls from the way it falls on the mountains and glaciers in the background. And the overall work remains true to the circumstances under which it was painted: Peterson did the owls in a Copenhagen zoo and added a background later. Owls and rocks together merely describe a silhouetted form against a standard Arctic scene. This does not reveal a weakness in the work but rather an insight into Peterson's intent. As Robert Bateman observes, "His goal did not seem to be creating a 'slice of life' as in a Vermeer or Degas or Brueghel but to create an 'arrangement' as in a Raphael or Japanese art or even a Picasso."[9]

The golden eagle painting has more of a narrative feel, a sense of drama that the snowy owl piece lacks. A beautifully detailed immature bird perched on a high crag dominates the painting, but it faces away from the viewer, looking out over a valley with a distant, meandering river. In the middle distance, an adult bird soars, much less detailed, but easily recognizable. And even though the color is a bit flat, with little movement within the painting itself, the concept is good. The feather detail is evident, but Peterson focused on the essence of the bird: a sense of imperious power and of the space it commands. The vastness of this space is enhanced by a use of perspective that evokes the Japanese ukiyo-e designers, who treated their foreground subjects in the flat and detailed Oriental manner, but placed them before a landscape that employed Western-style perspective. The arabesque of the river wanders through the valley until it simply vanishes into a background so generalized that it nearly becomes assumed.

A 1979 painting similar to the snowy owls, *Gyrfalcon*, shows what Peterson could do when he set out to make what he called "juicier, more painterly canvases." Influences here reach back to the Art Students League as well as to Audubon and Fuertes. Two white-phase gyrfalcons perch on two separate rocks in a field of yellow grasses. The near shoreline of a deep blue inlet intersects the angled lines of the falcons' postures, and a far shoreline adds a third angle that completes a design of active motion. A shadow on a distant glacier and deeper blue areas of water form a subtle nimbus that repeats the shape of the silhouette formed by the two falcons. A mountain range is given distance by its receding cool colors and indistinct ridges and snowfields. This same atmospheric perspective draws the birds closer to the viewer with Peterson's use of warm colors in the foreground. His brushwork there is rapid and impressionistic, and the muted tones of the grasses provide a strong contrast to the dramatically side-lit birds. It approaches a landscape as Peterson wanted to paint it: as the eye sees it, "bathed in light and shadow." With all of the piece's artistic attributes, however, it, like *Snowy Owls*, remains a bird painting. Peterson creates an "arrangement" with the gyrfalcons front and center and as precisely delineated as in any of his works, standing out as Peterson would have observed them through field glasses in their native environment.

30

In 1975, Peterson told an interviewer, "The last years of my life, I intend to indulge myself."[1] Such a change in attitude arose, in part, from his third marriage. A month after his divorce from Barbara, Peterson married Virginia Marie Westervelt, a friend from Old Lyme. All indications suggest that the early years of the marriage were good ones. He was happy in his work, and if he planned to "indulge himself," it wasn't reflected in his productivity. By 1980 he had published twenty-eight full-sized portraits with Mill Pond Press and finished the fourth edition of the eastern *Guide*. He formed a working partnership with Virginia, sharing the work on the range maps for the field guides. With her keen interest in flowers came numerous gardens to add the stimulus of color to Peterson's daily routine. She also rekindled his interest in butterflies when she designed a "butterfly garden" to, according to a *New York Times* article, "help her husband through an artistic block."[2]

In a letter to the Roger Tory Peterson Institute, she offered, in her words, her official vita:

> Professionally her life has been mainly concerned with research. In the 1940's, during World War II while at Harvard University, she was involved in underwater acoustic research.
>
> After the war, taking some years off, she raised a family of two attractive daughters, Linda Marie and Miriam Oliver Westervelt. Eventually, she resumed her career as a research chemist in a biochemical medical laboratory at Pfizer Inc., working specifically in diabetic research. Following this work she joined the chemistry branch of the U.S. Coast Guard Research and Development Center whose primary task was to develop a system that would prevent the pollution of the marine environment. Using infrared spectroscopy, within three years she helped develop a procedure that identifies the source of oil spills. She authored the U. S. Coast Guard's 'Infrared Field Manual for Oil Spill Identification.' For her work in enabling

the U.S. Coast Guard to detect those who pollute seas and waterways she received official commendation from the U.S. Government.

Currently she is actively engaged in producing books with her husband, author, painter Roger Tory Peterson.[3]

Virginia instituted a disciplined lifestyle. She quickly took control of Peterson's diet, ameliorating a prediabetic condition that had affected the circulation in his legs and that was controlled eventually by diet, exercise, and the prescription medication Orinase. Many friends tell of long, careful letters from Virginia on the "care and feeding of Roger" when he traveled without her. Typical of these was her instructional letter to Houghton Mifflin for the promotional tour on the fiftieth anniversary of the field guide:

> Roger is diabetic; he is 75 years old. . . . Diabetes affects eyes, limbs, and heart. Stress, especially at his age, is the most damaging to his condition. Rest at the proper time is a key factor in preventing damaging stress. People, many times, have innocently demanded or scheduled Roger's time (causing upset to his health) when he should have been resting. I have been 'in the field' or 'on stage' with Roger enough to know why, how, and when he gets into trouble.[4]

What follows is a careful arrangement of Peterson's time that would ensure his perfect ease when on the road. Other letters included dietary specifications suitable for the most advanced diabetic.

To keep him on task, she controlled his activities at home carefully, eliminating the all-night work sessions, managing his schedule, and limiting visits from members of the ornithological world. It was this supervision that enabled Peterson to complete the huge task of keeping up with field guide demands: the fourth editions of the western *Guide* and the eastern *Guide* and the fifth edition of the eastern *Guide*.

Peterson once told a friend that he always had a dominant woman in his life; between wives Barbara and Virginia, however, was a marked difference in management style and priorities. Both had an intense interest in Peterson's legacy, but while Barbara preferred to attend to everyday details and free Peterson to pursue his painting and writing, Virginia remained a constant presence. Barbara was content to stay in the background; Virginia wanted to share the limelight. With Peterson's marriage to Virginia came an increased concern with appearance, a turn from substance to style. But according to most observers and as later events would reveal, the principal difference between the two women was in their approaches to Peterson's legacy with regard to its impact on the natural world and preservation causes. Virginia concerned herself more with promoting and protecting "Peterson"—the name and its worth. The environmental concerns and the love of birds that Peterson shared with Barbara were secondary.

The matter of "legacy" would be a natural concern to someone of Peterson's renown. As early as 1964, he was thinking about writing an autobiography. In a letter to Paul Brooks, he somewhat self-consciously suggested a book, not about his life so much as about his life in the world of ornithology. And a decade later, he included an "autobiographical book" among a number of titles that he proposed to Houghton Mifflin.

> This would be an autobiographical book, not an autobiography, giving my eye-witness account of the rise of bird watching and the environmental movement as well as historical sketches of the National Audubon Society, National Wildlife Federation, World Wildlife Fund and other organizations with which I have played an important role. Also reflections on bird photography, bird painting, nature tourism, the lecture circuit, butterflies, field guides, botanizing, personalities, travels, etc.[5]

This was the direction the book would continue to take as he began actually writing it. He proposed that the book be done before 1978, when he turned seventy.

Peterson's plans were altered when he agreed to a biography, which was written by two journalists, John Devlin and Grace Naismith, and published in 1977. Because he took such an active role in the project, the biography actually moved his own book forward. In addition to giving the biographers a list of more than one hundred friends and colleagues to interview and submitting to long interviews himself, he composed typed memos, hundreds of pages of them, on topics of his choice and in response to questions from Naismith and Devlin. Many of these memos were appropriated by the biographers into their text while others found their way into Peterson's autobiography draft.

Naismith and Devlin's book, *The World of Roger Tory Peterson: An Authorized Biography,* was, by most standards, not very successful. Roger Pasquier, in the *New York Times Book Review,* panned it, saying, "Roger Peterson is a witty raconteur, and his writing is as carefully crafted as his art, so in reading this worshipful but clumsy biography, one keeps wishing he'd taken over the reins himself. Some of the mistakes made by Devlin and Naismith suggest they have never looked at the books and birds they discuss." The book is, indeed, riddled with errors and awkward prose, and it often is reduced to mere gossip. As Pasquier put it, "*The World of Roger Tory Peterson* is marred by a preoccupation with humanizing trivia."[6] As Peterson put it, more directly, in a letter to Paul Brooks, "They managed to get a lot of crap into the book that shouldn't have been included."[7] The book was "authorized" but not, as Peterson wrote to many of his friends, "bowdlerized." The result was a major disappointment to him. As he wrote to his longtime friend George Harrison, "I do not think journalists should write biographies. They are too superficial, do not get things straight, and they emphasize the wrong points in a subjective way. It's not quite the way things were. There is a vast difference between writing for newspapers and magazines and writing a book."[8] And to Robert Lewin, he wrote that journalists "try for the shock effect," adding, "A person such as myself should not be handled in the same way as a person in show business; where gossip seems to be the order of the day."[9] He even went so far as to suggest to Lewin that certain "prospects" might have been lost because of the book.

The direct result of the biography's failure was to urge Peterson on with his own book. In a 1982 letter to Austin Olney at Houghton Mifflin, he said he was averaging five hundred words a day on a book that would be called *Free as the Birds.* It would include "a lot more of my recent activities and adventures on other continents than the Devlin book," Peterson wrote. "Whereas a biographer can say things about a person that he could not or would not say about himself, an autobiography can take a somewhat different direction—telling more about other people and associates." He went on to propose a book "decorated throughout with marginalia—nice black-and-white drawings—interspersed with full page black-and-whites."[10]

The book was never finished. Peterson mentioned it off and on during the 1980s, still discussing it in 1989 with friends such as Joe Kastner and John Farrand. But in 1982 he did put together a draft of eighty-eight short pieces, totaling about three hundred pages of typescript. A foreword says, in part, "This is the story of my lifelong love affair with birds and birders, my personal fable, told my way."[11] There is some duplication of the memos he had written to Naismith and Devlin, but other new pieces about travel and colleagues indicate that he had been sticking to his plan as he outlined it to Brooks and Olney. He also added new stories from his childhood, as they pertained to birds and nature study, as well as several introspective reflections as he entered his later years. One such piece, a remembrance of his childhood friend Clarence Beal, is a fine example of his best expressive writing:

One evening in April, 1981, Lorimer Moe phoned to tell me some distressing news. Clarence Beal and Evangeline had just returned to Jamestown from a trip south to see their children and grandchildren. In preparation for the spring planting, he was burning off the grass, weeds, and brush in the field in back of the house when the fire got out of hand. Apparently in his attempt to get over the fence he became entangled in the barbed wire and was enveloped in the flames. He died on the way to the hospital.

It was a sad, gray morning, two days later, when I landed at the little hilltop airport not far from the Beals' home for the funeral. Large flocks of pectoral sandpipers were coursing over the grassy meadows beyond the runways, part of a major flight of these Arctic bound shorebirds that was noted elsewhere that week in western New York State.

That afternoon when we lowered the casket into its place in the Lakeview Cemetery I was within sight of the very spot where Clarence and I first met, but in nearly 60 years everything had changed. The cemetery itself had extended for fully a quarter of a mile since the old days, to accommodate the two more generations of citizens. Olson's Woods and Peterson's Pasture were gone. So were Beckerink's fields and the pig farm where we saw our first starlings. Suburbia was closing in. A broad interstate highway swept across the valley, speeding commerce on its way to Ohio. All the landmarks I knew were gone. Everything but memories.[12]

Passages such as this make one wish, with Roger Pasquier, that Peterson had, indeed, "taken over the reins himself."

31

In fact, the only evidence of the self-indulgence Peterson promised himself in 1975 can be seen in his increasing involvement with photography. Nature photographer and writer William Burt, a Peterson friend from Old Lyme, offered an observation about the importance of photography in Peterson's later years in his 2001 book, *Rare and Elusive Birds of North America*. "More than anything else on earth," Burt wrote, "Roger Peterson liked photographing birds; the mere talk of it perked him up, and put light in his eyes."[1] In fact, Burt and others have suggested that bird photography actually became more important than bird-watching; however, as Burt points out, Peterson could do a fair amount of bird observation through the long lenses that he favored.

Even from the beginning, bird photography and bird watching had been inseparable for Peterson; therefore his obsession with both grew and changed in parallel ways. As his early passion for birds was gradually enhanced by a deeper understanding of them and then by a desire to express both love and knowledge, his use of photography as a tool to record these feelings changed accordingly. Throughout his career as a photographer, he placed nature photography into the familiar artist/naturalist dichotomy: "Nature photography has two major approaches. The first is pictorial, concerned with composition, attractive pattern and values of light and shade, originality of concept and, when it can be achieved, emotional quality. . . . The second approach, the documentary, is less esthetic and more functional. The field biologist of today is seldom without a camera."[2]

Once Peterson's involvement with birds had gradually shifted during his teenage years from the emotional toward the intellectual, he made a strong case for photography as a tool for gathering information. He still took bird photos incessantly for pleasure, but the artist in him hadn't considered photography alongside painting as a means solely for expression. Photography, he insisted, is a record of a moment whereas drawing is a composite of an artist's experience. He wrote often that he thought photography taught him to see, that it helped develop his "awareness of the quality of light patterns and line." Yet he claimed that he used photographs only as a "memory jog," as a way to check on details of posture, plumage, and behavior or to help recall details for his writing. He never copied from them, leaving his painting to the guidance of his memory and experience, aided by study skins. When the Audubon Society published its bird guide, which was illustrated with bird photographs rather than drawings, Peterson dismissed it, calling it a "field guide in name only" and saying, "The reasons are obvious. A photograph captures a living instant—the vision of an individual bird in specific surroundings. For field identification this is as much a curse as a blessing. The individual bird's minor peculiarities are accentuated and often a distinguishing feature is hidden."[3]

He went on to say that "no film records a living organism's colors the same way throughout the day. The sun at dawn shines with a rosier glow than the glare of midday. A sparrow photographed in the woods has a different complexion than one caught in a yellow meadow, although their overall plumage may be identical."[4] Within this statement, however, also lie the possibilities of photography that Peterson began to explore as the photographs he published began to change. He told Henry Horenstein, in an *American Photographer* interview in 1986, that his photography was likely to play a larger role in his work and that he was using it to "tackle the problems he face[d] with his painting—three-dimensional activity, movement in space, and mood . . . the classic artistic problems of making photographs."[5]

It is doubtful, however, that Peterson ever really committed himself to the artistic problems of making photographs. As William Burt recalls,

> During the years that I knew Peterson [since 1963], I never knew him to plan for one particular photograph; or to set up for one and devote hours or days to it; or to go back and re-do one until he got it right. Rather, he would seek out opportu-

nities for long lenses at some distance, with lots of birds; and he would fire away (selectively, of course), and he would keep going, enthralled, seldom lingering or agonizing over any one shot.[6]

Back in 1949, Peterson wrote that "photography is not as grim a proposition to me as my painting, hence I enjoy it more—more, in fact, than anything else that I do with birds."[7] In his postscript to *Birds over America*, Peterson reacted to the photographs in the book by saying, "Every photograph [in the book] brings back memories."[8] They are the result of time spent with birds, a technological record of a powerful passion. Thirty-five years later, his tune hadn't changed: "Drawing, painting, writing demand such discipline that they can seem a sort of slavery. They call on everything you have ever seen or thought about a subject, a composite of your whole past experience, if you are to get the best possible result. And that can be very difficult." With a photograph, "you do the best you can to get a good picture, but then it's over."[9] He felt closed up in his studio, chained to his drawing board, but he was set free by his cameras.

Photography had become his therapy and escape. The camera lens replaced field glasses as a way to focus on birds and to force life onto the periphery. But then time and two cataract operations threatened to rob him of his only relief. He always said that his strength as a photographer was that he could "see" a photograph before he exposed it, referring to the concept that Ansel Adams called previsualization. Peterson's weakness, he said, lay in the mechanics of photography.

Any weakness with mechanics, however, didn't prevent Peterson from understanding the importance of the relationship between equipment and technique. He welcomed photography's advances, turning quickly to new cameras and accessories. When he was in the army, he was able to experiment with the new Kodachrome film before it was readily available. A Speed Graphic given to him for a shoot by *Life* magazine replaced his heavier Graflex, followed by the even smaller Hasselblads and Bronicas. With the introduction of 35 mm cameras, bird photography became easier and more convenient many times over. Peterson tried them all. And it was technology—the development of automatic focus—that saved him from his eye problems and, therefore, his focusing problems. Autofocus cameras, he said, "have given me young eyes again. I can depend on them."[10] Another of technology's boons was the motor drive, which turned Peterson from a conspicuous consumer of film into a voracious one.

The naturalist and artist came together in 1979 in *Penguins*. It is perhaps the quintessential Roger Tory Peterson book. The text is authoritative and well written, and it contains an environmental message. Dozens of drawings, mostly black-and-white washes, both decorate and illustrate. The seventy-one color photographs strike a balance between pictorial and documentary.

Although Peterson didn't concern himself with those elements of fine photography—such as balance, tension, motion of line and form—while he was in the field, the trained artist took over when he returned to his studio. As William Burt noted, "He would come back with hundreds and hundreds of exposures; then spend hours at the viewing station, selecting those that pleased, decisively, and dismissing the others without a second thought. Of course that ability to edit well, to see what works and what does not, that's part of the process, an important part; and he was good at it."[11]

While it's true that Peterson might have exposed thousands of shots to produce the photographs used in his later books, the fact remains that he *selected* these few to represent himself as a photographer. And some in *Penguins* are striking. In one, a dramatic study of ice floes and rugged terrain is reflected in shimmering water and framed by a melting iceberg that seems to give off its own light. In another, hundreds of emperor penguins, white and black with all the gray tones in between, stand in stark contrast to sea ice and a distant shore in shades of glacial blue—all under a remote half moon. Both images, like others in the book, achieve a certain "emotional quality" that Peterson wanted in his best photographs.

Many others have a more documentary rather than pictorial purpose, illustrating behavior or characteristics. But this in no way diminishes their visual appeal. Primarily descriptive, they often achieve a careful arrangement with dramatic results. Part of this is due to Peterson's creative use of his subject's natural coloring and design. In the book, he writes that penguins were his favorite bird family. Part of the reason might have been aesthetic: their stark and defined black-and-white coloring, occasionally muted with shades of gray or accented with splashes of orange or yellow, often standing against a bleak background. His photographs (and the drawings) are constantly mindful of these shapes and lines, especially as they are repeated in shots of couples or groups. The patterns and markings create form, silhouette, and negative space that suggest a natural abstraction, which Peterson employs to extraordinary effect.

Further evidence of the increasing appeal of Peterson's color photography can be seen in the seventy-eight pages of photographs he selected for his 1994 retrospective book, *Roger Tory Peterson: The Art and Photography of the World's Foremost Birder*. The overall impression of the works in the book is one of action, lavish color, and free design. The images range from extreme close-ups with the most minute of detail to groups of birds that, significantly, are so scant of detail that they are difficult to identify. A group of fifty willets stand in typical shorebird precision and uniformity on a sandbar. The photograph is shot with such a narrow depth of field that only one or two birds are in focus. The result is a portrait that suggests one organism rather than individuals in a group, a stationary image that implies the unity of shorebirds in flight. A flock of cormorants on a wave-battered rock are shot in such raking light that they become nonspecific—a part of a dramatic composition of surf and rocks and light. Even in the full-frame portraits, the representation of field marks often becomes secondary to design, with some features, such as beaks, truncated in Peterson's cropping of the images.

Perhaps the most interesting example of this de-emphasis of documentation is a striking photograph of a great egret, which invites anthropomorphism (which Peterson held in contempt) and misinformation (which he would not allow). The bird stands against a black background in a hunched-over posture typical of the species. Dramatic backlighting accentuates the windblown plumes that extend beyond the bird's tail during breeding season. The impression to the layman is of remarkable beauty found in a beleaguered bird, hunkered down against the cold. And, of course, it is anything but that, shot as it was in Florida in late spring. In this case, the beauty of the image overwhelmed any other considerations.

This photograph, however, remains a bird portrait rather than an artistically whole composition. Its lack of an integrated background reveals Peterson's central concern: to preserve the memories of the beauty of birds. Henry Horenstein closed his *American Photographer* piece with a prediction about Peterson: "It seems safe to predict that he will strive to reach the same high aesthetic levels that are the hallmark of his painting. Given his dedication to his first love, however, his many readers can rest assured that the siren song of the muse will never drown out the bird songs of realism, that accuracy will invariably win out over beauty for its own sake."[12] It is clear, however, that "beauty for its own sake" was also becoming no small consideration for Peterson's finished photographs.

In a 1983 interview, Peterson enumerated his four reasons to photograph. "One, relaxation and pleasure. Two, as background information for my artwork. Three, as note-taking for my writing. . . . And four, the top quality ones, for publication and lecturing."[13] In the Peterson Institute, one can see the remarkable result. In addition to folders of black-and-white prints is Peterson's huge collection of transparencies, all encoded and cataloged. The bulk of them, around 80 percent, are of birds of course—multiple shots arranged by species that range from "memory jogs" to careful studies to attractively composed and lighted portraits. Other categories can be classified in the same way. For example, there are nearly a hundred transparencies labeled "snow on evergreens," other sections of "branches and bark," "rocks and lichens," "trees and trunks," hundreds of wave and other water studies, more than three hundred slides of clouds alone, seven thousand landscapes from nearly every state and from every continent. These can be seen as useful tools, details for a painter or a writer to refer to. And many of them are simply beautiful. But were so many photographs necessary? There are more than two thousand transparencies of snow, ice, and icebergs, often breathtaking—carefully composed and brilliantly lighted. Clearly the first reason to photograph—relaxation and pleasure—superseded all the others. Among the classifications is one designated "locations." Here Peterson the curious traveler can be seen. These exposures seem almost random: shots of children from all around the world, interesting cultural behaviors and landmarks, architecture, friends, parties. He obviously couldn't stop.

Descriptions of Peterson at work with his cameras have two things in common: concentration and joy. This one by Downs Matthews, about a bird shoot at a white ibis rookery, is typical:

Suddenly a sunbeam pierces the clouds and illuminates the colony as if someone had turned on a floodlight. The clamor

of bird talk rises in volume as the flock comes to life. . . . Seeing the ibises doing something unusual, Peterson takes aim.
. . . fires in sustained bursts of several seconds' duration. . . .
His features relax into a smile of pleasure. . . . He moves constantly, making small adjustments in the framing of the scene before him, composing the elements, thinking visually. . . . His birds are performing for him in their timeless way. He, their portraitist and champion, seeks to capture their behavior to bring greater perfection to his own work and to celebrate . . .
Nature's most vivid life forms.[14]

Another striking story can be found in Burt's *Rare and Elusive Birds of North America.* Just one year before Peterson died, Burt had found a least bittern nest and thought immediately about how much Peterson would want to photograph the bird. But the nest was a difficult trudge through a deep cattail marsh. Burt was well aware of the danger of such an adventure to an aging man, but he understood well Peterson's passion for photography. "Even at home," Burt wrote, "incarcerated in Old Lyme, he was always looking for some chance to escape the studio with a camera. 'Let me know if there's anything around that *needs photographing*,' he would often tell his friends."[15]
So he called Peterson, who showed up within an hour, confirming with his enthusiasm the rightness of Burt's decision.

The resulting image powerfully depicts Peterson's lifelong approach to photography:

Out we went in our chest waders in the waist-deep water, slowly, cattails well above our heads, each saddled with a share of his equipment load. The peaty mud at bottom clung with a tenacity that would have impeded the sturdiest of younger men. I helped steady him now and then, and he progressed surely and with good humor, impatience voicing itself only when I told him the nest was nearby. 'Where is it?' he asked, with a no-nonsense urgency.

Six feet from the nest and the glaring bird, he stood there belly deep and bittern still and took his pictures coolly, half a roll or so, and it struck me how good a picture he would make there in the cattails, immersed in his element and focused as it were on the subject of his own life's work.[16]

Over a lifetime, joy took on the weight of obsession. The impulsive teenage photographer became the nearly compulsive adult, who carted pounds of cameras and equipment on nearly every outing. But the joy never went away. Peterson shot, by his own admission, an "appalling amount of film." Whereas Audubon called a day when he didn't kill at least 100 birds a failure, Peterson once claimed that he could do better: "On a bird photo safari, it's a poor day for me if I don't make several hundred exposures."[17]

"Photography can be fun," Peterson once said, "just plain fun."[18]

32

For Peterson, the fun was always brief; field guides intervened as usual. Three decades had passed since publication of the third edition of the eastern *Guide,* and two decades since the Golden Guide began to nudge Peterson and his guide out of the number one position. He began his response with his paintings for the Mexican *Guide,* and the changes that began with that 1973 book continued into the eastern *Guide*'s fourth edition. A good way to see the difference between Peterson's 1947 and 1980 efforts is to contrast birds with bold color patterns—the bay-breasted warbler, for example. In the 1947 painting, areas of color are simply that: areas that have been delineated, then filled with color from the outside in. The 1980 painting, on the other hand, depicts groupings of colored feathers that seem to expand to a pattern edge and blend with the adjoining pattern: chestnut to buff to black. Shading and countershading give the bird a rounder and fuller appearance. Better handling of the posture around the head and throat, as well as careful detail around the eye, suggest a live bird ready to fly.

The effect didn't come easily; Peterson approached his field guide plates in much the same manner as his gallery paintings. He began with a life-size drawing in pencil, working with sketches, files, photographs, and study skins to get every detail correct. This drawing was reduced mechanically to its working size, that is, to fit with the others on the plate.

When all the drawings were reduced and traced onto a drawing board that was twice the size of the printed page, he made tissue cutouts, which he manipulated until he had the desired composition for each plate. Here he remembered how his early idol Fuertes died before finishing his plates for the *Birds of Massachusetts.* Just in case another artist had to complete the fourth edition, Peterson blocked out the entire book in detail, making sure the design was perfect. Finally, he completed the final drawings and began to paint. Peterson always used water-based paint. First he laid down washes in transparent watercolors, then added opaque watercolors to saturate the color. Finally he put on a glaze of acrylics for modeling and shading.

True to the continued dual nature of his work, Peterson often deflected discussion of the new guide paintings from their artistic achievement and toward their practical and scientific purpose. Shortly after the 1980 edition was published, he wrote, "whereas my original intention [for the first edition] was simplification to allow recognition from a distance, many experts now want amplification." In response, he "leaned a bit more toward portraiture . . . while trying not to lose the basic abstraction that made the original book so practical—a difficult tightrope act."[1] This "tightrope act" reflected the balancing of Peterson's lives as artist and naturalist. And while he attempted to satisfy those who wanted a new kind of field guide, he also readjusted his reputation as an artist, even if he were to be judged by his guide paintings alone. The third edition of the *Field Guide to Western Birds* appeared in 1990, employing the same style and using many of the 1980 eastern *Guide* plates for birds that occur in both regions. These new plates in both books achieve the level of fine art, and as if to drive that point home, he published the twin, oversized volumes of *The Field Guide Art of Roger Tory Peterson,* the eastern birds and the western version, both in 1990.

These beautiful books present the plates as Peterson created them on his nine-by-fourteen-inch drawing boards—no text, no little arrows, and, most important, no reduction in size; just the brushwork, coloring, and impeccable detail that were lost in the printing of the field guides. Open any page and all doubt about Peterson's skill as a painter of birds disappears.

This skill is especially noticeable in his rendering of the small passerines, such as the warblers and sparrows. He is able to convey the essence of these birds—their weightlessness and softness, their vulnerability. Quick, light brushstrokes, especially around the heads and necks, help catch the feeling of holding a live bird in your hand: like capturing air or sensing the idea of flight. Careful counter-shading in the areas of darker plumage does the same, releasing the bird from the weight of even the most saturated colors. Rapid hatching and cross-hatching create a three-dimensionality that is tactile. Clearly, Peterson poured everything he knew about birds into these paintings. But they transcend mere knowledge. The closer they are examined, the more evident it becomes that they contain emotions as well—and a profound affection, the passion for birds that Peterson carried all his life and that, finally, even the scientist in him couldn't contain.

Peterson is equally adept at other essences. His page of crows and ravens in the western book, for example, is a portrait of potential energy and power. The three main figures—two species of raven and a crow—stand solidly on the page. Their feathering approaches portraiture, especially in the wings, drawing attention to the powerful rushing sound of these birds in flight. A small, overhead flight silhouette accompanies each painting, giving motion to the page. And the coloring is startling: black at a glance, but in reality, an admixture of black, blues, and browns. The birds seem to glow from inside with some regenerative force that finally escapes through the evocatively painted eyes.

One of the most remarkable pages is the plate of seven species of swifts, also in the western book. These are drab birds. Their coloring ranges from dull brown to gray to black, with various small, white markings. Peterson called them "cigars with wings." But the wings characterize the swifts—long and narrow, slightly bowed, and gracefully tapered—wings made for ceaseless flying. For his design of the plate, Peterson divided the page into two rectangular boxes, a white one above and a pale blue one below. He separated them with a bold, dark green line. Then having made containers for his birds, he let them escape. The three birds in the bottom half soar from lower right to upper left. The wing tips of the first two birds reach beyond the edge of the page. The right wing of the third swift actually extends into the upper box. The same technique is employed in the upper box as well, where the birds fly from lower left to upper right, up and away. With a poet's skill at imagery, Peterson put his most emotionally powerful attribute of birds—their freedom—into a painting of the most nondescript species.

It is easy to forget that these pages were meant to be instructional, that each bird was painted to show its field marks most clearly. Peterson's "tightrope act" was also a magic act; to these artistically satisfying bird paintings, just add arrows and labeling, reduce them to pocket size, and—presto—an efficient and accurate instrument for field identification appears. Nowhere is Peterson's genius for a synthesis of art and science more evident than in his work for the fourth editions of the *Field Guide*.

33

The decade of the 1970s saw Peterson at the peak of his career. Recognition flooded in. In 1975 he was elected to the National Wildlife Federation's Conservation Hall of Fame. His lifelong amalgamation of the two cultures of science and art was recognized by the Cosmos Club, which listed him as both artist and ornithologist in its announcement of his selection for its 1976 award. The Horatio Alger Award in 1977 honored him for overcoming the poverty and deprivation of his childhood. And the Leigh Yawkey Woodson Art Museum named him Master Wildlife Artist in 1978. In all, he received twelve national or international awards during the decade. However, as remarkable as the number of awards was, their diversity was even more notable; he was designated variously as educator, writer, conservationist, scientist, and artist. He capped this heady period of acclaim with the Presidential Medal of Freedom in 1980, the country's highest civilian honor. His renown can be gauged by the company he kept: he followed Helen Hays as the Cosmos Club awardee and preceded Pulitzer Prize poet Archibald MacLeish; he joined Aldo Leopold, John Muir, Jacques Cousteau, and others in the National Wildlife Federation Conservation Hall of Fame; and he shared the 1980 Medal of Freedom with Ansel Adams, Rachel Carson, Robert Penn Warren, and Eudora Welty, among others. As a more tangible form of recognition, the eastern *Guide* reached the

New York Times best-seller list in both paperback and hardbound editions, the paperback remaining there for more than six months.

Buoyed by this affirmation of his work and by finding a steady outlet for his painting at Mill Pond Press, he responded with steady productivity. During the years 1976–1978, for example, Mill Pond published seventeen lithographs of full-sized bird portraits. His production fell off abruptly, however. After painting a puffin group in 1979, he published only three more: wild turkeys in 1981, about which he said, "I do not like my turkey particularly, although I worked on it harder than any other painting I have done";[1] *Lord of the Air—Peregrine Falcon*, a 1986 work quite reminiscent of a 1977 peregrine falcon portrait; and a completely new snowy owl painting in 1983. He repeated the snowy owl subject at the request of Virginia, who attached a sentimental value to the first painting and was disappointed when Peterson sold it. And she influenced Peterson's treatment as well, asking him to paint a male and female bird instead of a single individual—a concept Peterson favored. For his own part, Peterson saw the painting as a "turning point" in that he considered it more "third dimensional, more painterly" than his earlier work.[2]

As they did in the 1976 work, two owls in an Arctic setting gaze out at the viewer. But there the similarity ends. Patches of rock done in a warm brown and showing through the snow, ice floes randomly floating in water saturated in color, mountains fading into a dramatic sky—all create interactive patterns and movement through space. Peterson's use of lighting and texture further separates this painting from the earlier one. Rocks and snow seem to glow in an otherworldly mood of a mysterious place apart, where these two lives burn and thrive. Significantly, Peterson titled the painting by its mood, *Arctic Glow*, rather than simply naming it after the species pictured.

In a letter to Susan Rayfield, he revealed his expectation for the work: "I picked the specific range of colors, textures, etc., to establish the mood of the painting simply because my own experience in the Arctic dictated it." By adding the element of mood to the painting, he faced the issue of how much delineation to employ as opposed to the usual question of accuracy. He went on to say that the most difficult part of the painting was the water: "just how it would reflect the mountains, background, etc., and to what extent it should be merely suggested or detailed." The matter of detail applied to the birds as well:

> In the male bird I have emphasized less detail but more of the fall of light and shade than in the bird in the foreground; partly because male snowy owls have less barring and patterning to begin with. One can work more purely with form. In the case of the female one must combine the two elements—form as indicated by light and shade overlaid with pattern which tends to obscure form to a certain extent. This is one of the dilemmas of painting birds.[3]

In his 1962 letter to George Sutton, Peterson had written of the necessity "to be true to ourselves and not worry too much about what other people think."[4] It was a theme he would come back to again and again, an old conflict often repeated, but Peterson's later work shows that he finally achieved, from time to time, the level of both naturalist and artist that he longed to attain. He often alluded to the longtime problem of bird painting by quoting critics who would invariably write either of two appraisals: "That's good art but poor ornithology" or "That's good ornithology but poor painting." As he reached the height of his long career, Peterson, in these full paintings, proved that good art and good ornithology were within reach. And one can view, at the very least, these later pieces as wonderfully and artistically satisfying extensions of his field guide art. Years of art training and practice, even more years of careful time spent with birds, can explain some of this success. A more profound reason is the passion that Virginia alluded to in a speech made after his death: "Most of his dreams were about birds. Even in his dreams he would see his hands as he painted birds."[5]

ROGER TORY PETERSON

1980–1996

Old Lyme

In spite of its popular and artistic success, the fourth edition, famil-iarly called RTP4, was castigated by many members in the upper levels of the bird-watching world. For the first time, Peterson felt the sting of such negative criticism. Reaction in the bad reviews generally fell into a pattern; critics were respectful of the Peterson legacy and praised the book as a guide for beginning and intermedi-ate bird students, but they were unanimous in their disappointment over perceived errors and omissions that would affect experienced birders' chances to make difficult identifications.

In its August 1981 issue, *Birding* collected a sampling of re-views of the book. Included were pieces by Henry Armistead, Ron Naveen, Claudia Wilds, Will Russell, and Lawrence Balch—along with a response by Peterson. Armistead wrote, for example, "RTP4 neglects many of the thornier identification problems and seems to have been written with little attempt to assimilate the fruits of the efforts of the continent's best field birders."[1] He went on to say that he "would like to see a field guide that reaches a compromise between over-simplification and over-elaboration, without being ir-responsible" (117). Naveen pointed out the impossibility of such a task: "As does the politician who plays for the most votes from the most constituents, Peterson had to find a common denominator. As a result, he may have won the election, but not everyone will be satisfied with his program" (118). Wilds identified the sources that Peterson neglected: "Skilled birders use information that is found in no guide at all, freely swapping each new piece of information with each other. . . . Much of this new information is found in regional journals and club newsletters but rarely reaches the average birder across the country" (119). She then stated what would be the most common complaint about RTP4: "While no field guide will ever be definitive, any guide published in the 1980's may be fairly judged by the degree to which it incorporates the identification discoveries of the 1960's and 1970's. And no contemporary author, however skilled as a field observer, can depend entirely on his own experi-ence and on national journals to produce the basic field guide that could now be written with the counsel of selected experts" (119). That Peterson failed to consult this elite group of "selected experts" was also identified by Russell as the basic weakness of the book: "Much of what is wrong with the fourth edition could have been corrected had the draft text and paintings been reviewed by any of a dozen highly skilled birders who live within a day's drive of Old Lyme" (121).

All of these reviewers pointed out specific problems in two areas: illustrations and descriptions that were not helpful at best and, at worst, misleading. But at the same time, they were of one accord in recognizing the importance of Peterson's work. Balch referred to the significance of each of the guides, from the 1934 edition on, as they "contributed greatly to the growth of the conservation movement by providing a focus for outdoor activity for millions of people" (121). And he suggested that the fourth edition would be no different: "The new guide has the same visual appeal and usefulness and is aimed at the same broad audience which the first guide reached, and, therefore, it should also be successful" (121). Each of these reviews concluded with such mild praise as that of Armistead, who wrote that until the ideal guide was written, "we can do much worse than to use Peterson's excellent new field guide" (118). Such underhanded praise must have come as cold comfort to Peterson.

One particularly galling critical reaction came from Kenneth Parkes of the Carnegie Museum of Natural History. Peterson had already developed a rather jaundiced view of reviewers, and of Parkes' style in particular, as he revealed in a letter to James Fisher in 1966. The letter was an attempt to calm Fisher, who was given to fits of fury over bad reviews. Peterson wrote, in part,

> As for reviews and reviewers, it seems to be the fashion to slaughter the big boys, and the more of a name someone enjoys the more likely he is to be clobbered. This, the nastiest sort of one-upsmanship, seems to be pervading our beloved science. Such reviewing is hardly the honesty that some of the practitioners insist that it is. Below the surface there is almost always selfish interest or personal antagonism involved. Take for example the attack by Ken Parkes on Ernst Mayr's latest book in THE WILSON BULLETIN. It could hardly be called a review; it was an attack.

Peterson went on, however, to advise Fisher to be temperate with such a reviewer: "I ignore him, and if he is a gentleman he probably feels a bit guilty. A hot letter, on the other hand, usually confirms him in his ways and his next review is likely to even nastier."[2]

In a letter to *Continental Birdlife*, Parkes took Peterson to task on many fronts, including the "abridgement of the text into plate captions," which made the omission of descriptions of some plumage varieties necessary. But what irritated Peterson most was the attack on him as an illustrator. Mention of taxonomic details such as the placement of the eyes in certain species and criticism of the choice of which plumages to illustrate were read by Peterson as affronts to his skills as a scientist. But Parkes really touched a nerve when he questioned Peterson's artistic abilities and intentions. At issue here was what Parkes called the fourth edition's "new artiness," its attempt to "pretty up the bird figures."[3] This, of course, hit at Peterson's main personal intent, which began in the Mexican *Guide:* to show the world that he was a better artist than his "little decoys" represented. Parkes points out, as an example, that the arrow on the black-capped chickadee plate points to a highlight on the bird's black cap. This slip, he argues, suggests that this identifying field mark is the bird's "glossy" cap rather than its black cap.[4]

Peterson was clearly angered. Early in 1982 he wrote to Ron Naveen, "I am still pissed off about Ken Parkes' review, which was off-base on almost every point."[5] And to Robert Sundell, a longtime friend and the authority on birds from Peterson's home region, he wrote, "I am so damned sick of these clowns who cannot draw themselves and yet arrogate themselves to a higher level by that kind of a review. If I like[d] fighting more I would hit back; but I suppose the thing to do is to ignore, or turn the other cheek. Fortunately, I have a great many friends like yourself who have some sense of proportion."[6]

Yet later correspondence shows that Peterson took his own advice about temporizing his response. He wrote a letter to Parkes in January 1982 that began:

> After reading your review in Continental Birdlife, following that of Kenn Kaufmann and the one by George Hall in the Wilson Bulletin, I am extremely depressed. Having worked so intensively for such a long period on the update of the book,

at its completion I had the feeling I had done a good job—the best I could do—and now I am left with the empty feeling that I may have failed. This is not easy to take at my time of life. However, there may be validity to some of your comments.

What follows is a calm response to Parkes's various assertions. He takes Parkes's point about the chickadees and simply defends himself on the others. For example, he writes, "The reason for the compromise between portraiture and schematics is that I have been under great pressure by the majority of birders to do exactly that." The letter's closing is neither defiant nor conciliatory, merely civil: "I have long valued our past association and realize that I should have consulted you. In spite of the criticism, everyone assures me that it is still the most effective field guide for identifying eastern birds that now exists. In due time I will upgrade it again."[7] Peterson's tone clearly left the door open for subsequent exchanges concerning ornithological points—which did, in fact, occur during the preparation of the revised western *Guide*.

Perhaps the most painful review was written by Kenn Kaufmann, one of the country's most respected young bird students at the time and a self-proclaimed "disciple" of Peterson's. The postreview correspondence that followed between the two reveals much about Peterson's—and Kaufmann's—character. Kaufmann concluded his review's three opening paragraphs of fulsome praise with a twist: "I would like to see a copy of this book in every household in eastern North America. I would also like the reader to remember I said that, because from here on I am going to be saying some harsh and critical things about the new Peterson."[8] He then outlined his general complaints with the book:

> The truly unfortunate thing is that it *could* have been a far better field identification guide *without* major changes in its convenient format . . . if only a plethora of errors had been edited out. If only a multitude of useful field marks had been written (and painted) in. If only the book reflected *current* knowledge of field identification, instead of being thirty years out of date for most species. If only the expert birders of North America had looked at the book before publication (instead of looking through it, groaning with disappointment and disbelief, *after* publication).[9]

A summary of advances in field identification followed before he began his specific complaints with this indictment: "Roger Tory Peterson—isolated at the pinnacle of the birding world, traveling the globe but rarely birding any more in North America—missed out. His new field guide reflects hardly a glimmer of the new sophistication in identification skills."[10] Three pages of close reading, nearly all of it negative, supported Kaufmann's thesis before he closed, condescendingly: "And if you should meet Roger Tory Peterson, do not criticize his latest Field Guide; just ask him to autograph your copy, and thank him for having done so much to promote bird study all over the world."[11]

The avalanche of criticism resulted in personal consternation. In a note attached to a copy of Kaufmann's review that Virginia sent to James Berry, president of the Roger Tory Peterson Institute, she wrote: "This is an unbelievable review. Sugar first—then acid aimed at destroying Roger's Field Guide."[12] And to his closest friends, like Victor Emanuel and Peter Alden, Peterson revealed how much he was hurt. It is natural to assume that someone of Peterson's acclaim could slough off criticism, but such was never the case. Dating back to Barbara Peterson's letters to her mother in the 1940s, one finds consistent references to dark periods; at their root, according to those who knew him best, was an insecurity that led to self-doubt. As Emanuel pointed out, it was often difficult for Peterson to focus on what he *had* achieved rather than what he *hadn't*. The reproachful voice of the father he could never please never really went away: "So you've been out after birds again! Haven't you seen them all before? I swear, I don't understand you."

In 1981, Peterson fired off impassioned letters to old and trusted friends that showed he shared Virginia's anger. In a letter to Harold Mayfield, he lashed out: "Kenn Kaufmann of *Continental Birdlife* and Will Russell have teamed up to do their own 'advanced field guide' and their strategy seems to be to cut the throat of the competition first."[13] To Olin Sewall Pettingill he wrote, "The review of the new Field Guide by Kenn Kaufmann in *Continental Birdlife* was absolutely revolting. . . . Some of these self-styled 'superstars' play dirty."[14] And to Joseph Hickey he wrote,

I thought I had done a very good job—my best—until several reviews (Kaufmann, Hall, Ken Parkes) made me feel I had failed. I became very depressed. I know that the new book is at least 300 percent better than the previous one; but there are a handful of modern Griscoms who would like a 1000-page field guide written specifically for themselves. I know that I can improve my rating with that crowd if I get the advice of my most likely critics first.[15]

The plan to consult his critics—which was precisely what some reviewers asked for—was the first indication that he would move forward rather than dwell on his anger. Obviously, he was deeply troubled; the self-doubt was genuine, and the disappointment in working so long and hard and then not living up to his peers' expectations was understandable. As he wrote to Mayfield, "Some points were undoubtedly valid; others not. I began to wonder if, after fifty years of effort put into the Field Guide, had I actually failed?" But true to his nature, he wasn't about to give up: "I am not going to subject myself to the same sort of thing with the new Western book. I will touch base with my most likely critics first and not wait for their comments in reviews."[16]

After allowing some time to reflect, Peterson reacted publicly with equanimity. In *Birding*, he wrote that he read reviews when he was ready to revise in order to be objective; however, he did complain that there were always "Young Turks out there ready to climb on my shoulders, but I can only hope that they do so wearing felt slippers and not with hob-nailed boots." He continued in general about the criticism of the fourth edition, focusing on the reviews' main complaint: that information about difficult identification was omitted or misleading. What reviewers wanted, he asserted, was impossible: "Theoretically, one could *prepare* the perfect book. In reality, he probably could not get it published because of technical limitations and economics." Chastising his critics for being "naïve about the realities of publishing," he pointed out that space was always a limiting factor, that authors were allowed "just so many signatures and just so many pages." Then he pointed out an article in *Birding* that discussed the plumages of the Thayer's gull—a topic that the reviews complained Peterson slighted. The article filled thirteen pages and ended with the author's disclaimer that his information might not all be correct. Peterson concluded by advising his critics to lighten up a bit—"Birding is not a grim do-or-die contest. It's a great game"—and requesting that they send specific comments or suggestions on three-by-five cards, as work on his western *Guide* revision was under way, and the promise of a fifth edition was waiting.[17] As he told Frank Graham, "I felt that I had done the best that I could do, and was quite pleased about the book, before being hit by some of the hardcore superstars." While asserting that he could rebuff much of the criticism, he admitted that "fifty percent" of it had some validity. And he made plans to change: "I am determined not to subject myself to this sort of thing in the update of the western book and am actively seeking the cooperation of a number of the best birders along the West Coast."[18] As Barbara Peterson observed, the only solution Peterson ever had to those difficult patches was to work harder. He applied the same solution after 1981, and his work on the revision of the western *Guide* progressed under a cloud of anger and depression that was compounded by the fact that the problem of how much detail to include—inherent in the fourth eastern *Guide*—remained in the western *Guide*. As he wrote in similar letters to reviewers Lawrence Balch, Ron Naveen, and Claudia Wilds,

> As an example, take the recent book by Grant on identification of gulls, which is of great interest to the avant guard [sic]. An average of 20 pages are given to each species. . . . If I were to treat all 500-plus western species as extensively, simple mathematics indicate that it would take more than 10,000 pages or a total of 20 to 25 books the size of the present field guide. How then, to reduce things to a 416-page book (the limit my publisher will allow) is the problem. However, within the limitations I can always improve the drawings and the text by continuing to look critically at certain species. Even this has its dangers. Some birders are so used to the way a bird looks in the present book that they may resent any changes. They are imprinted. It is a no-win game![19]

Meanwhile, Peterson and Kaufmann were privately and intelligently resolving their differences. After Peterson's piece appeared in *Birding*, Kaufmann took the first step, writing, "When I read your response to the book reviews in last August's issue of *Birding*, I was very impressed. No doubt the average person, faced with such an opportunity, would have been tempted to lash out in retaliation against his critics; but your response was carefully reasoned and courteous." He mentioned that he had been among Peterson's "admirers" since he was seven years old, and he expressed interest in helping with information on southwestern birds and in "going afield with you or discussing the local identification problems."[20] Peterson wrote back, thanking Kaufmann and discussing the points of the Parkes review; then, turning to the task at hand, he wrote, "Anyway, all that is very tiresome and what I plan to do now is to take advantage of anything valid amongst the criticisms, and there are some useful points. I would welcome the opportunity to show some of the maps and plates to you at a later date when they are more worthy of your scrutiny."[21] Thus, a mutual respect having been established, a warm and informative exchange followed that lasted until Peterson's death.

In one of the best responses to the critics, Peterson and Houghton Mifflin gave the manuscript of the western *Guide* revision to Peter Alden for a careful edit. Alden, an expert on southwestern birds, went through the book, species by species, and made hundreds of suggestions. Because of publishing deadlines, Peterson wasn't able to act on them all, but he made enough changes to satisfy the "Young Turks." The reception of the third edition of the western *Guide* in 1990 was much better from the critics, some of whom admitted privately that they were sorry for their harsh treatment of Peterson—not because they felt they were wrong but because they did little to temporize the tone of their reviews, turning evaluations into attacks. Privately, Kaufmann wrote to Peterson, "You are clearly a better and more reasonable man than your critics."[22]

The damage to Peterson's self-image—and to several of his relationships—was already done, however. Work on the fifth and final edition of the eastern *Guide* continued unabated. The public answer given to the question of why he attempted a fifth edition was his competitive nature. He *was* competitive, but he only competed with himself or, more specifically, with his image. Typical of his relationships with his "competitors," on the other hand, was his friendship with Robert Bateman. In the foreword to the fifth edition, Bateman tells of his first meeting with Peterson at a wildlife painting exhibit in 1975, the very exhibit where Peterson announced his plans to concentrate on "gallery" painting. Peterson took the younger artist aside, much as Fuertes had done with Peterson many years before, and talked with him about painting and about Bateman's work in particular. Later he would introduce Bateman to Robert Lewin and Mill Pond Press as well as to Lars-Eric Lindblad. As Bateman wrote, "He changed my life in immeasurable and positive ways."[23]

The main reason for the fifth edition of the eastern *Guide,* therefore, was probably similar to the reason for the fourth—the Peterson legacy. But it was his legacy as a naturalist, rather than as an artist, that he was defending. It fell to Noble Proctor, a longtime friend and fellow naturalist, to finish this legacy's final statement. As Proctor recalls, "The day before Roger died, I was at his studio, and he asked out of the blue, 'If I should die—will you finish the field guide?' Naturally my response, figuring he was going to live to 100, was 'Sure.' The next day he was gone."[24] Peterson had submitted data and maps to the best bird students in each state covered by the guide—he wasn't about to stand accused of ignoring the "experts" again. He had highlighted sections of the fourth-edition text and left marginalia. But he painted first; the text was left for later. Proctor's project, which took two years, was to synthesize the research and infer which changes Peterson wanted to make. The resulting text improved markedly on the fourth edition.

There was no artistic reason for a fifth edition, however. In the 1990 western *Guide* and the 1980 eastern *Guide,* Peterson established his mastery of the art form that he, essentially, created. The criticism of Kaufmann and others that prompted the fifth edition gave readers what amounted to an homage to Peterson's field guide art. Some new plates were added, some from 1980 were touched up, the black-and-white plates were all colored, and the larger size (five by eight inches) lessened some of the problems of reduction. But no new ground was broken artistically. Sentimentally, however, one priceless touch was added: the plate that Peterson was painting on the day he died.

It is a plate of "accidental flycatchers," birds that have been known to stray from their usual range into the southern United States. The paintings on the plate are in various stages of completion, ranging from several watercolor washes to only one or two. One bird stands empty, starkly white with only contour lines sketched in. In his elegiac foreword to the book, Robert Bateman tells a story of visiting an ancient tomb in Egypt:

One wall had beautifully delineated figures, birds, mammals, and inscriptions. They were finished in color. But as we proceeded through the tomb, some drawings were uncolored and were only outlines, then vague sketches, and finally emptiness. The royal personage had died, and work had stopped. It was so fresh you could imagine the artists would come in tomorrow and continue their work. I have the same vivid immediacy as I gaze at this plate of flycatchers.

Bateman saw in this parallel an image for the continuation of Peterson's work, work that would never end but rather continue like ripples on a pond: "That is the criterion for a person's importance. How big and lasting is the circle of ripples that his life has made? Roger Tory Peterson's life has been one of the most important lives of the last 100 years."[25]

35

Concurrent with his final triumphs in field guide illustration came an end to Peterson's painting career. Richard Lewin recalls visiting Peterson in his studio and showing him a Bateman painting of a cardinal that Mill Pond Press was publishing. Peterson examined it eagerly, then, as his mood darkened, said, "Oh dear. I could never do that."[1] During this time, Peterson repeatedly expressed his growing doubts about himself as a painter, doubts that rose from poor sales of the prints rather than any critical response. Although he admired and supported Bateman's work, Peterson seemed to come to the conclusion that his own painting was being eclipsed. In 1981 he wrote to George Sutton, "Bateman's compositions always make me say to myself, 'Why didn't I think of that?' Have you seen his new book? Don't miss it!"[2] Robert Lewin remained Peterson's sounding board during this period. About his puffin painting, Peterson wrote, "As for the puffins, it is very much the best piece of painting I have done and is a popular species. I have wondered what is wrong on that one."[3] And in 1984 he confessed, "I am getting discouraged about my ability to paint, particularly after the reception the snowy owl received, which is the best piece of painting I have done. Perhaps I should simply paint what I want to paint, whether it is suitable or not for reproduction or sale. I can always give things to the R.T.P. Institute and in that way they will have my best work."[4]

Finding the concepts and carrying through on them—his approach to his subjects—gave him the trouble. He wanted very much to do something novel, but his paintings continued to look much like his work of the 1970s. He worked extensively on a chickadee design that would be "as good as the one Bateman did several years ago, without seeming too derivative."[5] But before he got far along into the work, a similar design was published by Ron Parker. And in a 1981 letter to Richard Ellis that praised Ellis's new book of whale paintings, he wrote, "I think that it might be fun for me to try king penguins underwater in somewhat the same manner [as Ellis's]. They are a far cry from whales, but your superb paintings have suggested the idea to me."[6] But the ideas were never carried out. As he confessed in 1982 to Bateman, "Right now I am so obsessed and overwhelmed by the work on the Western field guide that I can hardly consider anything else. I will be so glad to have all that behind me so that I can get back to proper painting. Perhaps I have waited too long."[7]

Whether it was the realization that he could never attain the goals he set out for himself in 1975—to paint more "expansively" and "sensuously"—or simply more of the dreaded "field guide pressure" brought on by the reviews of RTP4, Peterson's "gallery" painting ended, for all purposes, in the mid-1980s. Speaking at Peterson's eightieth birthday party in 1988, his old friend Paul Brooks implored Peterson to return to painting. As another friend, Roland Clement, said later, "He was always frustrated that his work on publishing field guides prevented him from doing more easel-painting, but of course that was his own fault. He got so involved in publishing ventures that he didn't have much time to himself."[8] Clement remembers telling Peterson, "You just tell people to lay off. Stop promising your editors that you will continue to revise these handbooks." Friend and sculptor Kent Ullberg wrote in 1987,

I'm really looking forward to the time when you can paint exclusively what you feel for. A luxury that personally I feel you have earned many times over. . . . You never know what the final form of your art will be; but if you let it come to you naturally from your strength: a lifetime of painting and with intimate knowledge of your subject matter, I know it will be significant art, and to hell with the print market.[9]

As late as 1993, his close friend and old competitor Chandler Robbins mentioned the need for an update of the ranges for the Mexican *Guide*, then quickly added, "But, please, don't let this distract you from getting back to 'proper painting.'"[10] Despite entreaties from these and other friends, Peterson seemed unable to find time in the new schedule imposed on him for painting. Without motivation to pursue his artistic aims, Peterson turned almost exclusively to field guide work. And for respite, he turned more and more to his passion for photography.

In his published accounts of the travels that enlivened his later years, Peterson makes it clear that watching birds through field glasses had been replaced by bird photography. His 1992 essay "Birding the Gulf Islands" has much more to do with photography than with birding. His appraisal of the tour series he joined sets the focus of the piece and reveals plainly his new attitude toward field trips: "They [the tours] are restricted to no more than a dozen participants, most of whom go for the photography; they are not listers."[11] Although the description of each site he visits lists the birds there, it centers on the photographic conditions and evaluates each stop in terms of the shots he made. An essay recounting his last trip to the Antarctic and subantarctic, "The Falklands and South Georgia Revisited," features the conflict between his growing physical limitations and his desire to make as many photographs as possible. The Falkland Islands portion of the trip is seen almost entirely through the camera's lens. A sedge wren is compared to one he photographed in Minot, North Dakota; oystercatchers "made striking pictures"; kelp geese "posed for us"; night herons were "cooperative as they posed in the evergreens."[12] The highlight on one island stop was the chance to get pictures of a pair of red-backed buzzards: "While I stood on unstable legs below their cliff-side aerie I shot off two or three rolls of film as the birds hung in the blue sky above or power-dived at us below." A hazardous climb to photograph a nesting wandering albatross ends with a bruised knee and a bloody nose, but no pictures. In his summary of the trip, which was fraught with physical problems and ended with immigration and passport hassles, Peterson—no longer a "lister" but still competitive—wrote, "You can't win them all. Not even with 96 rolls of exposed film."[13] It is an appraisal reminiscent of his account of the first day of a Texas trip he made less than a year before his death: "September is not the best month to photograph some of these species, because they are in molt. Most of the green jays were scruffy, but one or two were in good condition. The same was true of the cardinals and pyrrhuloxias that patronized the hanging feeder. In all, I had a ten-roll day."[14]

This powerful hold that photography had on Peterson might have been simply a need to control and possess the object of his desire. Beset with vision problems, actual "birding" became more and more difficult and frustrating. But with the combination of long lenses, motor drives, and autofocus, it was still possible to "capture" a bird's image. Or perhaps photography presented an aesthetically pleasing and expressive form to record his time in the field; or, as he often claimed, was therapy for the hours imprisoned in his studio. It appears, as well, to be yet another example of the accommodation of the scientist and artist, making orderly sense of a naturally chaotic world—much as he did in his field guides. Whatever the cause or combination of causes, the result was a monumental amount of work that testifies to a man's happiest hours—time spent in nature and in the company of birds.

Photography served as a vehicle for much of Peterson's later writing. "The Llanos of Venezuela," for example, tells of a 1992 trip to the grasslands region of Venezuela, his last photography safari to South America. It reveals Peterson as an aging, but still eager, traveler. He begins with a good-natured complaint: "My eyes often give me an argument, my legs seem to lose flexibility, and I become irascible. The *golden* years? After 80 they become the *leaden* years."[15] But the bulk of the piece, packed with details of birds and adventures, shows that he had lost none of his enthusiasm for photography or his sense of wonder in nature. As he closes the essay, he shows no sign that he considers this his last international adventure: "Had we also visited the more forested areas . . . we would have had many additional woodland species. Next time perhaps."[16] Indeed, Greg Lasley, who traveled to Venezuela with him, tells of Peterson scrambling in and out of the back of the truck they traveled in, chasing down an anteater on foot, keeping company with anacondas and caimans—all to get more good photographs. He behaved, suggests Lasley, like a man afraid of slowing down, a man who wanted to get the most out of what was left of his life.[17]

Some writers, such as Devlin and Naismith, have suggested that Peterson's intense aversion to aging was based on vanity. He did, indeed, care a great deal about his appearance. In letters to confidants, he admitted that he was concerned about his image on camera and in photographs. He even went as far as to have some cosmetic surgery on his eyes in 1972. But more likely, the face he saw in the mirror, reflecting as it did the years of both nearly superhuman working habits and hours spent in the field under extreme conditions, served as a reminder that the passage of time was the real demon. In an address to the American Nature Study Society on 18 April 1988, he reflected on the fact that he was the oldest, living ex-president of the society, "the eldest of the elders." He went on to explain his curious concept of age: "Until recently I regarded anyone a year younger than I as young, and anyone a year older as old. I was somewhat in the middle. But inasmuch as my next birthday is my 80th, I must face the fact that in the usual concept I *am* old."[18] This realization came when he was asked to write a piece for a book about "the courage to grow old." He refused because "'the courage to grow old' is like whistling in the dark," he told his audience. "Quite frankly, I am angry and scared. There are too many things that I want to do and feel qualified to do that I have not yet finished, not just my new western field guide, but at least four other books; and more painting of the kind I was originally trained to do at the Art Students League and the Academy."[19]

In the closing piece of his 1982 draft of his autobiography, he told a story about returning to Jamestown not long after his seventy-fourth birthday to receive yet another honor:

> Next morning, Sunday, I awoke to the sound of chimes in the bell tower [at the Chautauqua Institution, where he spent the night]. I have always been upset by bells tolling away the hours (another hour of life gone—another hour closer to the grave). My thoughts drifted back to the night before; the hundreds of people in black tie and elegant gowns, strangers whom I had not known before. But none of the friends of my boyhood were there to see me. I burst into tears.[20]

But he wouldn't allow his thoughts to remain in that dark place. The rest of the essay concerns itself with the positive changes in the region since his childhood there. He mentions the return of deer, beaver, and wild turkeys. He writes about seeing birds on Lake Erie—glaucous gulls and double-crested cormorants—that he hadn't seen when he was a boy. This reaction was to become a theme in his later writing, which was intended, ultimately, to have been gathered into his last—but unpublished—books: *Wild Islands, Long after Audubon, In Search of Eden,* and his autobiography.

36

Wild America (1955) was Peterson's last "book," in the sense that his subsequent titles contained little interpretive intent or narrative. *The World of Birds* (1964), also coauthored with Fisher, was mostly Fisher's prose, edited by Peterson and with Peterson providing the illustrations. *Penguins* (1979), although its text contains chapters that tell the story of penguins from early depredation stories to life histories, is primarily a vehicle for Peterson's Antarctica photographs. However, his incidental pieces in *International Wildlife* and *Bird Watcher's Digest,* which he intended to collect into *Long after Audubon* and *Wild Islands,* reveal Peterson's mature style. He was, according to editors such as Bill Thompson III at *Bird Watcher's Digest,* the consummate professional, turning in clean copy seldom in need of editing, meeting every deadline, and not indulging in the usual writers' complaints. He had found a way to write that fit him and derived great pleasure from the process. And it was an activity, according to Thompson, that took him away from the despised field guide work.[1] As Peterson said in a letter to Austin Olney at Houghton Mifflin, the column "would be a pleasant turn-off from the grueling task of drawing all the time."[2] Easy-to-read but still clear and highly informative, the pieces fall into two categories: narratives—usually of photography trips—told in a relaxed and engaging voice—or authoritative, but gentle, argumentation. Peterson identified two types of writing, which he called "documentary" writing and "creative" writing. It is typical of him that his own writing synthesizes these categories, a reflection in his prose of his binary roles of naturalist and artist. His narratives document information while using the "creative writing" tools of plot, reconstructed dialogue, and setting to good effect. And his opinion pieces nearly always contain anecdotes or even extended narratives.

His bimonthly *Bird Watcher's Digest* columns (1984–1996) carry an overall optimistic tone about the long-range state of the environment; as he liked to say, "There is no future in pessimism." They are also heightened by elements of nostalgia and glimpses of mortality. At the suggestion of his editor there, Mary Beacom Bowers, Peterson eventually called the column *All Things Reconsidered*,[3] and as the name implies, he used the nearly eighty pieces to look back from his elevated and authoritative position on topics that had engaged him throughout his career. As was his practice, he recycled many previously published pieces, the champion being an essay about birding in New York City that was published originally in 1935, reappeared in *Birds over America* in 1948, and saw light again in 1991 in *Bird Watcher's Digest*. As he told Bowers, the column's title permitted this recycling. But much of the writing was new, and it provides a good sampling of Peterson's last written efforts. That the prose is familiar and predictable is not surprising. After all, he had nothing left to prove, so any edginess or risk taking found in earlier writing was gone for the most part. Further, he had written on a narrow range of subjects for more than fifty years. Small wonder that thoughts, phrases, and even whole sentences often resurface. Ironically, the same obsession that drove him to greatness proved ultimately to be a hindrance to achieve his ultimate writing goals.

Two paired columns—"Whatever Happened to the Junior Audubon Clubs?" (1984) and "Junior Audubon Comeback" (1992)—contain many of the elements of a Peterson piece. In the earlier essay, he tells some of the familiar and often-repeated stories: his introduction to Fuertes's bird portraits through a Junior Audubon Club in the fourth grade, his encounter with a sleeping flicker that sprang away when he touched it, changing the direction of his life. He reiterates his opinion that naming things precedes understanding them and adds the obligatory reference to the *Field Guide*.

The column centers on the history of the Junior Audubon Club program: its early, marginal existence, its resurrection under Peterson's direction during the late 1930s and early 1940s, its near demise in the 1960s, and the attempts under way to revive it a second time. The piece ends on a hopeful note, outlining Audubon's plans for change and adding, "If these efforts—admittedly costly—succeed, Audubon may regain its former preeminence in the area of nature education. . . . My own hope is that birds will continue to be a strong focal point."[4] Bowers suggested that Peterson was very cautious in print, and that closing sentence is a good example. Behind it lies Peterson's deeply held displeasure with the direction that the entire Audubon Society was taking—away from the study of birds and animals and toward a more general and political environmentalist view. As he wrote in 1991 to Peter Berle of the society, "Aren't we getting too far away from the original roots of the National Audubon Society? By taking the holistic approach aren't we spreading ourselves so thin that wildlife receives a minor role? We can't save the world. There are literally hundreds of other organizations into recycling, air pollution, population control and all the other 'in' things. Our distinctive focus and reason for being could be lost."[5] The letter was never sent. The 1992 piece is as cautious as the one written eight years before; after an introduction that asserts the success of recent changes to the Junior Audubon Clubs, it simply repeats—nearly word for word—more than three pages of the previous column. A two-paragraph conclusion, in spite of the letter to Berle written only a year before, assures Peterson's readers that the clubs are headed back in the right direction.

A similar duo is "The View from the Cedars" (1985) and "Update from the Cedars" (1995). In these, he longs for the habitat that drew him in 1953 to the Cedars, his new Connecticut home. He tells of the loss of the moth population over the years—due to gypsy moth control—and the nighthawks that depended on moths for survival, and he retells the story of the decline of the ospreys. But as a scientist, he can only indulge in nostalgia briefly. He concludes a section on other losses—bitterns, woodcocks, and meadowlarks—with the reciprocal gain in other species such as egrets, wild turkeys, and cardinals. Then he turns to a discussion of population dynamics and the fascination it holds for bird students. Again, the subject matter and treatment are not new, and the "update" is a near repeat of the earlier piece, but the perspective that Peterson brings gives authority to the piece, and the optimistic tone is common in his later writing.

A great deal of original work, however, enlivens the collection. Travel essays include trips to the Pribilofs, Kenya, Antarctica, the Falklands, and Botswana, for example. Informational essays cover such diverse topics as Audubon's errors in bird identification, western birds, wildlife art, and the state of ornithology in the Soviet Union at the time. In addition, two autobiographical essays—"My Evolution as a Bird Artist" and "Seventy Years behind the Camera"— are thoughtful and revealing. But in spite of his desire to be more "expressive" in his writing, Peterson only occasionally attempted to examine his "inner feelings" in his later work. Not surprisingly, the grim presence of mortality seems to drive those few pieces.

37

"The Maine Story" (December 1986), an example of a more expressive result in *All Things Reconsidered,* was written on the occasion of the fiftieth anniversary celebration of the founding of the Audubon Camp in Muscongus Bay on the Maine coast, the camp that was established after Peterson "scouted" it in 1935 and where he worked as the bird instructor for its first year. The celebration was marred, however, by the death that very day of Carl Buchheister—the camp's first director, a pivotal force in the Audubon Society's education program, and Peterson's close friend. What he didn't write in the essay was that his first wife, Mildred, whom he had divorced in 1943, had drowned while sailing alone on Muscongus Bay in 1977.

The first paragraph illustrates the heightened energy that Peterson brought to this particular piece:

> That day this past summer when I stepped from the car and
> stood on the hillside opposite the Audubon Camp in Maine,
> I could not fight back the tears. There were too many memories. Across the tidal inlet was Hog Island with its weathered
> buildings, looking much as they did 50 years ago—the old ship
> chandlery known as the 'Queen Mary' with its boat dock, the
> headquarters buildings, and, surrounded by spruce trees, the
> 'fish house' where we had slide lectures and classes.[1]

Sparked by the poignancy of the moment, this backward look continues with recollections of Buchheister and stories of camp life told in great detail and with a fondness that is sometimes humorous and sometimes wistful. It also includes a remembrance of Allan Cruickshank, who had been Peterson's close friend since his New York City days and had worked with him at the camp. As part of the celebration, the participants sailed to Eastern Egg Rock, which had been established as a wildlife sanctuary in Cruickshank's memory and where Peterson had given Cruickshank's eulogy.

"The Maine Story" then moves to a description and discussion of the species seen that day that had been absent when the camp was founded. This seems to be another form of the rebirth image that began with the famous flicker story from his youth. As he points out, "During these days of ecological enlightenment when we are bombarded with so much doom and gloom, it gives us a lift of spirit when we see a turnaround. Today, most of the birds of Maine's littoral are faring better than they did before the Audubon camp was opened in '34, and *far* better than they did at the turn of the century when these same birds were at their nadir."[2] He goes on to mention cormorants, eiders, laughing gulls, terns, and puffins as examples of breeding successes. Clearly, Peterson's return to this ongoing discussion of the recovery of various endangered or threatened species was a comfort to him.

A return to the camp in 1990 brought more than intimations of mortality; Peterson's brush with death there was frighteningly real. He had traveled with Judy Fieth and Michael Male of Blue Earth Films to the Audubon Camp to complete the filming of a PBS documentary, *A Celebration of Birds with Roger Tory Peterson.* The film was partly a recognition of Peterson and his contributions to bird identification and bird conservation and partly a recounting of the positive effects that the popularization of bird-watching had on bird populations. They had already filmed herons in Florida, shorebirds in the Delaware Bay, and ospreys in Connecticut. The Maine coast filming was to emphasize the recovery of seabirds in New England and to record Peterson's return to an area that he treasured as much as any other. It was a trip he eagerly anticipated; memories consumed him. He recalled stories and bird trips from a half century earlier and even showed the filmmakers the house in Wiscasset where he courted Mildred.

The plan was to spend three days camping on Eastern Egg Rock, the island at the mouth of Muscongus Bay where a long-term and successful recovery project had helped re-establish breeding populations of puffins, petrels, and terns. Bad weather threatened the trip, but Peterson was determined to go, despite the personal discomforts and difficulties such a trip entailed.

The party landed successfully on Eastern Egg but had to wait in fog for two days until the weather broke. On the last day, Peterson was able to photograph black guillemots and common and Arctic terns before the launch arrived for the return trip. On the way back to shore, they passed by the windward side of Western Egg Rock, a small rock ledge that was home to a large cormorant colony.

Meanwhile, far out to sea, the remnants of an offshore storm had built a powerful surf, and with no warning a huge wave lifted the twenty-three-foot boat and flipped it, throwing the five passengers and thousands of dollars of camera equipment into the water. While everyone aboard faced death by drowning or hypothermia in the dangerously cold water, their own life struggles were compounded by their responsibility for the eighty-two-year-old Peterson. They all reached the boat briefly but were swept away a second time. Close enough to shore by now to touch bottom, Michael Male managed to keep Peterson above water and, with the others, dragged him ashore, each of them too exhausted to do it alone. At this point, Male remembers, they all realized that Peterson was probably dying.

Once onshore, Peterson began to shiver uncontrollably, and Male lay on top of him, talking to him, encouraging him to hang on. Twenty frightening minutes passed until the combination of the sun-warmed rocks below, Male's body heat, and makeshift coverings washed ashore from the wreck warmed Peterson enough that his shivering subsided and he could be moved to a small tent.

Here Peterson rallied and, to their profound relief, began to talk with his rescuers, joking and reassuring them and expressing his concern for *their* well-being. He also talked about two other things. One was a butterfly that had alighted on the outside of the tent. The other was Mildred. When he was underwater, he said, he had seen the image of Mildred and understood that she was entreating him to remain with her there.

Eventually, a passing boat filled with bird-watchers saw the party and their distress signals and called the Coast Guard. Peterson and the others were finally taken from the island, four hours after their ordeal began, and Peterson was taken to hospital overnight for observation. In spite of a night made uncomfortable by various bruises, sinuses filled with saltwater, and wildly fluctuating blood sugar levels, he insisted on doing a telephone interview with the *New York Times* about the story—in which he called the event "the most critical incident of my life"—because it would make good publicity for his books. As Male and Fieth recalled, he seemed energized by the whole experience, proud of the proof of his vigor that his survival suggested, and eager to share the story of his adventure. He had been depressed and feeling old—a natural reaction to his failing health, combined with a nostalgic trip.[3] Thirty years before, in "High Seas in a Rowboat," he had written, "To take a chance once in a while and get away with it is to feel alive." His day at Western Egg Rock had reaffirmed this feeling.

Peterson's essay about the experience, "Capsized by a Rogue Wave," has the same sharpness of "Maine Story." He begins with the accident: "I was wrapped in eye-dazzling foam one moment, in murky green depths the next, with dark objects sinking around me—thousands of dollars of camera equipment. But no time to panic; another gulp or two of seawater could send me choking to the bottom where I could just drift away . . . to nothing."[4] For reasons known only to himself, he omitted the vision of his first wife. His account of the time he spent lying in the tent, however, is honest and revealing: "I fell into a deep sleep. Then awakening, with my one functioning eye I made out the shadow of a monarch butterfly as it alighted on the canvas above—but *was* it a monarch? The shape was more like that of a red admiral or an angle-wing butterfly. Was it the magnifying effect of the late sunlight on the canvas?"[5] The decision to include the personal detail of his reflexive curiosity about the natural world reveals the depth of his gift of focusing on his natural surroundings and gives the scene the weight of truth. Just as it does when he describes being carried off the island on a litter after help finally arrived: "I felt strangely peaceful; it was surreal. Lying on my back, helpless, unable to move and gazing straight up into the darkening heavens, I thought I saw a Leach's storm-petrel as it flew out of the mist."[6] The result is a compelling narrative that never slows down or loses its thread with digressions, as Peterson's stories sometimes did in the *Bird Watcher's Digest* articles. Then safely in a hospital, he returns, as he did in "Maine Story," to his theme of renewal, as if his rescue from likely death corresponded to the rescue of so many seabird populations along the Maine coast.

This juxtaposition may have been deliberate, subconsciously suggested to him by the fact that some of the same people who kept him alive were engaged in a project to reestablish Atlantic puffin breeding grounds, or merely an unconscious connection. The fact remains that these pieces written for the *Digest*— the record of his writing over the last twelve years of his life—balance concern over extinction and human threats to birds with a positive and optimistic view of population dynamics, while often turning, quite naturally, to thoughts of death. In the Blue Earth film, he admitted that concern over the birds' survival conflated more and more with concern over his own survival. For example, his 1990 tribute to Sir Peter Scott begins with a dream Peterson had the night he learned of Scott's death: "That evening on the plane I had a disturbing dream. Two of my dearest friends, Peter Scott and James Fisher, now both gone, were standing there. They said nothing; they were just there, standing side by side. Surrounding them was a tessellation of crystals, rather large triangular crystals, shifting about, glittering. Half-awake, I said to myself: 'I must hold onto this dream.' I repeated, 'I must hold on to this dream.' Then I awoke."[7] After recounting the dream, he returns to his rebirth theme; the first story he tells is about Scott's efforts to reestablish the osprey population in Scotland, and then he recalls Scott's project that saved the rare Hawaiian goose from extinction.

Peterson's interest in the renewal of species had its roots in his childhood. When he was in high school, he got in trouble for correcting his biology teacher, who told the class that egrets were endangered. He said they were making a comeback and went on to tell the teacher and class how populations could renew themselves if humans allowed them to—in this case, by outlawing the plume market. This was an idea that stayed with him, became more important as he grew older, and connected with his lifetime obsession with birds. Peterson had written the story of the flicker springing to life in dozens of essays but never with more passion than he did in 1992:

I thought [the flicker] was dead. Gingerly I poked it. Instantly it exploded into life, jerked its head free of its feathers, looked at me with wild eyes, then took off with a flash of golden wings. What had seemed like an inert, dead thing was very much alive. It was like resurrection—an affirmation of life. Ever since, birds have seemed to me to be the most vivid expression of life. The natural world became my 'real' world.[8]

His use here of the religiously charged word "resurrection"—and the fact that he chose the sentence "Birds are the most vivid expression of life" for his tombstone—gives the story the weight of an epiphany, in the spiritual sense of that word. Faced as he was with the deaths of friends and with his own mortality, this man of science appeared to gather natural emblems of rebirth that would bring comfort to him more completely than the anthropomorphic stories of organized Western religion might. For example, as a youth he saw butterflies as something beautiful "to be pursued and, hopefully, possessed"; in a 1993 *New York Times* interview, his view of them had changed to one more abstract and philosophical: "Here these things are little grubs for a while. And then they go into a little coffin. There they are in a sarcophagus, and then they come out and dance with the angels."[9] And with birds ruling as the principal icon in his life, the renewal of their numbers became a text that seemed to take on the importance of myth.

References to "God" are rare in Peterson's published writing, and in his correspondence they occur usually as part of another discussion. He clearly had abandoned the traditional Protestant dogma that he was exposed to as a child. For example, in a letter about the influence of his teachers, he referred to an article about him in the religious publication *Guideposts* magazine. The story, he said "was written according to their style which indicates that 'God made me do those things,' something I never thought of."[10] His was a larger view, as indicated in a letter about art critics: "'Art' is as difficult to define as the word 'God,' which, to most people, seems to be egocentric—concerned with the humanistic aspects of themselves rather than the more cosmic or holistic view of things."[11]

In 1991 he was asked to write a brief statement for *Life* magazine; it was to be part of a series of responses by well-known people to the question, What is the meaning of life? Peterson chose to tell the story of the flicker and how it "pulled him into the wider vistas . . . of the natural world." In an indirect response to *Life*'s vague question, he wrote,

> The meaning of life? What ignited the Life Force in the beginning? Certainly not a manlike being up there in the stratosphere. Our kind, *Homo sapiens,* the dominant primate, holds the whip hand; but need we be so egocentric as to think only of ourselves and dismiss the countless other forms of life? At the age of 83, having nearly drowned last summer, I have become ever more sensitive to the nuances of all living things.[12]

In 1994, Nancy Noel of the Buffalo Museum of Science asked Peterson directly what the flicker story meant to him. His reply was equally direct and can be read as an accompaniment to his more emotionally charged *Bird Watcher's Digest* pieces:

> In using the term 'resurrection' I perhaps did not make it clear that I meant the wholeness of the natural world—its renewal. Even though I was brought up as a God-fearing Lutheran I was never satisfied with most people's definition of the word 'God.' They cannot really define it or if they do, they seem to envision a humanistic being rather like us out there in the stratosphere somewhere. My own view is a holistic one in which life goes on but not in precisely the identical forms they were before they died. I prefer the term, 'life force,' because after we die there will be other people, other grasshoppers, other birds, other flowers, but all mixed up in a zillion ways and not in the same form as when we left this earth. The food we eat, the air we breathe, the water we drink are all composites of our ancestry.[13]

Many of the *Bird Watcher's Digest* series are workmanlike applications of formulas that Peterson had used successfully for decades; in the best of them, however, in the ones that really seemed to matter, he returned to a theme that revealed more of himself than he perhaps intended. In this way, he finally did approach his ambition to write in a way that would let his "inner feelings come through."

38

More than thirty years had passed since Peterson presided over the renewal of the Junior Audubon Societies, which he wrote about in *Bird Watcher's Digest*. He continued to see himself as a teacher — through his writing, lectures, and paintings and even in his free-lance illustrations. And his field guides were, first and foremost, instructional. But in the early 1970s, an opportunity was presented to him that would plunge him back into education in a significant and structured way. This opportunity led eventually to the Roger Tory Peterson Institute. And it represented a grassroots approach, one that was truly radical and subversive, not confronting the entrenched school structure but rather setting up an alternative system of education. It was, he later told former RTPI president Paul Benke, "the most fulfilling thing I have ever done."[1]

The first step in the evolution of the Roger Tory Peterson Institute took form in Peterson's hometown of Jamestown, New York, where he was lionized as the city's most famous citizen (along with Lucille Ball). H. Lorimer Moe, a friend of Peterson's since high school who had retired to Jamestown after a career in the diplomatic service, along with other leaders of the Jamestown Audubon Society, began meetings to discuss a working tribute to Peterson. These meetings advanced plans for the "Roger Peterson Nature Center" on land in the Audubon Society's Burgeson Wildlife Sanctuary. Moe advised Peterson of the plans in a 1971 letter in which he described the center as being "modest enough to command the support of the greater Jamestown community yet proud enough to bear your name." Moe continued, "It would be used primarily as a natural history teaching tool fashioned to appeal to all age groups, but with emphasis on youth. We envision an auditorium capable of seating 200 persons or somewhat more; this could be a multi-purpose room, with space to display specimens of our local fauna, special exhibits, etc. — perhaps even a Peterson original or two?" The letter was cautious, but enthusiastic; Moe chose his modifiers carefully to assure Peterson that the plans were not grandiose: "We should include an unpretentious nature library and reading room; a small workshop (an exciting banding operation is already conducted at the sanctuary); a small kitchen; . . . and—possibly—modest quarters for a resident naturalist-caretaker." In a postscript, Moe let Peterson know that everything was in place to proceed: "With your blessing, we will launch our fund raising effort right after the first of the year. Optimistic, as ever, we have already broached the proposal to a sympathetic architect. If all goes as we hope, we could start building in the spring."[2]

While planning was continuing on the building, the society's president, Henry Huston, and Moe approached Jamestown Community College in 1975 with a larger idea: the establishment of the Roger Tory Peterson School for Environmental Science. The school would be located on the Hundred Acre Lot, a parcel of wooded land on the college campus—an area that Peterson frequented often as a boy. What would be taught there was unspecified, and, at any rate, the idea generated little enthusiasm among the administration of the college. But Moe and the others were undeterred, and by now Peterson was fully engaged. In December 1975 he wrote to Moe, promising his unequivocal support and recalling his days in Jamestown:

> At the risk of sounding sentimental, I must say that the proposed Hundred Acre Lot site seems almost too good to be true. . . . I certainly never dreamed of a college campus there, nor a role for myself in making such a dream come true. Of course I am delighted. . . . I want to give whatever encouragement and help I possibly can as you proceed. . . . I must agree that an environmental studies building as part of a larger educational complex and easily available to a larger public would be a . . . suitable repository for memorabilia, etc. that I plan to provide.[3]

The next year, 1976, marked an important time in the expansion of the original idea. Early in the year, Peterson and Moe met in Hartford with John Hamilton, president of the Gebbie Foundation, a Jamestown-based funding source for nonprofit organizations. They discussed what further directions the "RTP Project" might take and considered how the project would be financed. In April of that year, in conjunction with groundbreaking ceremonies for the Roger Tory Peterson Nature Interpretive Building, another meeting among

Peterson, Moe, Hamilton, the Audubon Society, and the college advanced the project beyond a local level. A convocation of nationally known ornithologists and environmental education leaders was planned to coincide with the dedication of the Interpretive Building in October, and although nothing of substance was accomplished, the gathering alerted the natural history community across the country to Jamestown's fledgling plans.

Progress toward application for a charter as an educational corporation continued off and on, with the addition of Peterson's new wife, Virginia, and ornithologist and longtime friend Noble Proctor to the informal planning process, which had slowed somewhat. It was not given real impetus until Paul Benke was appointed president of Jamestown Community College in 1981. At that time, the RTP Project was formless and homeless. Peterson was interested in the overall concept but unwilling to commit to such an undeveloped idea. Benke became involved in the discussions and, at the urging of John Hamilton, began in earnest to shape the project into what would eventually become the Roger Tory Peterson Institute.

In the several discussions he had with Peterson and Virginia, Benke had two tasks. One was to convince them that an institute should be established in Jamestown, and the other was to find a focus, a final conflation of Peterson's ideas made manifest in a workable form. The first task was an act of persuasion. The Jamestown group was not the first to express interest in the Peterson papers. In the 1960s he had inquiries from such diverse sources as the Cornell Ornithology Laboratory, the University of Wyoming, and the Wisconsin State Historical Society. Virginia and others felt that Jamestown's rural location, far away from New York City or Boston, was decidedly deficient in glamour. She favored Yale for its visibility and its reputation. Benke argued that the institute might become lost among Yale's many peripheral academic attachments, whereas in Jamestown it would be a centerpiece of the community's culture. He also stressed the importance of natural history to the institute and the relevance of the specific natural history of the Jamestown area to Peterson. His case was significantly aided by a $2.5 million grant from the Gebbie Foundation. But in 1981, Peterson was still "a bit cautious about firming things up in Jamestown," as he wrote in a letter to Charles Nichols. He was still actively pursuing the idea, however, "inasmuch as I would like a proper repository for my illustrations and art work as well as my library, correspondence, and photograph collections."[4]

The second task involved a process of integrating Peterson's deeply held educational principles into a concept for an actual institution. Throughout his discussions about the location of the proposed institute, he went back to his goals, as he did in a letter to Ernest Brooks Jr.: "As for the function of such an institution, it would be based on good old-fashioned 'natural history' which is so ignored in the biology departments of most universities where the students can often tell you what a creature's liver looks like but do not know the animal in life nor anything about its ecology or environment."[5] During their meetings, Peterson enunciated two ideas to Benke. First, he expressed dismay at the demise of the naturalist in the scientific community, which he had mentioned to Ernest Brooks. In an age of specialization, the generalist character of naturalists' work had moved the perception of them away from scientists to something approaching dilettantes. One of Peterson's goals, therefore, was to restore the designation of "naturalist" to its former position of respect. The second idea, repeated often, was a simple one, but the driving force of all of his thinking. In a 1976 speech in Stockholm before an audience of Nobel laureates and other notables, he paraphrased one of his favorite writers, Henry Beston, when he said, "We live in a world which is also populated by what we condescendingly call 'lesser animals.' But these other creatures with which we share the earth should not be measured simply by our standards. They are not underlings. They are other nations—sharing with us the basic problems of survival. They are not inferior."[6] It is a basic biocentric idea, but one, if accepted fully and earnestly, that overturns much of Western thought.

Benke met with the Petersons in 1982 and made his formal proposal: the establishment of the Roger Tory Peterson Institute for the Study of Natural History. Peterson's correspondence during this time shows him moving carefully toward a final decision. In a January 1982 letter to Russell Peterson, president of the National Audubon Society, he broached the question, Why Jamestown?: "This is a valid question because, in the first place Jamestown is a bit off the beaten path; secondly, it is a two-year college, and thirdly, it might not have quite the ecological variety for field work as some locality nearer the coast."[7] As a result, he retained Noble Proctor to "be my emissary to explore things in Jamestown and elsewhere so as to develop a feasible plan for the maximum use of my personal materials, memorabilia, etc., for the purpose of teaching natural history somewhat in the traditional way rather than the 'total environment' which seems to be the main thrust in many universities. There is a great need to give young students a more thorough field knowledge of the ecological components—birds, plants, butterflies, etc.—and also to instruct them in such subjects as biological illustration, nature photography, nature writing, etc."[8] He went on to point out that entire collections of paintings and photographs had been lost at large institutions such as Yale and the National Audubon Society.

He also considered the idea of a compromise, a "double-barreled affair," with a base in Jamestown and one somewhere along the northeast coast. As he wrote to his old friend Carl Hammerstrom, "The question is: Are my roots where I was born or where I have done most of my productive work?"[9] Meanwhile a steady stream of letters from Lorimer Moe kept Peterson informed about developments in Jamestown while encouraging him to give approval.

Finally a decision was made. On 30 August 1993, Peterson spoke at the dedication of the RTPI Museum building at what he called the "greatest moment of my life." In his address he said, "The function of the Institute is not just to house my memorabilia, and it will, but also to reflect my philosophy by putting in the hands of teachers the media and tools needed to teach."[10] The moment was the culmination of a decade of planning and work. In a letter to Cornell in December 1983, he had ended any doubt about the disposition of his materials. "Our announced intent to have the Institute in Jamestown went out in September and we are now planning the next steps which involve financing, buildings, programs, etc. Inasmuch as practically all of my memorabilia and materials will be going to Jamestown, that practically eliminates the possibility of them going to Cornell."[11] And on 14 February 1984, Peterson wrote to Paul Benke, identifying the ornithological materials to be contributed to the Institute. A board of trustees formed, which approved the purchase of land for a building and appointed the institute's first president. But before an institutional educational philosophy could evolve, Peterson's idea had one last skirmish with established education.

Among the ideas that Benke presented to Peterson was a graduate program of study that would result in a degree in natural history. Jamestown Community College would teach the first two years and pass students along to the State University of New York at Fredonia, a nearby liberal arts college, for the next two years of study. Graduate work would take place at the institute. Thomas Erlandson, a naturalist and biology professor at Jamestown, was given the job of putting the program together.

The problems Erlandson encountered in trying to implement this program suggest that not much had changed in education since the factory system was installed. The generalist character of a natural history curriculum made it unwieldy, causing problems that the two colleges could or would not solve. Additionally, it was a genuinely new idea; in his research Erlandson could find no other program like it.[12] Neither college could understand the nature of natural history and how to accommodate it as a course of study. They simply suggested that students enroll in courses already in place. Finally, there was no chance for agreement about which institution would get state reimbursements for students who might enroll. Stymied by these obstacles, the plan was abandoned. The failure of this particular version of Peterson's vision underscored the need to approach nature study from outside the system with an alternative program that could intersect with mainstream education without having to overcome bureaucratic impediments.

A degree-granting program spoke well to Peterson's concerns about natural history. And in its early years, the institute was primarily involved with research grants. But there were two other precepts that, according to Benke, had lain dormant for years and reemerged as the institute evolved. These were Peterson's theories from his Audubon Camp days: that the most effective nature instruction centered on teaching the teachers and that nature study should take place outside the physical school. Gradually, and by consensus, the emphasis of the board of trustees and the institute staff turned to children's education—and appropriately so—because Peterson had believed all along that a biocentric concept was best taught when students were young, a challenge that he felt the National Audubon Society was failing to meet.

By 1990, money that had been allocated for research grants was being shifted over to educational program development and administration. Two educators, Bill Sharp and Mark Baldwin, joined the staff and planning began for the programs that would inform the place-based educational philosophy of the institute. Baldwin began conducting workshops in what was to become the foundation of the institute's educational efforts: training teachers in the creation of nature journals. This gradual distillation of Peterson's ideas was incorporated in the institute's original mission statement, which was written by Paul Benke: "To create passion for and knowledge of the natural world in the hearts and minds of children by inspiring and guiding the study of nature in our schools and communities."[13] Benke's language reflects Peterson's educational concerns closely. The parallel goals of creating "passion in the hearts" and "knowledge in the minds" repeat Peterson's own progress toward an understanding of the natural world and his teaching approach as well. And by teaching the teachers, nature study could be "guided" without a direct confrontation with educational bureaucracy. The task of putting the mission statement into practice fell to Sharp and Baldwin, and the result was called the Selborne Project. It remains the finest expression of the institute's mission.

The name and, to a degree, the model came from Gilbert White's 1789 classic, *The Natural History of Selborne*. In what could be called a close reading of a place, White spent his life detailing the flora, fauna, people, customs, and antiquities of his small town of Selborne, England. A second archetype, one hundred years later, was Thoreau's exploration of the land around Concord. For a contemporary influence, the staff turned to the One Square Mile series planned by Mary Kennan Herbert at the publisher Walker and Company. In the series, naturalists from each of four regions of the country were engaged to examine in depth one square mile in their home places.

The Selborne Project, now renamed Teaming with Nature, creates a study area of one square kilometer around each participating school, which becomes what the institute calls "an outdoor laboratory for interdisciplinary learning." Teachers attend summer training programs at the institute or staffers travel to train interested groups. These sessions give teachers the tools and abilities to instruct their students in field observation skills, field journal writing, and principles of ecology. Training also includes preparing interdisciplinary teams, curriculum integration, and public relations.

The Roger Tory Peterson Institute, Jamestown, New York, dedicated in 1993.

Teachers return to their schools and lead their students in an array of activities that follow Peterson's steps to understanding the environment. Each lesson begins with observation and culminates in a wider ecological lesson. To lay the groundwork, the students first learn to use field guides by studying birds and having scavenger hunts for leaves and trees. Once they have the basic skills of identification, the activities become more complex. They graph growth rates using core samples from trees, compare them to graphs of climatological data, and then construct a timeline that includes cultural history as well. They create cloud-watching data sheets that involve learning the principles of fractions and ratios, weather journals that include the concept of fronts and pressure systems, and natural plant dyes that illustrate the process of pigmentation. Using U.S. Department of Agriculture soil survey maps and soil samples, teams of students evaluate an area for wise development. Each team is assigned a specific suitability issue—roads, septic systems, foundations, or landscaping—and makes a presentation. Appropriately, one of the bird activities is among the most ambitious. Students identify birds in the area and natural food that is available. These data extend to an understanding of food chains and then to the creation of food webs, when the nitrogen-carbon cycle is added. Ultimately, students are able to create an energy pyramid that graphically completes the picture of the natural relationship of animals and plants in the community. The result is what Peterson would have wished: an excitement about the natural world that promotes learning and, in turn, results in ecological awareness. And the Selborne Project/ Teaming with Nature has succeeded. Along with other similar programs at the institute, it has reached thousands of teachers in hundreds of communities nationwide.

39

In September 1995, just after his eighty-seventh birthday, Peterson traveled to Wyoming and Texas: to Wyoming to receive the Rungius Medal from the National Museum of Wildlife Art in Jackson Hole, and then to Texas to speak at a gathering to honor the legendary Texas birder Connie Hagar at the opening of the Connie Hagar Cottage Sanctuary. Of course, bird photography was involved as well. The day before his speech, Peterson visited several sites where his friend Greg Lasley and others had set up blinds for him to shoot from. It was a hot day, filled with photography, and Peterson insisted on taking full advantage. Lasley remembers waiting with the others in the truck while Peterson was on his knees outside shooting hundreds of butterflies that had gathered in a rain pool. Friends have suggested he didn't keep himself hydrated, and because he tended to "misbehave" when he was on his own, he didn't eat the several small meals he needed to keep his blood sugar levels under control.

He spoke the next day from a platform in the late morning sun in temperatures over ninety degrees. Shortly after he returned to his chair, he fell to the platform, unconscious. On 15 February 1996 he wrote a letter to Barbara, describing the incident:

> For the last several months I've been suffering from a heat stroke which I experienced in Texas. I was committed to speak from the platform and it was hot, hot, hot—the hottest day that Texas had all last year—over 100 degrees in the shade and the

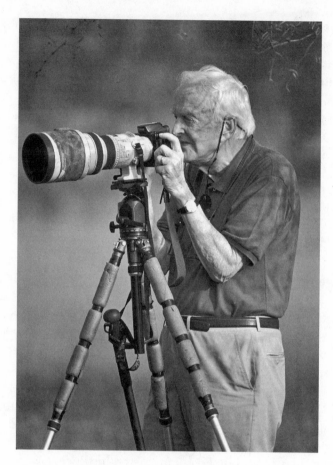

Still in the field at age eighty-seven.

ceremony was at high noon and there was no cover. I managed
to speak my piece for ten minutes. I cut the ribbon and then
sat down, thankful that my voice held out and suddenly everything went blank. I fell on my face, retching violently.[1]

He was taken to a hospital, where he was diagnosed as being de-
hydrated, treated with IVs, and held for observation. As he wrote
later, his blood sugar levels fluctuated each day from 80 to over 300
mg/dl.

When he arrived home several days later, his activities were
severely curtailed. His careful daily routine for years—work at the
studio at nine, snack (a rice cake with peanut butter and bananas) at
ten, lunch at noon, nap, then work again—always began with a slow

walk up the hill from his house to his studio. Each day he would observe. He noted the coming and going of the birds and butterflies. He kept track of the flowers and their blossoming. After the episode in Texas, these walks ended; he had to be driven to the studio. Shortly after, he was hospitalized briefly with what was called a "mild stroke." He wrote to former Delaware governor and Audubon president Russell Peterson in November 1995: "At the present time I am recovering from a number of small strokes which have left the right side of my body somewhat paralyzed and I don't like it one bit. I can't afford to give up at this point because there is too much that remains to be done on the update of the Eastern Field Guide."[2]

For months he was confined to the house, unable to paint. He had to limit his work to researching and writing text and his activity to watching birds and butterflies through the windows. A family friend set up lights and cameras so Peterson could photograph the wild turkeys that came to eat cracked corn each day. Through it all, he continued to labor, drawing on what was left of his strength to finish the fifth edition. He closed his letter to Barbara in a tone of fear and determination: "I seem to be improving. I've simply got to get that Eastern book done and at my age, my 88th year, I question whether I'll make it. I simply must."[3] When he could finally return to his studio, he worked on range maps and painted on the unfinished plates, until he literally gave up his life to his field guides on 28 July 1996.

40

On 30 August 1993, Peterson, along with Virginia and the officers of the Roger Tory Peterson Institute in Jamestown, New York, signed a retention agreement, leaving his life's work to the institute. In the September/October 1994 issue of *Bird Watcher's Digest*, he summarized the materials included in this contract, listing "my field guide originals . . . some of my paintings reproduced as limited edition prints . . . other more painterly paintings in watercolor, gouache, acrylics, oil, or mixed media . . . a lifetime of writing . . . including correspondence with practically everyone who was involved in the

earlier stages of the environmental movement . . . hundreds and thousands of transparencies."[1]

With the retention agreement, he realized his dream of establishing a tangible presence that would reflect his contributions as a teacher and his philosophy that education is the key to conservation. Here would be educational materials for study, housed in ideal archival accommodations at a perfect location—the wooded area where he studied the natural world as a child. A new building was up and running, and his materials were promised. But this accomplishment, which, among all the others, he called "the most fulfilling," was destined to be threatened.

When Peterson died in 1996, he had every reason to believe that his legacy was secured. But during the year after his death, Virginia Peterson, while still sitting on the institute's board, began to move to cut the institute out of a large portion of Peterson's estate. On 10 October 1997 she established a revocable trust that divided Peterson's work between her two daughters and the institute.

The institute didn't learn of the trust until shortly after Virginia's death in April 2001 and began efforts to view the trust document because of rising concerns that its contents might affect institute collections. These efforts were unsuccessful until July 2004, when the board of trustees finally obtained a copy. They were astounded to learn the details of the estate's division. According to the institute's president, James Berry, the document specified that the institute was to receive only 634 pieces of artwork, most of them ink or scratchboard book illustrations; 506,685 photographic images (only one-third arrived); and various artifacts such as Peterson's medals, study skins, 16 mm films, and personal belongings. Virginia Peterson's daughters received approximately 1,030 pieces of art, including all of his "painterly" works and field guide originals for all but the first two editions of the guides. The Peterson family was astounded as well. Peterson's oldest son, Tory, said, "I think he [Peterson] would have been horrified. It totally goes against his stated wishes."[2]

It was a division that retained for Virginia Peterson's daughters what James Berry called "the most commercially and educationally valuable items."[3] The institute's lot amounted to what Tory Peterson termed the "dregs" of the collection, whose total value he estimated at over $2 million.[4]

As for the "lifetime of writing," it arrived in 120 boxes along with a letter from Virginia Peterson—unsigned—informing the institute that the boxes were to remain unopened until 2020. Institute lawyers determined that the unsigned letter was not a valid document, and the correspondence has been opened for researchers to study, but it was clear by 2004 that the former spirit of cooperation between Peterson's estate and the institute had become moribund.

Based on the perception that Virginia Peterson unilaterally changed the retention agreement by retaining the majority of the artworks and most of the photographic images, the institute's board of trustees hired a litigator in July 2004 to serve notice of breach of contract. Further, according to a 7 December 2004 press release, the institute filed a complaint on 3 December of that year in the Superior Court of Hartford, Connecticut, "to secure the items previously promised by Dr. Peterson and set forth in the 1993 agreement."[5]

The legal question concerned two documents. The institute claimed that the retention agreement contract had been illegally breached. The Virginia Peterson Estate claimed that the revocable trust superseded the contract, a move the estate felt was permitted by the retention agreement's wording. Depositions were taken during the spring of 2005, and a trial date was set for September 2006.

According to the institute, an issue larger than the legal one involved the public interest. At risk were opportunities for future students, scholars, and enthusiasts: to view the body of work of one of the twentieth century's most influential wildlife artists; to study the worksheets and original art of the field guides that changed field study forever; and to learn about the milieu of environmentalism's beginnings.

The institute saw itself as a public resource under duress. In pursuing what it considered its legal and moral obligations to its founder, it had to spend extra time, resources, and money. Further, its dependence on fundraising dramatically raised the importance of the value and integrity of its collections. According to Berry, the promise of Peterson's work was central to obtaining more than $12 million in loans and grants to establish the institute, whose reason for existence was to house and maintain the very materials it was seeking in the complaint. Before the litigation went to trial, however, both sides agreed to a mediated settlement. By the terms of the agreement, the details are to remain confidential.

This litigation provided a sad denouement to a conflicted life and to a remarkable career whose legacy found itself depending, in part, on legal procedures. But it is not surprising that things came to this pass. As Peterson wrote to his lawyer, Edward Schlesinger, "I am one of the least legal and least political people you can imagine — very naïve about structured things."[6] Although he courted and enjoyed fame and recognition, he never set out to become the most significant naturalist of his time. As he repeatedly pointed out, the achievements and events of his life all grew from a single fact: his obsession with birds. It began as a youthful ache for the freedom that birds represented to him, a physical freedom to go anywhere they wanted. And where Peterson wanted to go was where there were birds; that simple and profound desire drove his life.

In the film by Michael Male and Judith Fieth, he reminisced that "birds symbolized to me a freedom I would have given my soul to have."[7] While it's impossible to know what he meant by the phrase "given my soul," it is fair to say that much of what is present in the lives of ordinary people Peterson gave away over a lifetime. Operating with an obsession as his only basis for making choices, he left the parts of his life outside his obsession in the control of others, often damaging people closest to him in the process. Some would use the control that Peterson freely gave up to his benefit; others would abuse it.

<h1 style="text-align:center">41</h1>

Over his lifetime, Peterson produced a body of work that was remarkable both for its quantity and quality. However, in the natural passing of things, much of his production has been equaled or even surpassed. To that part of the world that has only peripheral contact with nature, "Peterson" has been morphed from a person into a name. While he was laboring on his final field guide revisions, he was being marketed relentlessly. His bird images appear on porcelain bird eggs, vases, plates, and bells. A "First Day Cover" was published for stamp collectors by the Postal Commemorative Society. Various spin-offs were created, licensed, and marketed by Virginia's daughters and their husbands, such as the Roger Tory Peterson Nature Cards and the Birding Game with Roger Tory Peterson. The extreme of the uninformed public's perception is related by Peterson's last editor at Houghton Mifflin, Harry Foster. He tells of an acquaintance expressing astonishment that he had worked with Roger Tory Peterson; she had no idea there was such a person but thought he was merely a brand name, "like Betty Crocker."[1]

To the millions who are engaged with the natural world, however, the first edition of *A Field Guide to the Birds* stands as the most important contribution to bird (and nature) study in the twentieth century. Yet bird students today rely on a plethora of guides: books by David Sibley and Kenn Kaufmann as well as guides-by-committee published by the National Audubon Society and National Geographic. A "peterson" is no longer *the* field guide but one of the field guides. The posthumous publication of the fifth edition caused little stir in comparison with the release of its 1980 predecessor. Reviews were respectful and generally not critical. Pete Dunne, who helped in the completion of the book, placed it in a larger context, calling it "the functional link between the man whose name is synonymous with the century that spawned birding and those birders who will come to this avocation in the century ahead." He defended the book's simplicity and Peterson's adherence to his original idea by pointing out that "every beginning birder (in existential fashion) relives the formative age of birding."[2] Likewise, many contemporary wildlife painters, often with the encouragement and support of Peterson, have achieved much of what he wanted to achieve in his own painting. As he told his assistant Mary Dowdell, "I came along at the right time."[3] He recognized that he was not the best painter or writer or photographer, but he was able to do all three. In that sense, he represented the last generation of generalists, much like the naturalists he so admired and who were subsumed by a wave of specialists. In a letter he wrote to art historian David Lank, he replied to a question about the five most important influences on his life. Peterson's list of names clearly reveals the breadth of his accomplishments, the complexity of his nature, and the "two worlds" he lived in: (1) Willem Dieperink von Langereis, who encouraged him to leave Jamestown and attend art school in New York; (2) Alexander Maley, who helped him "form his views and to develop the techniques of teaching"; (3) William Vogt, his editor at *Bird-Lore* and the man who proposed the field guide; (4) James Fisher—"James revealed to me some of the techniques of scholarship and had I known him 20 years earlier, I too might have been a scholar"; (5) Guy Emerson—"as a civilized human being." Peterson was unable to stop at five. He also listed Ludlow Griscom, his birding mentor; Paul Brooks, his editor at Houghton Mifflin; Robert Lewin, who handled his painting career after 1975; and "the women to whom I have been married."[4] These people, and many others, ministered to both sides of Peterson's binary life: artist and naturalist, hedonist and puritan, dreamer and worker. But it remained for Peterson himself to accommodate the strong and conflicting forces of emotion and reason that drove him. From time to time he managed this reconciliation—always during a productive period and always in the company of birds.

In addition to his groundbreaking 1934 guide, his lasting legacy will be as a teacher. He taught millions of people to identify birds and thereby involved them with the natural world by giving them a reason to go outdoors. With each new program the Roger Tory Peterson Institute adds, Peterson's teaching methods and passion for his subject continue to live. What is being perpetuated is a basic educational philosophy. As Peterson's life and work suggest, the root purpose of natural history study should be to create environmentalists.

Notes

Cataloging of the Peterson Papers was under way but in its early stages at the time of this writing. Thus a number of documents in the collection are untitled, undated, and/or unattributed in the notes cited below.

1908–1926 | Jamestown, New York

CHAPTER I

1. David Clapp, quoted in Scott Allen, "He Showed That a Bird in the Bush Is Just Where It Belongs," *Boston Globe*, 10 October 1994.
2. Noble Proctor, quoted in "Roger Tory Peterson, Our Century's Audubon, Dies," *Hartford Courant*, 30 July 1996.
3. Frank Graham Jr., "Field Guide for America," *Audubon* (September/October 1996): 120.
4. Roger Tory Peterson (hereafter cited as "RTP"), memo to John Devlin and Grace Naismith, "Jamestown, NY," n.d., Peterson Papers, Roger Tory Peterson Institute of Natural History (hereafter cited as "RTPI"), Jamestown, NY.
5. Barbara Coulter Peterson (hereafter cited as "BCP"), conversation with the author, 25 April 2003, Kennett Square, PA.
6. BCP to her mother, 1943, Barbara Peterson papers, private collection.
7. RTP to Phillip Reed, 17 November 1979, Peterson Papers.
8. RTP, "Evolution of a Field Guide," *Defenders of Wildlife* (October 1980): 282.
9. RTP, autobiography, Peterson Papers.
10. RTP, "Evolution of a Field Guide," 282.
11. RTP, preface to *A Field Guide to the Birds* (Boston: Houghton Mifflin, 1934).
12. Blanche Hornbeck to RTP, 10 May 1950, Peterson Papers.
13. Ibid.
14. Hornbeck to RTP, 8 April 1951, Peterson Papers.
15. RTP, quoted in Laura Riley, "Roger Tory Peterson at Home," *Bird Watcher's Digest* (July/August 1983): 19.
16. RTP, memo to the Devlins, "Jamestown, NY," n.d., Peterson Papers.
17. Clarence Beal, "My Recollections of Roger Tory Peterson," unpublished paper, 17 February 1948, Peterson Papers.
18. Untitled paper, n.d., Peterson Papers.
19. Quoted in Riley, "Roger Tory Peterson at Home," 22.
20. RTP, "Fourth Year of Bird Study," journal, 1922, Peterson Papers.
21. RTP, *Birds over America* (New York: Dodd, Mead, 1964), 5.
22. RTP, "Evolution of a Field Guide," 283.
23. RTP, *Birds over America*, 5.
24. Gustav Swanson to Robert A. McCabe, 14 August 1990, Peterson Papers.

25. RTP, *The Bird Watchers' Anthology* (New York: Harcourt, Brace, and World, 1957), 45.
26. RTP, "Fourth Year of Bird Study."
27. RTP, Peterson Papers.
28. Edwin Way Teale, "Artist at Work," *Audubon Magazine* (November/December 1942): 352.
29. RTP, Peterson Papers.
30. RTP to "Mr. Nichols," 12 October 1924, Peterson Papers.
31. Frank Chapman, editorial, *Bird-Lore* (March/April 1922): 109.
32. RTP, "The Carolina Wren and Tufted Titmouse at Jamestown, N.Y.," *Bird-Lore* (March/April 1926): 128.
33. Beal, "My Recollections."
34. William Bergstrand, "America's No. 1 Birdwatcher," *Lutheran Source* (May 1973).
35. Margaret Peterson Lager, "Tales of an Early Bird," *Chemung Valley Audubon Society Bulletin* (February 1975): 3.

CHAPTER 2
1. Quoted in Scott L. Montgomery, *Minds for the Making* (New York: Guilford Press, 1994), 134.
2. RTP, school notebook, Peterson Papers.
3. RTP, Peterson Papers.
4. *Jamestown Post-Journal*, 24 June 1925.
5. RTP, autobiography.
6. RTP, "Symbols of Nature in Art," *Audubon Magazine* (September/October 1941): 404.
7. *The Red and Green*, Jamestown (NY) High School yearbook, 1925.
8. RTP, *Birds over America*, 12.

CHAPTER 3
1. RTP, "Immortal Audubon," *Bird Watcher's Digest* (July/August 1990): 12.
2. RTP, autobiography.
3. Ibid.
4. RTP, "In Memoriam: Ludlow Griscom," *Auk* (October 1965): 601.
5. RTP, "Bird Art," *Natural History* (September 1983): 68.
6. RTP, quoted in William Zinsser, "A Field Guide to Roger Tory Peterson," *Audubon* (November/December 1992): 94.
7. *First American Bird Art Exhibition* (Los Angeles: Cooper Ornithological Club, 1926).
8. Frank Chapman, editorial, *Bird-Lore* (September/October 1925): 353.
9. Ibid.
10. Lee Peterson, conversation with the author, 25 April 2003, Oxford, PA.
11. Beal, "My Recollections."

1926–1934 | New York City and Boston
CHAPTER 4
1. RTP to Gustavus Bentley, 19 April 1927, Peterson Papers.
2. Henrietta Bader Peterson (hereafter cited as "HBP") to RTP, 18 March 1927, Peterson Papers.

3. HBP to RTP, February 1927, Peterson Papers.
4. RTP to Margaret Lager, n.d., Peterson Papers.
5. RTP, "Warbler Ways," *Bird-Lore* (May/June 1929): 183–186.
6. RTP, "Bird Art," 68.
7. RTP, "My Evolution as a Bird Artist," *Bird Watcher's Digest* (September/October 1996): 18.
8. RTP, memo to John Devlin, "Art Students League," Peterson Papers.
9. RTP to HBP, n.d., Peterson Papers.
10. RTP to HBP, n.d., Peterson Papers.
11. RTP, quoted in Patricia Van Gelder, *Wildlife Artists at Work* (New York: Watson-Guptill, 1982), 130.

CHAPTER 5
1. RTP to HBP, n.d., Peterson Papers.
2. Frank M. Chapman, *Handbook of Birds of Eastern North America* (New York: D. Appleton-Century, 1895), 411.
3. Elliot Coues, quoted in RTP, "Books of a Feather," *National Wildlife* (December/January 1983): 22.
4. RTP, quoted in Frank Graham Jr., "A-birding in the Bronx," *Audubon* (May 1982): 12.
5. Allan Cruickshank to Clarence Allen, 11 November 1967, Peterson Papers.
6. RTP, *Birds over America*, 16.
7. RTP to HBP, 10 June 1927, Peterson Papers.
8. Alexander Sprunt, *Carolina Low Country Impressions* (New York: Devin-Adair, 1964), 178–179.

CHAPTER 6
1. RTP to Bentley.
2. RTP, "An American Tragedy—A Plea for Our Birds of Prey," *New York State Bulletin* (April 1930): 190.
3. RTP, handwritten manuscript, Peterson Papers.

CHAPTER 7
1. Allan Cruickshank to RTP, n.d., Peterson Papers.
2. Clarence Allen to RTP, 17 February 1930, Peterson Papers.
3. Don Hudson, letter to the author, 17 July 2002.
4. Ibid.
5. RTP, memo to John Devlin.
6. Clarence E. Allen, "The Birds Were Glad," *Florida Naturalist* (April 1969).
7. Conversation between RTP and Alexander Maley, summer 1975, tape recording, Peterson Papers.
8. C. E. Allen, "The Birds Were Glad."
9. Sinclair Hart, letter to the author, 18 July 2002.
10. Bart Chapin, quoted in *Chewonki Foundation Chronicle* (Spring 1997): 12.
11. Conversation between RTP and Maley, summer 1975.
12. C. E. Allen, "The Birds Were Glad."
13. RTP to "Harold," n.d., Peterson Papers.
14. Clarence Allen to Edwin Way Teale, 16 February 1949, Peterson Papers.

15. "Deposition of Alexander Maley to Mr. John Devlin," 2 June 1975, Peterson Papers.
16. RTP to Lager, n.d., Peterson Papers.
17. Ibid.
18. Elliott Richardson, "Rara Avis," *Yankee* (September 1995): 50.
19. Elliott Richardson, quoted in Alex Stephens, "A Teacher to Millions: Roger Tory Peterson's Years at Rivers," *Riparian* (Spring 1995): 7.
20. Richardson, "Rara Avis."
21. Elliott Richardson, transcript of speech delivered to the American Association of School Administrators, Atlantic City, NJ, 23 February 1974, Peterson Papers.

CHAPTER 8
1. RTP, "Evolution of a Field Guide," 282.
2. RTP, autobiography.
3. William Vogt, "From Bird-watching, a Concern for Nature," *New York Times Book Review* (11 June 1961): 6–7.
4. RTP to Richard Westwood, date illegible, Peterson Papers.
5. RTP, "Half a Mile Away: Field Characteristics of Eastern Gulls," *Nature Magazine* (February 1932): 105–106.
6. Ibid.
7. RTP, "Sea Ducks," *Field and Stream* (September 1932): 15.
8. RTP, "Marsh Ducks," *Field and Stream* (October 1932): 32.
9. RTP, "Bay Ducks," *Field and Stream* (November 1932): 26.
10. RTP, memo to the Devlins, "Field and Stream, Field Guide, etc.," 8 December 1975, Peterson Papers.
11. Beal, "My Recollections."
12. Allen Thomas to John Devlin, 5 September 1975, Peterson Papers.

1934 | The *Field Guide,* First Edition

CHAPTER 9
1. RTP, "Evolution of a Field Guide," 284.
2. RTP, *A Field Guide to the Birds* (1934), 1.
3. Ibid., 2.
4. Houghton Mifflin, promotional material, n.d., Peterson Papers.
5. RTP, autobiography.
6. RTP, "Sea Ducks," 14.
7. RTP, *Field Guide* (1934).
8. Ludlow Griscom, quoted in William E. Davis Jr., *Dean of the Birdwatchers: A Biography of Ludlow Griscom* (Washington, DC: Smithsonian Institution Press, 1994), 114.
9. RTP, quoted in Frank Graham Jr., "Roger Peterson Builds a Blockbuster," *Audubon* (September 1980): 59.

CHAPTER 10
1. William Vogt to RTP, n.d., Peterson Papers.
2. RTP, *Field Guide* (1934), xvii.
3. Ibid., xviii.

4. Griscom, quoted in Davis, *Dean of the Birdwatchers*, 111.
5. Davis, *Dean of the Birdwatchers*, 110.
6. Ibid., 111.
7. RTP, "Evolution of a Bird Artist," *Birder's World* (April 1989): 55.
8. RTP, *Field Guide* (1934), xviii–xix.
9. Ibid., xviii.
10. Ibid.

CHAPTER 11

1. Paul Brooks, "A Field Guide to Roger Tory Peterson," *Country Journal* (December 1985): 36.
2. RTP, "Evolution of a Field Guide," 283.
3. Lewis Gannett, "Books and Things," *New York Herald Tribune*, 1934, photocopy included among Peterson Papers.
4. Quoted in Brooks, "Field Guide," 37.
5. W. S[tone], review of *A Field Guide to the Birds*, by Roger Tory Peterson, *Auk* (July 1934): 407–408.
6. Francis H. Allen, review of *A Field Guide to the Birds*, by Roger Tory Peterson, *Massachusetts Audubon Bulletin* (May 1934).
7. Frank M. Chapman, review of *A Field Guide to the Birds*, by Roger Tory Peterson, *Bird-Lore* (July/August 1934): 253.
8. Frank M. Chapman, *Bird-Lore* (July/August 1934): 253–255.
9. P. M. Silloway, quoted in Joseph Kastner, *A World of Watchers*, 106.
10. RTP, quoted in Riley, "Roger Tory Peterson at Home," 29.
11. RTP, autobiography.
12. John Yrizarry, conversation with the author, 3 November 2006.
13. RTP, autobiography.
14. RTP, "Evolution of a Field Guide," 283.
15. Alice G. Marquis, *Hope and Ashes: The Birth of Modern Times, 1929–1939* (New York: Free Press, 1986).
16. RTP quoted in John O'Reilly, "Bird Watching," *Audubon Magazine* (March/April 1949): 100.

1934–1942 | New York City

CHAPTER 12

1. RTP, interview by Carl W. Buchheister, 21 October 1975, transcript, Peterson Papers.
2. Frank Graham Jr., *The Audubon Ark* (Austin: University of Texas Press, 1990), 16.
3. Ibid., 128.
4. Barbara Coulter Peterson, conversation with author, 25 April 2003.
5. Robert Allen to Teale, n.d., Peterson Papers.
6. RTP, interview by Buchheister, 21 October 1975.
7. "Nature-Training Camp in Maine," *Bird-Lore* (November/December 1935): 140–141.
8. RTP, "The Maine Story," *Bird Watcher's Digest* (November/December 1986): 76.
9. Ibid., 80–81.

10. RTP, "Junior Audubon Comeback," *Bird Watcher's Digest* (May/June 1992): 18.
11. "Staff Additions," *Bird-Lore* (November/December 1934): 397.

CHAPTER 13
1. RTP, "Junior Audubon Comeback," 16.
2. RTP, "The Belted Kingfisher," National Association of Audubon Societies Leaflet no. 19.
3. RTP, National Association of Audubon Societies Leaflets: "The Loon," no. 78; "The Canada Goose," no. 106; and "The House Wren," no. 39.
4. RTP, "The Ruby-Throated Hummingbird," National Association of Audubon Societies Leaflet no. 56.
5. RTP, "The Canada Goose."
6. RTP, "The American Goldfinch," National Association of Audubon Societies Leaflet no. 17.
7. RTP, "The Snowy Egret," National Association of Audubon Societies Leaflet no. 54.
8. RTP, interview by Buchheister, 21 October 1975.
9. RTP, "How Should Nature Be Taught?" *Bird-Lore* (May/June 1938): 193.
10. Ibid., 195.
11. Ibid., 201.
12. RTP, "Forests," *Bird-Lore* (September/October 1939): 304.
13. RTP, "Down the Santee in a Folding Boat," *Bird-Lore* (May/June 1938): 179.
14. Ibid., 181.
15. RTP, "Symbols of Nature in Art," 403.
16. RTP, "Tricks of Bird Photography," *Bird-Lore* (March/April 1940): 175–182.
17. RTP, quoted in Graham, *Audubon Ark*, 136–137.
18. Carl Buchheister, quoted in John C. Devlin and Grace Naismith, *The World of Roger Tory Peterson* (New York: Times Books, 1977), 74–75.
19. Joseph Hickey to RTP, 26 February 1963, Peterson Papers.
20. Robert Allen to Teale, n.d., Peterson Papers.
21. RTP, memo to the Devlins, "Field Trips," Peterson Papers.
22. RTP to HBP, n.d., Peterson Papers.
23. RTP to HBP, n.d., Peterson Papers.
24. Clarence Allen to Teale, 16 February 1949, Peterson Papers.
25. Joseph Hickey to Teale, 26 January 1949, Peterson Papers.
26. Clarence Allen to Teale, 16 February 1949.
27. RTP, "Report by Mr. Roger Tory Peterson on the Association's Education Programs, Annual Meeting, 1938," *Bird-Lore* (January/February 1939): 41.
28. RTP, autobiography.

CHAPTER 14
1. RTP, "Evolution of a Bird Artist," 54.
2. Frank M. Chapman, review of *A Field Guide to Western Birds*, *Bird-Lore* (March/April 1939): 177.
3. G. M. Allen, "Recent Literature," *Auk* (July 1939): 348–349.
4. Alden H. Miller, review of *A Field Guide to Western Birds*, *Condor* (July 1941): 204–205.
5. Ludlow Griscom, review of *A Field Guide to Western Birds*, *Audubon Magazine* (May/June 1941): 378–379.

6. Donald Culross Peattie, "The Nature of Things," *Bird-Lore* (July/August 1941): 346.

CHAPTER 15
1. RTP, "My Evolution as a Bird Artist," 18.
2. Ibid.
3. Willem Dieperink von Langereis to RTP, n.d., Peterson Papers.
4. RTP, "Immortal Audubon," 19.

CHAPTER 16
1. RTP, quoted in Devlin and Naismith, *World of Roger Tory Peterson*, 118.
2. Graham, *Audubon Ark*, 141.
3. RTP, "The Maine Story," 79.
4. RTP to John Baker, n.d., Peterson Papers.
5. RTP to Baker, n.d., Peterson Papers.
6. RTP, "Birds and Floating Oil," *Audubon Magazine* (January/February 1942): 217–221.
7. John Baker, "The Director Reports to You," *Audubon Magazine* (January/February 1943): 246.
8. RTP to Baker, n.d., Peterson Papers.

1942–1953 | Washington, D. C.

CHAPTER 17
1. BCP, conversation with the author, 25 April 2003.
2. Brooks, "Field Guide," 39.
3. Susan Nichols, "Mrs. Peterson: Portrait of an Active Woman," *New Haven Register* (18 November 1968).
4. BCP, transcript, n.d., BCP papers, private collection.
5. RTP to Baker, n.d., Peterson Papers.
6. U.S. Army discharge papers, Peterson Papers.
7. RTP to Baker, n.d., Peterson Papers.
8. RTP to George Sutton, 7 November 1944, Peterson Papers.
9. Ibid.
10. RTP to Baker, n.d., Peterson Papers.
11. RTP to Joseph Kastner, 23 May 1945, Peterson Papers.
12. Quaker State Lithograph Co., promotional materials.
13. RTP, autobiography.
14. BCP to her mother, n.d., BCP papers, private collection.
15. Ibid.
16. RTP, autobiography.
17. RTP, *Birds over America* (1948).
18. RTP, autobiography.
19. RTP to Beal, n.d., Peterson Papers.
20. RTP to Baker, 30 November 1944, Peterson Papers.

CHAPTER 18
1. Nathan Copple, "A Field Guide to the Words . . . of Roger Tory Peterson," *Living Bird* (Winter 1996): 32.
2. RTP, *A Field Guide to the Birds* (1947).

3. Ibid., 231.
4. Kastner, *World of Watchers,* 201.
5. RTP, "Evolution of a Field Guide," 285.
6. Devin A. Garrity, "Bird-Lovers' Bible Revisited," *New York Post* (28 July 1947).
7. Leonard Dubkin, "Revised Edition of Peterson's Guide to Birds," *Chicago Tribune* (20 July 1947).
8. Ludlow Griscom to RTP, 11 July 1947, Peterson Papers.

CHAPTER 19
1. John Baker to RTP, 7 September 1944, Peterson Papers.
2. RTP to Baker, 17 November 1944, Peterson Papers.
3. Baker to RTP, 23 November 1944, Peterson Papers.
4. RTP to Baker, 30 November 1944, Peterson Papers.
5. Baker to RTP, n.d., Peterson Papers.
6. RTP to Baker, n.d., Peterson Papers.
7. RTP to Kastner, 17 April 1956, Peterson Papers.
8. Baker to RTP, 1 February 1946, Peterson Papers.
9. RTP to Baker, 14 January 1948, Peterson Papers.
10. BCP, conversation with the author, 25 April 2003.
11. RTP, quoted in Riley, "Roger Tory Peterson at Home," 21.
12. Ibid.
13. RTP, "Wildlife Art," *Bird Watcher's Digest* (January/February 1993): 8.
14. RTP, quoted in Devlin and Naismith, *World of Roger Tory Peterson,* 117.
15. John K. Terres, review of *Birds over America,* by Roger Tory Peterson, *Audubon Magazine* (November/December 1948): 379.
16. RTP, *Birds over America* (1983).
17. Arthur Allen to R. T. Bond, 8 November 1948, Peterson Papers.
18. Ludlow Griscom, handwritten note, 12 December 1948, Peterson Papers.

CHAPTER 20
1. RTP, *Wildlife in Color* (Cambridge, MA: Riverside Press, 1951), 7.
2. RTP to Paul Brooks (hereafter cited as "PB"), 11 October 1944, Peterson Papers.
3. RTP, editor's note in *A Field Guide to the Shells of Our Atlantic Coast* (Boston: Houghton Mifflin, 1947).
4. RTP, preface to *A Field Guide to the Butterflies* (Boston: Houghton Mifflin, 1951).
5. RTP to Richard Grossenheider, 19 October 1950, Peterson Papers.
6. John O'Reilly, "All the Birds This Side of the Iron Curtain," *Audubon Magazine* (September/October 1950): 316–317.
7. Peter Farb, "Twentieth Century Audubon," *Audubon* (November/December 1961): 316.
8. RTP, "The Old World and the New," *Audubon* (May/June 1953): 103.
9. Guy Emerson to RTP, 27 January 1950, Peterson Papers.

1954–1974 | Old Lyme, Connecticut
CHAPTER 21
1. "Announcing a Feature by Roger Tory Peterson," *Audubon Magazine* (July/August 1952): 210.

2. RTP, "A Night in a Channel Lighthouse," *Audubon Magazine* (September/October 1952): 279.
3. Ibid.
4. Ibid., 280.
5. RTP, "Reflections on Flowers," *Audubon Magazine* (November/December 1955): 248.
6. Ibid.
7. Ibid., 249.
8. Ibid., 259.
9. RTP, "High Seas in a Rowboat," *Audubon* (January/February 1962): 20–21.
10. RTP, *Bird Watcher's Anthology*, ix–x.
11. Walter Harding, review of *The Bird Watcher's Anthology*, edited by RTP, *Richmond News Leader* (27 November 1957).
12. David McCord, review of *The Bird Watcher's Anthology*, edited by RTP, *Saturday Review* (7 December 1957): 27.

CHAPTER 22
1. RTP, autobiography.
2. RTP to PB, 22 February 1953, Peterson Papers.
3. RTP and James Fisher (hereafter cited as "JF"), *Wild America* (Boston: Houghton Mifflin, 1955), 250.
4. Rick Wright, "Fifty Years Down a Long Road: On Re-reading *Wild America*," *Birding* (April 2003): 183.
5. RTP and JF, *Wild America*, 3.
6. Wright, "Fifty Years," 186.
7. RTP to PB, Peterson Papers.
8. RTP, autobiography.
9. Ibid.
10. RTP to JF, 2 April 1954, Peterson Papers.
11. Ibid.
12. Ibid.
13. Cyril Connolly, review of *Wild America*, by RTP and JF, *Sunday Times*, 14 October 1956.
14. Edwin Way Teale, review of *Wild America*, by RTP and JF, *New York Times Book Review*, 16 October 1955.
15. Irston Barnes, review of *Wild America*, by RTP and JF, *Atlantic Naturalist* (November/December 1955).
16. Teale, review of *Wild America*.

CHAPTER 23
1. Charles Wurster, quoted in Harmon Henkin, Martin Merta, and James Staples, *The Environment, the Establishment, and the Law* (Boston: Houghton Mifflin, 1971), 57.
2. RTP, "The Osprey: Endangered World Citizen," *National Geographic* (July 1969): 56.
3. BCP, New Year's letter, 1962, Peterson Papers and BCP papers, private collection.
4. RTP to Carl Buchheister, 25 August 1962, Peterson Papers.
5. RTP to Allen Morgan, 4 November 1962, Peterson Papers.

6. RTP to Joseph Hickey, 5 February 1963, Peterson Papers.

7. RTP to Alexander Sprunt, 23 January 1964, Peterson Papers.

8. BCP, New Year's letter, 1965.

9. RTP to William Vogt, 11 July 1964, Peterson Papers.

10. This and subsequent quotations are from RTP, statement to Ribicoff Committee, April 1964, copy among the Peterson Papers.

11. RTP, "The Osprey Story," *Bird Watcher's Digest* (September 1988): 41.

12. RTP and Joseph Hickey, mass mailing, 1956, Peterson Papers.

13. This and subsequent quotations are from RTP, address at Andover School, Andover, Massachusetts, 1964, Peterson Papers.

14. This and subsequent quotations are from RTP, address to the Advancing Science/Serving Society Convention, San Francisco, February 1974.

15. William Zinsser, "Watching the Birds," in *Peterson's Birds: The Art and Photography of Roger Tory Peterson,* edited by Roger Tory Peterson and Rudy Hoglund (New York: Universe Publishing, 2002), 16.

16. RTP, "Keeping Watch on the Needs of Wildlife," *National Wildlife* (April/May 1989): 7.

17. RTP, "Mexico: Exciting and Depressing," *Audubon Magazine* (September/October 1955): 230.

18. Ibid.

19. RTP, untitled "Bird's-Eye View" column, *Audubon Magazine* (January/February 1956): 6.

20. Ibid.

21. RTP, "Tragedy of the Albatross," *Audubon Magazine* (November/December 1959): 249.

22. RTP, "A Plea for a Magic Island," *Audubon* (January/February 1968): 50.

23. Ibid., 51.

24. Ibid.

25. Lars-Eric Lindblad, *Passport to Anywhere* (New York: Times Books, 1983), 184.

26. RTP, "The Tourist as a Conservationist," *Audubon* (March 1972): 48.

27. RTP quoted in Riley, "Roger Tory Peterson at Home," 29.

CHAPTER 24

1. RTP, Red Rose Tea card, ser. 4, no. 23.

2. RTP, *Birds over America,* 9.

3. RTP, "Illustrating Nature Books," *Nature* (August 1950): 388.

4. RTP to Mrs. John Baker, n.d., Peterson Papers.

5. Subsequent quotations are from text of speech in RTP, "Illustrating Nature Books."

CHAPTER 25

1. RTP to PB, 18 April 1963, Peterson Papers.

2. Ibid.

3. RTP to Harold Mayfield, 17 December 1968, Peterson Papers.

4. RTP to PB, 18 April 1964, Peterson Papers.

5. Chandler Robbins to RTP, 5 June 1966, Peterson Papers.

6. Ibid.

7. RTP to Robbins, 15 June 1966, Peterson Papers.

8. RTP, "Evolution of a Field Guide," 285.

CHAPTER 26

1. Lee Peterson, conversation with the author, 25 April 2003.
2. BCP, New Year's letter, 1959.
3. RTP, "How I Photographed All the Flamingos of the World," *International Wildlife* (January/February 1971): 42.
4. Ibid., 45.
5. RTP, "Exploring Antarctica with Roger Tory Peterson," *International Wildlife* (November/December 1971): 30.
6. Ibid., 31.
7. RTP, notes, n.d., Peterson Papers.
8. RTP, "Exploring Antarctica," 31.
9. Ibid.
10. RTP, autobiography.
11. RTP, script for the film *Wild Africa,* Peterson Papers.
12. BCP, letter to her mother, BCP papers, private collection.
13. BCP, New Year's letter, 1964, Peterson Papers.
14. RTP to JF, 12 October 1964, Peterson Papers.
15. RTP to Lorimer Moe, 12 October 1970, Peterson Papers.
16. RTP to JF, 16 August 1967, Peterson Papers.
17. BCP, New Year's letter, 1970.
18. Irston Barnes, "Larcenous Cave Rat a Winsome Creature," *Washington Post* (5 October 1952).
19. RTP, James Fisher memorial speech, Copinsay, Scotland, 7 July 1973, Peterson Papers.
20. BCP, New Year's letter, 1964.
21. RTP, "Bird Painting in America," *Bulletin of the Massachusetts Audubon Society* (June 1942): 115–116.
22. RTP, quoted in John Diffily, "A Field Guide to Roger Tory Peterson," *American Artist* (April 1977): 72.
23. PB to RTP, 29 March 1962, Peterson Papers.
24. Guy Emerson to RTP, n.d., Peterson Papers.
25. RTP to PB, 4 May 1972, Peterson Papers.
26. BCP, New Year's letter, 1970.

1974–1980 | Old Lyme

CHAPTER 27

1. RTP, autobiography.
2. RTP to PB, 20 April 1956, Peterson Papers.
3. BCP, New Year's letter, 1967.
4. Guy Emerson to RTP, 27 October 1943, Peterson Papers.
5. George Sutton to RTP, 17 July 1944, Peterson Papers.
6. BCP, New Year's letter, 1965.
7. Houghton Mifflin, press release, March 1963, Peterson Papers.
8. RTP to PB, 28 December 1971, Peterson Papers.
9. RTP to Francois Bourliere, 8 March 1965, Peterson Papers.
10. RTP to John Terres, 15 December 1964, Peterson Papers.
11. R.C.C., "Soaring but Bumpy Flight," *Christian Science Monitor* (24 February 1965).

12. RTP to JF, 16 August 1967, Peterson Papers.
13. RTP, memo to PB, 25 March 1973, Peterson Papers.
14. RTP, memo to John Devlin, "Painting—Mill Pond Press."
15. RTP, speech to Society of Wildlife Artists, New York, 16 March 1979.
16. Robert Lewin to RTP, 8 June 1970, Peterson Papers.
17. RTP to Robert Lewin, 15 August 1973, Peterson Papers.
18. Ibid.
19. RTP to Lewin, 12 December 1975, Peterson Papers.
20. RTP, "Immortal Audubon," *Bird Watcher's Digest* (July/August 1990): 14–15.
21. RTP to Martha Hill, 4 May 1979, Peterson Papers.

CHAPTER 28
1. Lee Peterson, conversation with the author, 25 April 2003.
2. RTP to PB, 5 December 1972, Peterson Papers.
3. BCP to JF, 28 January 1962, Peterson Papers.
4. RTP, quoted in Riley, "Roger Tory Peterson at Home," 25.
5. BCP to Helen Barsky, 3 April 1974, Peterson Papers.
6. BCP to Robert Gillmor, 10 March 1974, Peterson Papers.

CHAPTER 29
1. RTP, "Illustrating Nature Books," 389.
2. RTP, "Bird Art," 73–74.
3. RTP to John Terres, 24 February 1962, Peterson Papers.
4. RTP to Sutton, 22 July 1962, Peterson Papers.
5. Ibid.
6. RTP to John Terres, 24 February 1962, Peterson Papers.
7. RTP to Sutton, 22 July 1962, Peterson Papers.
8. RTP, Mill Pond Press promotional material, Peterson Papers.
9. Robert Bateman, letter to the author, 18 December 2002.

CHAPTER 30
1. RTP, memo to John Devlin, n.d., Peterson Papers.
2. Lisa Foderaro, "In the Studio with Roger Tory Peterson, Reluctant Earthling," *New York Times* (26 August 1993).
3. Virginia Marie Peterson to Lynn Walker, 9 September 1988, Peterson Papers.
4. Virginia Marie Peterson to Carolyn Amussen, 5 January 1984, Peterson Papers.
5. RTP to PB, 25 March 1973, Peterson Papers.
6. Roger F. Pasquier, "Nature and Naturalists," *New York Times Book Review* (11 December 1977).
7. RTP to PB, 8 January 1982, Peterson Papers.
8. RTP to George Harrison, 13 November 1979, Peterson Papers.
9. RTP to Robert Lewin, 21 December 1979, Peterson Papers.
10. RTP to Austin Olney, 17 February 1982, Peterson Papers.
11. RTP, autobiography.
12. Ibid.

CHAPTER 31
1. William Burt, *Rare and Elusive Birds of North America* (New York: Universe Publishing: 2001), 73.

2. RTP, foreword to Russ Kinne, *The Complete Book of Nature Photography* (Philadelphia: Chilton Book Co., 1971), 11.
3. RTP, "Evolution of a Field Guide," 287.
4. Ibid., 288.
5. Henry Horenstein, "Watching the Birdies," *American Photographer* (July 1986): 73.
6. William Burt, letter to the author, 18 September 2003.
7. RTP, *Birds over America*, 329.
8. Ibid., 330.
9. RTP, quoted in Riley, "Roger Tory Peterson at Home," 25.
10. Downs Matthews, "Bird Shoot with Roger Tory Peterson," *Popular Photography* (July 1993): 124.
11. Burt, letter to the author, 18 September 2003.
12. Horenstein, "Watching the Birdies," 73.
13. Riley, "Roger Tory Peterson at Home," 24.
14. Matthews, "Bird Shoot," 124.
15. Burt, *Rare and Elusive Birds*, 73.
16. Ibid.
17. Matthews, "Bird Shoot," 32.
18. Riley, "Roger Tory Peterson at Home," 24.

CHAPTER 32
1. RTP, "Books of a Feather," 28.

CHAPTER 33
1. RTP to Robert Lewin, 18 April 1983, Peterson Papers.
2. RTP to Susan Rayfield, 13 June 1984, Peterson Papers.
3. Ibid.
4. RTP to Sutton, 22 July 1962, Peterson Papers.
5. Virginia Marie Peterson, notes, n.d., Peterson Papers.

1980–1996 | Old Lyme

CHAPTER 34
1. Henry Armistead, Ron Naveen, et al., "Bird Book Wars: The Emperor Strikes Back," *Birding* (August 1981): 117.
2. RTP to JF, 3 March 1966, Peterson Papers.
3. Kenneth Parkes, "Letters," *Continental Birdlife* (June 1981): 94.
4. Ibid.
5. RTP to Ron Naveen, 17 March 1982, Peterson Papers.
6. RTP to Robert Sundell, 10 February 1982, Peterson Papers.
7. RTP to Kenneth Parkes, 28 January 1982, Peterson Papers.
8. Kenn Kaufmann, "Abridged Too Far . . . ?" *Continental Birdlife* (February 1981): 22.
9. Ibid., 23.
10. Ibid.
11. Ibid., 27.
12. Virginia Marie Peterson to James Berry, n.d., Peterson Papers.
13. RTP to Harold Mayfield, 30 November 1981, Peterson Papers.
14. RTP to Olin Sewell Pettingill, 2 December 1981, Peterson Papers.

15. RTP to Joseph Hickey, 30 December 1981, Peterson Papers.
16. RTP to Mayfield, 30 November 1981.
17. Armistead et al., "Bird Book Wars," 125–127.
18. Frank Graham Jr., "The New Peterson," *Audubon* (May 1990): 13.
19. RTP to Lawrence Balch, Ron Naveen, and Claudia Wilds, 21 December 1982, Peterson Papers.
20. Kenn Kaufmann to RTP, 26 January 1982, Peterson Papers.
21. RTP to Kaufmann, 2 April 1982, Peterson Papers.
22. Kaufmann to RTP, 16 April 1982, Peterson Papers.
23. Robert Bateman, foreword to *Birds of Eastern and Central North America,* 5th ed. (Boston: Houghton Mifflin, 2002), xvi–xvii.
24. Noble Proctor, letter to the author, 4 November 2003.
25. Bateman, foreword, xvii.

CHAPTER 35
1. Richard Lewin, conversation with the author, 20 September 2003.
2. RTP to Sutton, 29 December 1981, Peterson Papers.
3. RTP to Robert Lewin, 18 April 1983, Peterson Papers.
4. RTP to Lewin, 10 February 1984, Peterson Papers.
5. RTP to Lewin, 13 July 1979, Peterson Papers.
6. RTP to Richard Ellis, 22 December 1981, Peterson Papers.
7. RTP to Bateman, 12 May 1982, Peterson Papers.
8. Roland Clement, quoted in "Roger Tory Peterson, Our Century's Audubon, Dies," *Hartford Courant.*
9. Kent Ullberg to RTP, 5 October 1987, Peterson Papers.
10. Robbins to RTP, 1 January 1993, Peterson Papers.
11. RTP, "Birding the Gulf Islands," *Bird Watcher's Digest* (November/December 1992): 8.
12. RTP, "The Falklands and South Georgia Revisited," *Bird Watcher's Digest* (May/June 1995): 26.
13. Ibid., 29.
14. RTP, "Wyoming to Texas—Again," *Bird Watcher's Digest* (January/February 1996): 18.
15. RTP, "The Llanos of Venezuela," *Bird Watcher's Digest* (September/October 1992): 12.
16. Ibid., 17.
17. Greg Lasley, conversation with the author, 15 October 2003.
18. RTP, speech to American Nature Society, New York, 18 April 1988, transcript, Peterson Papers.
19. RTP, autobiography.
20. Ibid.

CHAPTER 36
1. William Thompson III, conversation with the author, 27 June 2005.
2. RTP to Austin Olney, 28 July 1983, Peterson Papers.
3. Mary Beacom Bowers, conversation with the author, 17 August 2005.
4. RTP, "Whatever Happened to the Junior Audubon Clubs?" *Bird Watcher's Digest* (September/October 1984): 92.
5. RTP to Peter Berle (unsent), 21 January 1991, Peterson Papers.

CHAPTER 37

1. RTP, "The Maine Story," *Bird Watcher's Digest* (November/December 1986): 76.
2. Ibid., 81.
3. Judith Fieth and Michael Male, conversation with the author, 21 October 2003.
4. RTP, "Capsized by a Rogue Wave," *Bird Watcher's Digest* (November/December 1990): 8.
5. Ibid., 9–10.
6. Ibid., 10.
7. RTP, "Memories of Sir Peter Scott," *Bird Watcher's Digest* (March/April 1990): 12.
8. RTP, "Junior Audubon Comeback," 15.
9. RTP, quoted in Foderaro, "In the Studio with Roger Tory Peterson," sec. C, 1.
10. RTP to Charles Kaplan, 21 December 1984, Peterson Papers.
11. RTP to Lex Hedley, 29 June 1993, Peterson Papers.
12. RTP, notes for *Life* feature titled "The Meaning of Life" (1991), Peterson Papers.
13. RTP to Nancy Noel, 15 July 1994, Peterson Papers.

CHAPTER 38

1. Paul Benke, conversation with the author, 19 February 2002.
2. Lorimer Moe to RTP, 22 November 1971, Peterson Papers.
3. RTP to Lorimer Moe, 12 December 1975, Peterson Papers.
4. RTP to C. W. Nichols Jr., 4 February 1981, Peterson Papers.
5. RTP to Ernest Brooks Jr., 16 December 1982, Peterson Papers.
6. Henry Beston, *The Outermost House* (Penguin Books 1988), 25.
7. RTP to Russell Peterson, 4 January 1982, Peterson Papers.
8. Ibid.
9. RTP to Carl Hammerstrom, 4 August 1982, Peterson Papers.
10. RTP, RTPI dedication address, 30 August 1993.
11. RTP to Charles Wolcott, 6 December 1983, Peterson Papers.
12. Thomas Erlandson, letter to the author, 19 April 2004.
13. Paul Benke, RTPI mission statement, February 1997.

CHAPTER 39

1. RTP to BCP, 15 February 1996, Peterson Papers.
2. RTP to Russell Peterson, 3 November 1995, Peterson Papers.
3. RTP to BCP, 15 February 1996.

CHAPTER 40

1. RTP, "The Roger Tory Peterson Institute," *Bird Watcher's Digest* (September/October 1994): 21.
2. Tory Peterson, quoted in "Bird-watching Author's Work Lands in Court Fight," *Charlotte Observer* (9 December 2004).
3. James Berry, letter to the author, 8 June 1996.
4. Tory Peterson, quoted in "Bird-watching Author's Work."
5. Press release, Roger Tory Peterson Institute, 7 December 2004.
6. RTP to Edward Schlesinger, 7 September 1993, Peterson Papers.

7. Michael Male and Judith Fieth, *A Celebration of Birds with Roger Tory Peterson*, Blue Earth Films, 1992.

CHAPTER 41
1. Harry Foster, conversation with the author, 12 May 2005.
2. Pete Dunne, "The One and Only: Roger Tory Peterson's Fifth Edition . . . ," *Birder's World* (August 2002): 22.
3. Mary Dowdell, conversation with the author, 28 September 2003.
4. RTP to David Lank, 20 April 1976, Peterson Papers.

Works Cited

Primary Works by RTP, in Chronological Order

"The Carolina Wren and Tufted Titmouse at Jamestown, N.Y." *Bird-Lore* (March/April 1926): 127–129.

"Warbler Ways." *Bird-Lore* (May/June 1929): 183–186.

"An American Tragedy—A Plea for Our Birds of Prey." *New York State Bulletin* (April 1930): 189–190.

"Half a Mile Away: Field Characteristics of Eastern Gulls." *Nature Magazine* (February 1932): 105–108.

"Sea Ducks." *Field and Stream* (September 1932): 14–15.

"Marsh Ducks." *Field and Stream* (October 1932): 32–33.

"Bay Ducks." *Field and Stream* (November 1932): 26–28.

A Field Guide to the Birds. Boston: Houghton Mifflin, 1934, 1939, 1947, 1980, 2002.

"The American Goldfinch." National Association of Audubon Societies Leaflet no. 17.

"The Belted Kingfisher." National Association of Audubon Societies Leaflet no. 19.

"The House Wren." National Association of Audubon Societies Leaflet no. 39.

"The Snowy Egret." National Association of Audubon Societies Leaflet no. 54.

"The Ruby-Throated Hummingbird." National Association of Audubon Societies Leaflet no. 56.

"The Loon." National Association of Audubon Societies Leaflet no. 78.

"The Canada Goose." National Association of Audubon Societies Leaflet no. 106.

"Down the Santee in a Folding Boat." *Bird-Lore* (May/June 1938): 179–183.

"How Should Nature Be Taught?" *Bird-Lore* (May/June 1938): 193–203.

"Report by Mr. Roger Tory Peterson on the Association's Education Programs, Annual Meeting, 1938." *Bird-Lore* (January/February 1939): 41.

"Forests." *Bird-Lore* (September/October 1939): 301–304.

"Tricks of Bird Photography." *Bird-Lore* (March/April 1940): 175–182.

The Audubon Guide to Attracting Birds. With John H. Baker. New York: National Audubon Society, 1941.

A Field Guide to Western Birds. Boston: Houghton Mifflin, 1941, 1961, 1990.

"Symbols of Nature in Art." *Audubon Magazine* (September/October 1941): 403–412.

"Birds and Floating Oil." *Audubon Magazine* (January/February 1942): 217–221.

"Bird Painting in America." *Bulletin of the Massachusetts Audubon Society* (June 1942): 113–120.

Birds over America. New York: Dodd, Mead, 1948; Dodd, Mead, and Co., 1964, 1983.

How to Know the Birds. Boston: Houghton Mifflin, 1949.

"Illustrating Nature Books." *Nature* (August 1950): 388–389.

Wildlife in Color. Cambridge, MA: Riverside Press, 1951.

"A Night in a Channel Lighthouse." *Audubon Magazine* (September/October 1952): 278–280.

A Field Guide to the Birds of Britain and Europe. With Guy Mountfort and P. A. D. Hollom. London and New York: Collins Publishers and Houghton Mifflin, 1953, 1959, 1993.

"The Old World and the New." *Audubon Magazine* (May/June 1953): 103.

Wild America. With James Fisher. Boston: Houghton Mifflin Company, 1955.

"Mexico: Exciting and Depressing." *Audubon Magazine* (September/October 1955): 6ff.

"Reflections on Flowers." *Audubon Magazine* (November/December 1955): 248–249ff.

Untitled "Bird's-Eye View" column. *Audubon Magazine* (January/February 1956): 6.

The Bird Watcher's Anthology. New York: Harcourt, Brace, and World, 1957.

"Tragedy of the Albatross." *Audubon Magazine* (November/December 1959): 8, 249.

"High Seas in a Rowboat." *Audubon Magazine* (January/February 1962): 18–21.

The World of Birds. With James Fisher. New York: Doubleday, 1964.

"In Memoriam: Ludlow Griscom." *Auk* (October 1965): 601.

A Field Guide to Wildflowers of Northeastern and North-Central North America. With Margaret McKenny. Boston: Houghton Mifflin, 1968.

"A Plea for a Magic Island." *Audubon Magazine* (January/February 1968): 50–51.

"The Osprey: Endangered World Citizen." *National Geographic* (July 1969): 53–66.

"How I Photographed All the Flamingos of the World." *International Wildlife* (January/February 1971): 42–45.

"Exploring Antarctica with Roger Tory Peterson." *International Wildlife* (November/December 1971): 28–35.

"The Tourist as a Conservationist." *Audubon* (March 1972): 44–45.

A Field Guide to Mexican Birds. With Edward L. Chalif. Boston: Houghton Mifflin, 1973.

Penguins. Boston: Houghton Mifflin, 1979.

"Evolution of a Field Guide." *Defenders of Wildlife* (October 1980): 282–288.

"Bird Art." *Natural History* (September 1983): 66–74.

"Books of a Feather." *National Wildlife* (December/January 1983): 22–28.

"Whatever Happened to the Junior Audubon Clubs?" *Bird Watcher's Digest* (September/October 1984): 86–93.

"The Maine Story." *Bird Watcher's Digest* (November/December 1986): 76–85.

"The Osprey Story." *Bird Watcher's Digest* (September 1988): 41.

"Evolution of a Bird Artist." *Birder's World* (April 1989): 52–57.

"Keeping Watch on the Needs of Wildlife." *National Wildlife* (April/May 1989): 7.

The Field Guide Art of Roger Tory Peterson. Norwalk, CT: Easton Press, 1990.

"Memories of Sir Peter Scott." *Bird Watcher's Digest* (March/April 1990): 12–19.

"Immortal Audubon." *Bird Watcher's Digest* (July/August 1990): 12–19.

"Capsized by a Rogue Wave." *Bird Watcher's Digest* (November/December 1990): 8–19.

"Junior Audubon Comeback." *Bird Watcher's Digest* (May/June 1992): 12–19.

"The Llanos of Venezuela." *Bird Watcher's Digest* (September/October 1992): 12–19.

"Birding the Gulf Islands." *Bird Watcher's Digest* (November/December 1992): 8–18.

"Wildlife Art." *Bird Watcher's Digest* (January/February 1993): 8–18.

"The Roger Tory Peterson Institute." *Bird Watcher's Digest* (September/October 1994): 20–24.

"The Falklands and South Georgia Revisited." *Bird Watcher's Digest* (May/June 1995): 22–29.

"Wyoming to Texas—Again." *Bird Watcher's Digest* (January/February 1996): 16–20.

"My Evolution as a Bird Artist." *Bird Watcher's Digest* (September/October 1996): 16–24.

Birds of Eastern and Central North America. 5th ed. Boston: Houghton Mifflin, 2002.

Personal Papers

Peterson, Barbara. Papers. Private collection.
Peterson, Roger Tory. Papers. Roger Tory Peterson Institute of Natural History, Jamestown, NY.

Secondary Works

Allen, Clarence E. "The Birds Were Glad." *Florida Naturalist* (April 1969).
Allen, Francis H. Review of *A Field Guide to the Birds,* by Roger Tory Peterson. *Massachusetts Audubon Bulletin* (May 1934): 6.
Allen, G. M. "Recent Literature." *Auk* (July 1939): 348–349.
Allen, Scott. "He Showed That a Bird in the Bush Is Just Where It Belongs." *Boston Globe* (10 October 1994).
"Announcing a Feature by Roger Tory Peterson." *Audubon Magazine* (July/August 1952): 210.
Armistead, Henry, Ron Naveen, et al. "Bird Book Wars: The Emperor Strikes Back." *Birding* (August 1981): 116–128.
Baker, John. "The Director Reports to You." *Audubon Magazine* (January/February 1943): 246.
Barnes, Irston. "Larcenous Cave Rat a Winsome Creature." *Washington Post* (5 October 1952).
———. Review of *Wild America,* by Roger Tory Peterson and James Fisher. *Atlantic Naturalist* (November/December 1955).
Bergstrand, William. "America's No. 1 Birdwatcher." *Lutheran Source* (May 1973).
"Bird-watching Author's Work Lands in Court Fight." *Charlotte Observer* (9 December 2004).
Brooks, Paul. "A Field Guide to Roger Tory Peterson." *Country Journal* (December 1985): 34–41.
Burt, William. *Rare and Elusive Birds of North America.* New York: Universe Publishing, 2001.
Chapman, Frank M. Editorial. *Bird-Lore* (March/April 1922): 109–110.
———. Editorial. *Bird-Lore* (September/October 1925): 353–354.
———. *Handbook of Birds of Eastern North America.* New York: D. Appleton-Century, 1895.
———. Review of *A Field Guide to the Birds,* by Roger Tory Peterson. *Bird-Lore* (July/August 1934): 253–254.
———. Review of *A Field Guide to Western Birds. Bird-Lore* (March/April 1939): 177.
Connolly, Cyril. Review of *Wild America,* by Roger Tory Peterson and James Fisher. *Sunday Times,* 14 October 1956.
Cooper Ornithological Club. *First American Bird Art Exhibition.* April 1926.

Copple, Nathan. "A Field Guide to the Words . . . of Roger Tory Peterson."
  Living Bird (Winter 1996): 30–33.
Davis, William E., Jr. *Dean of the Birdwatchers: A Biography of Ludlow
  Griscom.* Washington, DC: Smithsonian Institution Press, 1994.
Devlin, John C., and Grace Naismith. *The World of Roger Tory Peterson.*
  New York: Times Books, 1977.
Diffily, John. "A Field Guide to Roger Tory Peterson." *American Artist*
  (April 1977): 31–33ff.
Dubkin, Leonard. "Revised Edition of Peterson's Guide to Birds." *Chicago
  Tribune* (20 July 1947).
Dunne, Pete. "The One and Only: Roger Tory Peterson's Fifth Edition . . ."
  Birder's World (August 2002): 22–24.
Farb, Peter. "Twentieth Century Audubon." *Audubon* (November/December 1961): 312–317.
Foderaro, Lisa W. "In the Studio with Roger Tory Peterson, Reluctant
  Earthling." *New York Times* (26 August 1993).
Gannett, Lewis. "Books and Things." *New York Herald Tribune,* 1934.
Garrity, Devin A. "Bird-Lover's Bible Revisited." *New York Post* (28 July
  1947).
Graham, Frank, Jr. "A-birding in the Bronx." *Audubon* (May 1982): 12.
———. *The Audubon Ark.* New York: Alfred A. Knopf, 1990.
———. "Field Guide for America." *Audubon* (September/October 1996):
  120.
———. "The New Peterson." *Audubon* (May 1990): 12–13.
———. "Roger Peterson Builds a Blockbuster." *Audubon* (September
  1980): 59–63.
Griscom, Ludlow. Review of *A Field Guide to Western Birds. Audubon
  Magazine* (May/June 1941): 378–379.
Harding, Walter. Review of *The Bird Watcher's Anthology,* edited by Roger
  Tory Peterson. *Richmond News Leader* (27 November 1957).
Henkin, Harmon, Martin Merta, and James Staples. *The Environment, the
  Establishment, and the Law.* Boston: Houghton Mifflin (1971).
Horenstein, Henry. "Watching the Birdies." *American Photographer* (July
  1986): 66–73.
Kastner, Joseph. *A World of Watchers.* New York: Alfred E. Knopf, 1986.
Kaufmann, Kenn. "Abridged Too Far . . . ?" *Continental Birdlife* (February
  1981): 22–27.
Kinne, Russ. *The Complete Book of Nature Photography.* Philadelphia:
  Chilton Book Co. (1971).
Klots, Alexander. *A Field Guide to the Butterflies.* Boston: Houghton Mifflin
  Company, 1951.
Lager, Margaret Peterson. "Tales of an Early Bird." *Chemung Valley Audubon Society Bulletin* (February 1975): 1–5.

Lindblad, Lars-Eric. *Passport to Anywhere.* New York: Times Books, 1983.

Male, Michael, and Judith Fieth. *A Celebration of Birds with Roger Tory Peterson.* Blue Earth Films, 1992.

Marquis, Alice G. *Hope and Ashes: The Birth of Modern Times, 1929–1939.* New York: Free Press, 1986.

Matthews, Downs. "Bird Shoot with Roger Tory Peterson." *Popular Photography* (July 1993): 30–32ff.

McCord, David. Review of *The Bird Watcher's Anthology,* edited by RTP. *Saturday Review* (7 December 1957): 27.

Miller, Alden H. Review of *A Field Guide to Western Birds. Condor* (July/August 1941): 204–205.

Montgomery, Scott L. *Minds for the Making.* New York: Guilford Press, 1994.

Morris, Percy. *A Field Guide to the Shells of Our Atlantic Coast.* Boston: Houghton Mifflin Company, 1947.

"Nature-Training Camp in Maine." *Bird-Lore* (November/December 1935): 140–141.

Nichols, Susan. "Mrs. Peterson: Portrait of an Active Woman." *New Haven Register* (18 November 1968).

O'Reilly, John. "All the Birds This Side of the Iron Curtain." *Audubon Magazine* (September/October 1950): 316–317.

———. "Bird Watching." *Audubon Magazine* (March/April 1949): 100.

Parkes, Kenneth C. "Letters." *Continental Birdlife* (June 1981): 93–95.

Pasquier, Roger F. "Nature and Naturalists." *New York Times Book Review* (11 December 1977).

Peattie, Donald Culross. "The Nature of Things." *Bird-Lore* (July/August 1941): 346–347.

Peters, Harold S., and Thomas D. Burleigh. *Birds of Newfoundland.* Boston: Houghton Mifflin, 1951.

R.C.C. "Soaring but Bumpy Flight." *Christian Science Monitor* (24 February 1965).

Richardson, Elliott. "Rara Avis." *Yankee* (September 1995): 50.

Riley, Laura. "Roger Tory Peterson at Home." *Bird Watcher's Digest* (July/August 1983): 17–34.

"Roger Tory Peterson, Our Century's Audubon, Dies." *Hartford Courant* (30 July 1996).

Sprunt, Alexander. *Carolina Low Country Impressions.* New York: Devin-Adair, 1964.

"Staff Additions." *Bird-Lore* (November/December 1934): 397.

Stephens, Alex. "A Teacher to Millions: Roger Tory Peterson's Years at Rivers." *Riparian* (Spring 1995): 4–7.

Stone, W. Review of *A Field Guide to the Birds,* by Roger Tory Peterson. *Auk* (July 1934): 407–408.

Teale, Edwin Way. "Artist at Work." *Audubon Magazine* (November/ December 1942): 352–355.

———. Review of *Wild America*, by Roger Tory Peterson and James Fisher. *New York Times Book Review* (16 October 1955).

Terres, John K. Review of *Birds over America*, by Roger Tory Peterson. *Audubon Magazine* (November/December 1948): 379.

Van Gelder, Patricia. *Wildlife Artists at Work.* New York: Watson-Guptill, 1982.

Vogt, William. "From Bird-watching, a Concern for Nature." *New York Times Book Review* (11 June 1961).

Wright, Rick. "Fifty Years Down a Long Road: On Re-reading *Wild America*." *Birding* (April 2003): 182–186.

Zinsser, William. "A Field Guide to Roger Tory Peterson." *Audubon* (November/December 1992): 91–96.

———. "Watching the Birds." In *Peterson's Birds: The Art and Photography of Roger Tory Peterson*, edited by Roger Tory Peterson and Rudy Hoglund. New York: Universe Publishing, 2002.

Index

Page numbers in *italics* refer to illustrations. Roger Tory Peterson is referred to as RTP.

dedication, 41, 48; environmentalism, 3; field identification, 112–113; fifth edition, 204, 230–231, 261; fiftieth anniversary, 204; first edition, 55–70, 93, 133, 261, 262; fourth edition, 114, 174, 203, 204, 215, 218, 223–231; "gulls" plate, 60; "How to Use This Book," 58, 61, 64; painting style, 115; preface in early editions, 5; reviews of, 65, 91, 116, 142, 192, 223–231; revision, 112; royalties, 65; second edition, 91; as text in ornithology, 89; third edition, 62, 174, 215; writing style, 113–115. See also *Field Guide to Western Birds*

Field Guide to the Birds of Britain and Europe (RTP, Mountfort & Hollum), 132, 134–135, 136, 166

Field Guide to the Butterflies (Klots), 111, 133

Field Guide to the Fish (Herald), 111

Field Guide to the Mammals (Burt), 134

Field Guide to the Shells of Our Atlantic Coast (Morris), 133

Field Guide to the Trees (Petrides), 133

"Field Guide to the Words . . . of Roger Tory Peterson" (Copple), 114

Field Guide to Western Birds (RTP), 60, 91, 92, 100, 101, 172, 173, 231; fourth edition, 204; painting style, 115; reviews of, 92–93; second edition, 113, 175; third edition, 216, 230

Field Guide to Wildflowers (McKenny), 140, 166, 189–192

field identification, 33–34, 39, 56, 59, 65, 112

field marks, 33, 39, 48, 49–50, 55, 56, 57–58, 59, 68, 133, 135; of flowers, 140

Fieth, Judith, 241–243, 260

"Fifty Years Down a Long Road: on Re-reading *Wild America*" (Wright), 143–144

films, 69, 119, 179, 241, 260. See also Audubon Screen Tours; individual titles

First American Bird Art Exhibition, 21

Fish and Wildlife Service, U.S., 111, 156

Fisher, James, 135, 142–150, 176, 181–184, 224–225, 244, 262; death, 181, 183. See also Copinsay Nature Reserve

flicker, 8, 20, 244–246

Forbush, Edward Howe, 20, 33, 47, 49

Forest and Stream, 73

Forest Service, U.S., 68. See also Pinchot, Gifford

Foster, Harry, 261

"Fourth Year of Bird Study" (RTP, journal), 9, 10

Franklin and Marshall College, 132

Free as the Birds (RTP, proposed autobiography), 206

Fuertes, Louis Agassiz, 7, 13, 19–20, 67, 86, 94–95, 97, 98, 128, 201; death of, 183, 216; influence on Singer, 174; RTP writing on, 183–184

Galápagos, 163, 179. See also *Wild Eden*

Gannett, Lewis, 65

Garrity, Devin, 116

Gebbie Foundation, 248–249

Glen Echo, Maryland, 112

Golden Books, 172, 173. See also *Birds of America*

Golden Eagle (RTP, painting), 201–202

Golden Guide. See *Birds of America*

Golden Press, 173. See also *Birds of the World*

Graham, Frank, Jr., 3, 75, 87, 99, 121, 229

Graves, Morris, 200

Greenwich Village, 88, 89, 100

Grinnell, George Bird, 73

Griscom, Ludlow, 20, 32–34, 35, 38, 47, 57, 62, 64, 102, 116, 130; at Harvard, 63; letter from, 62; letter to, 59; reviews by, 93; RTP's birding mentor, 262

Gromme, Owen, 166

Grossenheider, Richard, 134. See also *Field Guide to the Mammals*

Guide to the Birds of New England and Eastern New York (Hoffmann), 56

Gyrfalcon (RTP, painting), 202

Hagar, Connie, 255

"Half a Mile Away: Field Guide Characteristics of Eastern Gulls" (RTP, essay), 38, 48–49

Hall, George, 225, 227

Hamilton, John, 248–249

Hammerstrom, Carl, 251

77; nonprofessional life, 73, 197–198; ornithologist, 63, 75; painting, 20, 21, 29–32, 43, 47, 57, 93, 94, 96–98, 110, 112, 115–116, 118, 120, 164–171, 174–175, 184, 191, 193–197, 199–202, 209, 216; painting career, end of, 232–233; painting technique, 195, 215–216; photographs, 12, 128–129, *129*, 135, 171, *176*, *178*, *185*, 237; photography, 9, 21, 28, 85–86, 100, 141, 171, 208–214, 234–235; radio, 69, 86, 89; reasons to photograph, 213; religion, 246; research, 56, 85; retention agreement with RTPI, 257–259; reviews, 142, 192, 223–231; skills, 47–48, 216–217; as teacher, 39–44, 46–47, 63, 162, 247; time capsule, 99; tombstone, 245; "trade mark," 16; travel, 100, 134, 135, 142–150, 175–181, 197, 213, 240; turning points in life, 7–8, 17, 20, 151, 155, 197–198, 219; wildlife protection, 159; WOR radio, 86; writer's block, 198; writing, unpublished, 237; writing style, 79, 113–115, 120–121, 128, 130–131, 237–238. *See also* awards; speeches

Peterson, Russell, 250, 257
Peterson, Tory (eldest son), 111, 117, 175, 258
Peterson, Virginia (third wife), 203–205, 219, 220, 227, 249, 257, 258, 259; complaint against estate filed in Superior Court of Hartford, CT, by RTPI, 259; daughters, 258, 260–261; death (2001), 258; revocable trust, 258
Peterson Field Guide Series, 111, 133–134
Peterson Field Guide System, 172
Peterson Institute. *See* Roger Tory Peterson Institute for the Study of Natural History
Petrides, George, 133. See also *Field Guide to the Trees*
Pettingill, Olin Sewall, 227
Phillips, Helen, 149
"Photographic Postscript" (RTP, essay), 128
Pinchot, Gifford, 68
plagiarism, 172–173
"Plea for a Magic Island" (RTP, essay), 161–162
Postal Commemorative Society, 260
postcards, 94–95, 164
Potomac River, 112

Pough, Richard, 75, 115, 118
preservationist, 68, 83, 85, 135, 155–156, 205
Presidential Medal of Freedom, 218
Proctor, Noble, 3, 231, 251

Quaker State Lithographing Company, 109, 110, 115, 119, 164, 166

"Rain Shadows of the Mexican Border" (RTP, essay), 126–128
Rare and Elusive Birds of North America (Burt), 208, 214
Rayfield, Susan, 219
realism (in painting): academic, 31, 199–200; intellectual, 201; objective, 199, 201; photographic, 199
Red Rose Tea cards, 164
Reed, Chester A., 34, 38–39, 117, 118
"Reflections on Flowers" (RTP, essay), 140
Ribicoff, Abraham, Senator, 154
Richardson, Elliott, 46–47
Richmond News Leader, 143
"Riddle of Migration" (RTP, film), 119, 179
Rivers School, 44–46, 56, 57, 77
Robbins, Chandler, 172, 173, 234
"Roger Peterson's Bird's-Eye View" (RTP, column), 132, 139–142, 159–163
Roger Tory Peterson Institute for the Study of Natural History, 9, 43, 193, 227, 233, 247–255, 254, 262; board of trustees, 251, 258–259; complaint filed in Superior Court of Hartford, CT, 259; mission statement, 253; photography archive, 213
Roger Tory Peterson Nature Cards, 261
Roger Tory Peterson Nature Interpretive Building, 248–249
Roger Tory Peterson School for Environmental Sciences, 248
Roger Tory Peterson: The Art and Photography of the World's Foremost Birder (RTP), 212
Royal Society for the Protection of Birds, 182, 183
"Ruby-throated Hummingbird" (RTP, leaflet), 80
Rungius Medal, 255

Saturday Review, 142
Schlesinger, Edward, 260

White, Gilbert, 253

Wild Africa (RTP, film), 179–180

Wild America (RTP & Fisher), 142–150, 237; film by RTP, 119, 179; illustrations for, 96, 169, 170; proposed spin-offs, 192–193

Wild Eden (RTP, film), 179

Wild Europe (RTP, film), 179

Wild Islands (RTP, unpublished), 237

Wildlife in Color (RTP), 131–132, 133

wildlife protection, 159

Wilds, Claudia, 229

Wilson Bulletin, 224–225

Wilson Ornithological Society, 175

World of Birds (RTP & Fisher) 157, 166, 191–192, 237

The World of Roger Tory Peterson: An Authorized Biography (Devlin & Naismith), 205–206

World of Watchers (Kastner), 115

Wright, Rick, 143–144

Wurster, Charles, 151

Yrizarry, John, 67

Zinsser, William, 159